No Turn Unstoned

No Turn Unstoned

The Worst Ever Theatrical Reviews Compiled by

DIANA RIGG

Silman-James Press
Los Angeles

Designed by Craig Dodd

First Silman-James Press Edition

Published by arrangement with Doubleday, a division of Bantam Doubleday
Dell Publishing Group, Inc.

Library of Congress Cataloging-in-Publication Data

No turn unstoned: the worst ever theatrical reviews/
compiled by Diana Rigg
p. cm.
Reprint, Originally published: New York: Doubleday, 1983.
Includes index.
1. Theater--Reviews.   I. Rigg, Diana.
[PN1707.N58 1991]   91-11430
792.9'5--dc20   CIP

ISBN: 1-879505-03-7

Cover design by Heidi Frieder

Printed and bound in the United States of America

SILMAN-JAMES PRESS
Distributed by
Samuel French Trade
7623 Sunset Blvd.
Hollywood, CA 90046

Contents

Acknowledgements

I would particularly like to thank all the critics who not only generously allowed me to use their texts, but also gave great encouragement; Molly Sole of The Old Vic; John Goodwin of The National Theatre Press Office; Levi Fox of The Shakespeare Institute; Angus Mackay for his tireless research and profound knowledge of matters theatrical; John Lonsdale and Colin Wilson of The Times Library for help with research, and John Lonsdale for the index; John Adrian, Frank Muir and Bevis Hillier; Martin Tickner and Sheridan Morley; Frances Koston; Dorothy Swerdlove of The New York Metropolitan Museum Theatre Library. Jenny Pearson comes at the end of this paragraph only because I wish to say a great deal more about her and her contribution. Jenny is a writer, yet out of friendship and enthusiasm for the project undertook to help not only research, but the wearisome business of transcribing tapes, sourcing, and generally pulling the book into shape. It was her gentle guidance that kept me going when I flagged, her skill that transformed my plodding prose into the readable. In short, without Jenny there would have been no book.

I, and my publishers, would also like to thank the following for permission to use copyright material:

Punch Publications Ltd for many illustrations and some extracts; George Harrap Ltd for the illustrations by Nerman from *Caught in the Act*; Raymond Mander and Joe Mitchenson Theatre Collection for all the other illustrations. *The Daily Telegraph*, in particular for the reviews of W. A. Darlington; The Society of Authors as the literary representative of the Estate of St. John Ervine and the Estate of George Bernard Shaw; the Trustees of the British Museum, the Governors and Guardians of the National Gallery of Ireland and Royal Academy of Dramatic Art for the letter from George Bernard Shaw to Wendy Hiller, © 1982; Walter Kerr and Brandt and Brandt Inc, New York; Clive James (from *Visions Before Midnight* published by Cape and Picador and *Glued to the Box* published by Cape); The Literary Executors of James Agate and George Harrap Ltd; Mrs Eva Reichmann and the Estate of Max Beerbohm; *The Observer* and Robert Cushman; *Times Newspapers Ltd* for reviews by Irving Wardle and Ned Chaillet; Random House Inc for the extracts by John Simon from *Singularities*; Mrs George Jean Nathan for the extracts by George Jean Nathan from *The Theatre Book of the Year* 1943-44 through 1950-51; Harper and Row Publishers Inc. for the extracts by Stanley Kauffman from *Persons of the Drama*; Express Newspapers Ltd for the extracts by Hannen Swaffer; the Estate of Kenneth Tynan for extracts from *A View of the English Stage* published by Davis-Poynter, *Curtains*, *He That Plays The King* and *Tynan Right and Left* published by Longmans; John McCarten in *The New Yorker* © 1945, 1973, reprinted by permission; and Andrew D. Weinberger for the extracts from *The Portable Dorothy Parker*, © 1973 The National Association for Advancement of Colored People, first published in *The New Yorker*.

Every effort has been made to trace the copyright holders, but, should there be any omissions in this respect we apologise and shall be pleased to make acknowledgement in any future editions.

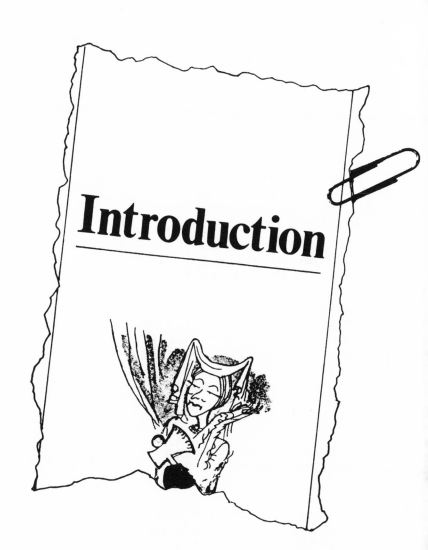

Introduction

'A critic is a man who leaves no turn unstoned,' as my friend the Reverend Joseph McCulloch once remarked to me, and from this maxim came my idea for the book. It followed, surely, that everyone in my profession must, at some time, have been given a bad notice. So I wrote to all the well-known actors and actresses of today and asked them to donate their worst/funniest review. A delicate task. I was, quite simply, asking them to dredge up what they might well have preferred to forget. For my part, I still remember distinctly the dismay and hurt I felt on reading John Simon's review (page 42) but after some weeks I began to see the funny side of it, and not much later was quoting it freely. I hoped to discover that this attitude prevailed among my betters and peers.

I was not disappointed. The replies rolled in and much encouragement with them. Some sent several cuttings to choose from. Just a few didn't reply. Others couldn't remember, but urged me to research.

I then realized how big a task I had undertaken. To do credit to the generosity of my contemporaries I felt I must, in fairness, demonstrate how their predecessors had fared similarly: how adverse criticism had been visited on one and all, even the most legendary. So I set to work, researching back to the earliest sources of comment on actors and their art.

Critics as a formally appointed body of men and women whose job is to express a view of what is happening in the theatre are a comparatively recent phenomenon: they didn't really get going until the eighteenth century. But remove the capital 'C', the formal designation, and it turns out that from the very beginning the audience has contained people who insist upon making their reactions felt, both during and after the performance.

As Ralph Richardson said in an article for the old *Vic-Wells Magazine,* 'A member of the audience, if he's worth anything at all, when he gets home after a performance, will criticise the entertainment he has seen. It is in the nature of things that he should and it hasn't done him any good if he does not.'

In this sense we are all critics, and so it has been since the very beginning. Turns, I discovered, have been stoned by many people down the years for extremely varied reasons.

Bad notices go back as far as acting itself. When Thespis, the Greek poet who founded our profession, made history by stepping out of the chorus to impersonate one of the characters in the story that was being told, not everyone greeted this brilliant departure with the enthusiasm it deserved. (I wonder what prompted him to take this revolutionary step? Even today, directors complain that actors always want to improve their parts: but we have an ancient precedent and the instinct remains strong!)

When Thespis brought his invention to Athens around 560BC, Solon, the lawgiver, denounced it as a dangerous deception. This was more than a personal view: it was the expression of a deep social anxiety over the representation of godlike qualities by a mere man.

On this first confrontation, however, the critics were overridden by the success of the enterprise. (And not for the last time either.) By 543BC the practice was so well established that a competition in tragic acting was held in Athens, and Thespis, now an old man, was awarded first prize.

At this early stage all the parts in a play were performed by one man, usually the author. Aeschylus, the great actor-dramatist, then added a second actor to the cast in his plays, Sophocles added a third, and so the profession was established.

From that dawn until the present day it has continued in the teeth of a daunting opposition, ranging from the intellectual and civic leaders of classical antiquity through the saints and Church Fathers to the Puritan opposition of relatively modern history.

Plato (429-347 BC) would have exiled the acting profession entirely from his ideal *Republic*:

> And therefore when any of these pantomimic gentlemen, who are so clever that they can imitate anything, comes to us, and makes us a proposal to exhibit himself and his poetry, we will fall down and worship him as a sweet and holy and wonderful being; but we must also inform him that in our state such as he are not permitted to exist; the law will not allow them. And so after we have annointed him with myrrh, and set a garland of wool upon his head, we shall send him away to another city.

The first instance of 'don't call us, we'll call you'?

When the dramatic tradition of Ancient Greece was carried across to Italy under the Roman Empire, standards were not maintained. Ovid (43BC-AD18) may well have been accurate when, in his *Ars Amatoria,* he gives us a glimpse of audiences of his day: 'Adulterers, Whore-masters, Panders, Whores and such like effeminate, idle, unchaste, lascivious, graceless persons were the most assiduous Play-hunters in their time.' In other words (expressing a view which has persisted down the ages) nice people don't go to the theatre.

There were a few good Roman dramatists such as Plautus, Seneca, and Terence, but in general the theatre offered a very mixed fare of bawdy rhymes, broad farce and elaborate spectacles — often serving as curtain-raisers to a chariot race or a gladiator's display.

Actors at the time were invariably slaves: Roscius, greatest of Roman actors (d.62BC) was granted freedom as a result of his success. But he was the odd one out: the profession as a whole had a bad time of it.

The poet Lucian (AD 120-200) left a description of the Roman style of acting at its worst:

> Let us consider . . . the hideous, appalling spectacle that the actor presents. His high boots raise him up out of all proportion; his head is hidden under an enormous mask; his huge mouth gapes upon the audience as if he would swallow them; to say nothing of the chest-pads and stomach-pads with which he contrives to give himself artificial corpulence, lest his deficiency in this respect should emphasise his disproportionate height. And in the middle of it all is the actor, shouting away, now high, now low — chanting his iambics as often as not; could anything be more revolting than this sing-song recitation of tragic woes?

The Emperor Augustus Caesar (63BC-AD14) had the actor Epiphanus whipped three times around the palace and banished for daring to give a performance in his presence on a public holiday. And the Emperor Marcus Aurelius (AD 121-180) carried on the tradition of official discouragement: 'I have seen nothing more unprofitable to the Commonwealth . . . than to learn of these Players, triflers and other such jugglers . . .'

Finally, to the double bombardment of aesthetic and official disapproval was added a third voice, more powerful and lasting in its condemnation than either of the other two: the voice of the recently established Christian Church.

Up to this moment, the critics had more or less confined themselves to saying '*I* don't approve.' Now they began to declare, with mounting conviction, that 'God doesn't approve.'

And still, marvellous to relate, the actors of the day clung to their occupation. Attacked, reviled, excommunicated, denied burial in Holy ground, they nevertheless persisted in clambering on to (often makeshift) stages to entertain people by playing parts.

The arguments of the Church Fathers against our beleaguered profession make fascinating reading. While some of them have a remote and foreign ring, unlike anything that would be said today, others are all too familiar: the basic thinking of censorship.

Tertullian (AD 155-222), an African Church Father who left copious writings in Latin, makes the rather simple objection that an actor must be immoral because in pretending to be someone else on stage he has to tell lies.

We are no longer threatened in quite these terms. But when Origen (AD 185-245) head of the Christian school of Alexandria wrote, 'Christians must not lift up their eyes to Stage-plays, the pleasurable delights of polluted eyes, lest their lusts be inflamed by them,' we surely hear the voice of Mrs Mary Whitehouse (see page 169). It is a line of thinking that echoes right down the ages.

St Augustine of Hippo (AD 345-430), himself a keen theatregoer before his conversion to Christianity, added his voice to the campaign: 'Stage plays are the most petulant, the most impure, impudent, wicked, unclean, the most shameful and detestable atonements of filthy Devil-gods.'

Likewise St Chrysostom (AD 347-407) — except that his words inadvertently bear witness to the very thing I want to celebrate here: the triumphant survival of the drama. Clearly the discovery of Thespis and his kind had answered some deep human need which, once awakened, would never allow itself to be stifled. St Chrysostom's voice has a plaintive ring: 'How many sermons have we bestowed, admonishing many stupid ones that they would utterly relinquish and abandon theatres, and the lascivious things proceeding from thence. And they did not abstain, but always even unto this day run to the unlawful spectacles of plays and dances . . .'

Many years ago, whilst working in America, I was given a medallion inscribed with the words 'St Genesius. Patron Saint Of Actors.' The story told of him is that, in the course of an entertainment given to the Roman Emperor Diocletian (AD 245-313) he played the part of a candidate in a mocking representation of Christian baptism. But the Grace of God touched him and afterwards, when presented to the Emperor, he declared that he had been converted suddenly to Christ during the performance. As a result of this confession he was put to the torture, but he would not recant and so his head was struck off. 'Whether there was ever a martyr named Genesius at Rome has not been decided for certain,' says the *Dictionary of Saints.* Why not, I wonder? There must surely have been Christian actors, and that some chose to reveal their faith is evident. No officially accepted Patron Saint of Actors exists. It is a sad omission — and, one can't help feeling, a critical one.

By the end of the sixth century AD, what remained of the classical theatre tradition was fractured beyond repair by the barbaric invasions of the Huns. A theatre is called 'dark' when no regular performances are given, and so it was through the theatre as a whole in the Dark Ages. There only remained the ragged troupes of mimics, acrobats and ballad singers who, like migrating birds, carried the seeds of theatre around Europe.

The old classical dramas survived through this bleak period only because they had been written down, and as such they retained a select audience among people of education in the Church, though it would seem they were studied under plain brown cover.

A nun called Hrotsitha (or Roswitha), who lived in Saxony from AD 925-1002 and herself wrote plays about the Christian martyrs, delicately reveals her debt to the plays of the great Roman comedian Terence, though she tactfully disassociates herself from their subject matter. 'There are many Catholics, and we cannot entirely acquit ourselves of the charge, who, attracted by the polished elegance of the style of pagan writers, prefer their works to the holy scriptures. There are others who, although they are deeply attached to the sacred writings and have no liking for most pagan productions, make an exception in favour of the works of Terence, and, fascinated by the charm of the manner, risk being corrupted by the wickedness of the matter.'

Her own plays were part of a new dramatic tradition which arose, paradoxically, within the Church itself. It had begun with the priests chanting brief Latin dialogues during religious observance. This led naturally on to the development of a liturgical drama, and gradually its performance became infiltrated by an artistic awareness.

Bible stories were re-enacted, first in Latin, and then translated into the vernacular. Sets and costumes were devised and the presentations became more and more elaborate. At first the actors were clerics, with choirboys and junior clerics in the women's parts. Then laymen were invited to join the cast and play the non-Christian parts, lusty opponents to the forces of good. The mixture became uneasy . . .

The emergence of a new and vigorous drama became embarrassing to the sober clergy and too exuberant to be contained by the Church. It burst out into the streets where it found a ready audience and patrons in the form of guilds and other civic authorities. They were in fact the first 'angels', funding and mounting plays and insisting upon discipline and standards.

At Valenciennes in 1547 actors had to sign a contract before a public notary. It stated the days on which the actor had to perform (only illness being admitted as an excuse for not doing so); the part, or parts allocated, which he must accept without argument; and that he must not indulge in recriminations with the producer, not get drunk, and so on. It reads like a normal West End contract.

Civil authorities now took it upon themselves to stone actors with sanctions when they felt they had been let down. At Beverley in 1520, the Painters' Company was fined two shillings 'Because their play of *The Three Kings of Colleyn* was badly and confusedly played, in contempt of the whole community, before many strangers.' Good old Yorkshire civic pride.

Nevertheless standards declined once more as the drama was carried on to a large extent by uneducated people, separated from the learning and discipline of the Church. A drama which had been joyously played out as a collective act of worship deteriorated, in many places, to the level of rather shoddy amateur theatricals. Sometimes the actors didn't even bother to learn their parts. Here's an account by Richard Carew, a contemporary of Shakespeare's, of a performance he watched in Cornwall in 1602. 'The players conne not their parts without book, but are prompted by one called the Ordinary, who followeth at their back with the book in his hand, and telleth them softly what they must pronounce aloud.'

No doubt Shakespeare himself was a witness to this kind of rustic incompetence: hence the 'Pyramus and Thisbe' interlude in *A Midsummer Night's Dream.*

Through the latter part of the Middle Ages, an alternative or 'fringe' theatre had been steadily growing. These were the strolling players, troupes of actors who considered themselves professionals and travelled from place to place equipped with costumes, props and a portable backdrop, performing plays and improvising to suit the occasion. The strongest development in this genre was the *Commedia dell' arte all' improviso,* in Italy: improvised comedy in which a company of professional and highly accomplished entertainers would play a number of stock characters within a loosely constructed story line. So high was their standard that the actors achieved recognition as artists and began to analyse and record their methods of work. And here, *at last* women were brought into the cast, playing their legitimate parts.

General enthusiasm for *Commedia dell' arte* spread out of Italy across Europe. Audiences loved it. Actors admired and imitated it.

In spite of their talent and popularity, the players of the sixteenth century were often in great difficulty over finding a place to stage their performance. Laws governing public assembly could be tightened up and turned against them by disapproving civic authorities and this did happen, so that acting once again became a hazardous occupation.

Within the City of London, companies of players were banding together and performing wherever they could find a suitable place: often in the courtyards of inns. But the disapproving City Fathers and Puritan preachers did their best to prevent them finding a foothold. The laws were tightened up to a point where it was dangerous to stage a performance unless you had the protection of a powerful patron. By 1572, a player staging a casual performance risked brutal consequences: 'to be grievously whipped and burnt through the gristle of the right ear with a hot iron of the compass of an inch about, manifesting his or her roguish kind of life.' Second offences were judged to be felonies and third offences entailed death 'without benefit of sanctuary or clergy.'

Such was the power of the critics in those days. To give them their due, the Puritan opponents of the theatre went about their task with a rare dedication. *Histrio mastix*, a book running to 1006 pages, was published in 1632 by one William Prynne, who as a young man attended four dramatic performances in London. He was so shocked by what he saw that he devoted the next seven years of his life to collecting under one cover all that had been said against the theatre in the scriptures and the writings of the Church Fathers — indeed, much of the saintly disapproval I quoted earlier was found in Prynne's book. A later Puritan critic, Jeremy Collier, was so assiduous in attending and writing up the theatre he disapproved of that he left behind him a considerable body of criticism at a time when live performances were hardly ever described. His writings have been quoted in the main body of the book.

While players were being persecuted by the City authorities, Queen Elizabeth was taking an evident delight in the entertainments provided at court by her Master of Revels. She watched as many as eight plays in one Christmas season. At first these were performed by boy players, but when she discovered the skill of adult professionals her favour swung towards them. In 1574 she granted a patent to the Earl of Leicester's Company, permitting him to perform regularly in London. Later the same year the Court of Common Council of London passed an act discouraging competition: 'No play, Comedy or Tragedy . . . shall be openly played within the liberties of the city which shall not first be perused . . . by such persons as by the Lord Mayor and Court Aldermen.'

This censorship cannot have been viewed with much joy by the playwrights and actors. By now the dramatic art was developing fast and needed room to breathe. The simple solution lay outside the 'liberties of the city' in Shoreditch. In 1576, a joiner turned impresario, James Burbage, took a huge gamble and borrowed money to construct a building whose sole purpose would be to present plays. It was called the Theatre.

Success was immediate. Within twenty-two years four similar ventures got off the ground. The theatre in England was established. It grew roots firm enough to withstand the ravishings of the plague, civil war and Puritan rule. In 1660 Charles II granted patents to Sir William Davenant and Thomas Killigrew, permitting them to build theatres and organize companies, since when its survival has never been in question.

I offer this slender account of the early theatre and some of its enemies as a background to what follows — and as evidence of the miracle of the theatre's survival.

It will always be a point of controversy and criticism. Whether arguments rage over style of acting, writing, content of plays or directorial approach, at the very least something will be happening to engage heart and mind.

And whenever a theatre has contented itself with bland fare a critic somewhere, thank God, has denounced it. I think particularly of the long years when drawing-room comedy held the West End in its grip, and to lend example I quote four of them spanning fifty years, who shared an intense dislike of the vogue:

Max Beerbohm, 1905: In the course of a theatrical season, the critic's proud spirit is gradually subdued. Twaddling play succeeds twaddling play, and as the wearisome procession goes by, the critic's protests become fainter . . .

Ivor Brown, 1926: Out of nothing nothing comes. The mind of the dramatic critic returns despairingly to the Lucretian tag. Night after night we spend some two and a half hours watching the process whereby a dull young woman is transferred from wedlock with a dull young man to wedlock with one still duller.

James Agate, 1932: When a play is crashingly dull the critic has only two resources. One is sleep, in justification whereof I shall quote William Archer's dictum that the first qualification for a dramatic critic is the capacity to sleep while sitting bolt upright.

Bernard Levin, 1959: These plays are inimical to our theatre, because they declare that the stage need not be concerned with life, and they are dangerous to our society, because they imply that it is perfect and invincible.

The stale convention died out. It can be argued that if it took so long to do so, the critics can't have been all that powerful. Nonetheless, they set their shoulders to the task of heaving the torpid giant out — because they were bored, yes, but also because they cared for the state of the theatre.

Other and more positive examples of this care have occurred when critics have championed the cause of a new playwright or actor — for instance, Bernard Shaw and William Archer proclaiming the genius of Ibsen in the face of widespread opposition.

For actors survival in the theatre under criticism is hardest of all. By survival I don't mean making a living. I mean the hazard of keeping a reputation through succeeding generations. It is in the nature of our profession — perhaps a vital source of stimulation — that a great actor or actress is recognised but must eventually be eclipsed by another. Leigh Hunt wrote, 'We believe it was the opinion of a great many besides ourselves that Kean did extinguish Kemble: at all events we hold it for certain that Kean hastened his going out . . . Garrick's nature displaced Quin's formalism: and in precisely the same way did Kean displace Kemble . . . It was as sure a thing as Nature against Art, or tears against cheeks of stone.'

Styles of acting have radically changed over the years, and these days naturalism predominates. Much is talked of playing the 'truth' of a character or situation as if it were the exclusive discovery of the twentieth century — well, it isn't, as the following prove:

Colley Cibber 1671-1757: What made the merit of Kynaston and Betterton was that they both observed the rules of truth and nature.

David Garrick 1717-1779: The only way to arrive at great excellency in characters is to be very conversant with human nature . . . by this way you will more accurately discover the workings of spirit . . .

Sarah Siddons 1755-1831: When a part is first put before me for studying, I look it over in a general way to see if it is in Nature, and if it is, I am sure it can be played.

William Charles Macready 1793-1873: Whatever might extend my experience of the various aspects of human nature I regarded as needful and imperative study. Under this persuasion I braced my nerves to go through the lunatic asylum . . . I watched every movement, every play of features of those stricken creatures. I was reading one of the most harrowing pages out of Nature's book, and so faithfully conned over that every character was impressed indelibly on my memory. I took from thence lessons, painful ones indeed, that in after years added to the truth of my representations.

I remember listening to an ancient recording of Sarah Bernhardt as Phèdre, a part in which we are told she excelled, and whilst I applauded her vocal technique in passionate delivery, I felt nothing more. Worse, young actors and actresses listening to it with me laughed, and I began to wonder what on earth would happen if, by magic, we could summon up other legendary figures and place them on a contemporary stage. Perhaps the emotional truths of one generation would inevitably become the laughing-stock of the next. And anyway, as in the case of this book, why dig up their old reviews and reassess them in such a negative light? Precisely because criticism is the thread that gathers them together. So, by juxtaposing Shaw and Levin, Plato and Tynan, all jumbled up according to arbitrary factors like the alphabetical ordering of plays, or actors' names, I hope I have created a mixture which will give readers a laugh and, at the same time, pause for thought. The best critics have always done this. If they weren't entertaining, they would soon lose their readers — in the same manner as a boring play. Indeed, a number of critics have themselves been writers of plays and other theatrical productions — and you will notice that these have not been immune from attack by their fellows.

Where famous names in the theatre are missing from these pages, let me hasten to say that it is not because they have had no bad reviews. It has been my guiding principle, not once disproved in the course of my researches, that everyone has a bad notice somewhere. But there were times when the specimen I found was so dull that it didn't seem worth giving space to it.

I should also add a warning to the scholarly. You may find occasional lapses in accuracy in some of the reviews that follow. When they came pouring through the post as a result of my original request, I tracked down as many as I could to check that the wording was right. But some eluded me, often because the actor or actress in question, while retaining an all too vivid impression of the painful phrase, had lost track of the details: writer, publication date, even place or play. But I decided to use them anyway, the important thing being what they remembered over the years.

If the longer reviews are not organised on the page exactly as they originally appeared (in terms of punctuation, paragraphing and so on) this is because many have been sent in by kind friends in the profession in a form that comes more easily to us than typing, i.e., performed into a cassette recorder.

There are so many wonderful qualities to be found in the theatre, and courage predominates. At the risk of appearing to bang the professional drum, I think it takes guts to act. Certainly no life is at stake stepping on stage, simply a reputation should one fail, and the rewards of success are a boost to the ego and bank balance alike. Yet the courage I speak of is there every time an entrance is made, every time an actor or actress undertakes the daring and delicate task of making an audience believe. And another great quality is generosity of spirit, of which the modern part of this book stands evidence.

I therefore dedicate it to all thespians — the lauded, aspiring, failed, past, present and, all joy to them, the future.

CHAPTER ONE

Actors and Actresses in Britain

James Agate, in one of his kinder moments, addressed these words to the acting profession: 'You remind me of a disused pack of cards — all knaves and jokers.'

In abusing us he was in line with a centuries-old tradition. Actors and actresses habitually counter this tradition by turning it into a kind of in-humour. When they get together for dinner, at some point in the evening the talk invariably turns to capping each other's worst reviews.

I like to think of this first section of the book, which is also its foundation, as an extension of that custom, letting the reader in on the joke. It is made up of bad notices for actors and actresses spanning some three centuries of theatre in Britain.

Of the contemporary reviews, a good number were generously contributed at my request by friends and colleagues, starting with my good friend Alec McCowen and, over a dinner table when the idea was new, the conductor Georg Solti (included in the Miscellany section at the end of the book, as he is not an actor).

All quotes which were volunteered are marked with a star, to which I add my thanks to those who sent them. The rest, the unstarred entries (the majority, since they are drawn from the larger time range) have been found by research. If any of the subjects are upset at re-reading their worst reviews, let them pause and consider: we are in good company. We stand alongside the great of all the ages. None have been immune.

As you read through this section, you will see that every device of criticism — sarcasm, ridicule, insidious comparison, or not-even-a-mention — has been levelled against actors over the years, and still they have survived. For the great ones who have gone on what is called the Eternal Tour, their achievement cannot be denied. For those of us who remain in the arena, the battle goes on. How well I know that sinking feeling as one opens the first of the morning-after papers . . .

Max Adrian (1902-73) as Feste in Shakespeare's *Twelfth Night* Aldwych, 1960. Reviewed by Caryl Brahms.

Max Adrian's Feste astonishingly transported that really very fine actor to a kind of cloud cuckoo garden for aged psychos.

Henry Ainley (1879-1945) as Prospero in Shakespeare's *The Tempest*, Sadlers Wells, January, 1934. Reviewed by James Agate in the *Sunday Times.*

Mr Ainley played the old codger like a toastmaster celebrating his golden wedding.

Maria Aitken as Lottie in *When we are Married* by J. B. Priestley. Reviewed in the *Manchester Evening News.*

* Maria Aitken played Lottie inadequately and loudly, heavily padded and resembling nothing so much as a man in drag.

Patrick Allen as the Ghost in BBC TV's production of Shakespeare's *Hamlet,* May, 1980. Reviewed by Clive James in the *Observer.*

Clad in complete steel and a flying panel of what looked like tulle, Patrick Allen, voice-over in a thousand commercials, was a good ghost, although you would not have been stunned to hear him recommend Danish bacon.

Judith Anderson as Irina in *The Seagull* by Anton Chekhov, Old Vic, 1960. Reviewed by Mervyn Jones.

At no single point is she on the same stage as the rest of the company. Nor for that matter is she in Chekhov's play.

Peggy Ashcroft as the Duchess in *The Duchess of Malfi* by John Webster at the Theatre Royal, Haymarket, April, 1945. Reviewed by James Agate.

* Something more than plaintiveness, however touching, is wanted if 'I am Duchess of Malfi still' is not to sound like 'I am still little Miss Muffet'.

and as Imogen in Shakespeare's *Cymbeline,* Stratford-on-Avon, 1957. Reviewed by Kenneth Tynan.

. . . I was prepared to be entranced by Peggy Ashcroft's Imogen until I began to be obsessed by this actress's ocular mannerisms. We all know that she blinks: it was my misfortune to discover that her blinks coincide with the words she intends to emphasize. Having spotted this trick, I watched only for her blinking, and am thus in no position to assess her performance . . .

Richard Attenborough in the film of *Brighton Rock,* by Graham Greene, 1947. Reviewed by Leonard Mosley in the *Daily Express.*

This book is not really about films, but when colleagues have sent amusing film reviews I have put them in.

* The piece was headed 'Brighton Rock doesn't taste right' and Mr Mosley went on to say that Mr Attenborough's Pinkie was about as close to the real thing as Donald Duck to Greta Garbo.

Dorothea Baird (1875-1933) as Rosalind in the Shakespeare Anniversary Celebration, Metropole, Camberwell, April, 1896. Reviewed by George Bernard Shaw in the *Saturday Review.*

Miss Baird's Rosalind is bright and pleasant, with sufficient natural charm to secure indulgence for all its shortcomings. Of these the most serious is Miss Baird's delivery of the lines. Everybody by this time knows how a modern high school mistress talks — how she repudiates the precision, the stateliness, the awe-inspiring oracularity of the old-fashioned schoolmistress who knew nothing, and cloaks her mathematics with a pretty little voice, a pretty little manner, and all sorts of self-conscious calineries and unassumingness. 'Poor little me! What do *I* know about conic sections?' is the effect she aims at. Miss Baird's Rosalind has clearly been to the high school and modelled herself upon her pet mistress, if not actually taught there herself . . .

If I had been Dorothea Baird I would NOT have felt that the flattery in the first sentence atoned for what followed.

Tallulah Bankhead (1902-68) in *He's Mine,* Lyric, October, 1925. Reviewed by Hannen Swaffer in the *Daily Express.*

A plonking, damp squib of a review, the kind of thing an actress least *likes to read over the morning toast . . .*

. . . Although Tallulah did not undress, as usual, she lay down on the bed and she got into it, and a maid showed some underclothing. Her plan was to trap her lover into her bedroom to force him to marry her. Then they found another man in the cupboard!

This scene was in the approved Tallulah style — tantrums, and fake tears, and coaxings, and blazing indiscretions. Still, it didn't come off.

Ronnie Barker as Yepihodov in *The Cherry Orchard* by Chekhov, Playhouse, Oxford, 1951. Reviewed in the *Oxford Times.*

* The most monumental bit of mis-casting this week is Ronald Barker as Yepihodov.

Never has anyone been so much at sea since Columbus. He cried when he should have laughed, clowned when he should have been serious, and generally had everything back to front, including his guitar in the second act, and his lady-friend's favours in the third.

Jill Bennett as the Queen in *The Eagle has Two Heads,* by Jean Cocteau, adapted by Ronald Duncan, Chichester Festival Theatre, 1979. Reviewed by Nicholas de Jongh in the *Guardian.*

* . . . a deaf and dumb servant looks like someone guarding the doorway of a Turkish restaurant in London, the Chief of Police looks like Shylock, while Jill Bennett in the leading role is acted off the stage by her costumes.

and as Gertrude in Shakespeare's *Hamlet*, Royal Court, 1980. Reviewed by Irving Wardle in *The Times*.

. . . Jill Bennett's Gertrude is the most unmaternal performance I have ever seen of that role . . .

Mr Bensley, an eighteenth century English actor as Glanville, discussed in *The Devil's Copybook, 1786.*

Mr Bensley's Glanville only operates to awaken those sentiments in the mind which will occur when we are confined to the mortification of seeing and hearing him performing, namely sentiments of amazement that a man so weakly gifted and repulsive in almost every faculty that is necessary to the completion of an actor should have interest and effrontery sufficient to appear before a rational audience. It may be a compliment to the charity of the nation that such a man is permitted to perform, but it likewise conveys the awkward implication that a British audience can be insulted with impunity.

Survive that one if you can.

Constance Benson (1860-1946), wife of F. R. Benson and leading actress in his touring company, of which she left a lively record in her book *Mainly Players*. As Titania in Shakespeare's *A Midsummer Night's Dream.* (From *Mainly Players*)

Another drawback of *The Dream* was the fairies. Anyone who has knowledge of 'super' children on tour will realize that they are none too clean, especially in some of the Scottish towns. When I played Titania, in preparation for my fifteen minutes of sleep on the stage, I used to arm myself with a tin of Keatings' [flea-powder], and during the lullaby I soundly peppered the bank 'whereon the wild thyme grows'. But this comforting practice had to be abandoned, as in one criticism we read, 'evidently fairyland is not entirely free from earthly evils, if we are to judge by Titania's action before she retires to sleep.'

For information about 'supers' see page 168.

F. R. Benson (1858-1939). Actor-Manager who founded the touring company which bore his name. They played Shakespeare for many years in the provinces and at the Stratford Festival. As Caliban in Shakespeare's *The Tempest*, Stratford Festival, 1896. Described by Constance Benson.

She didn't mean this as a criticism but, reading it, one suspects the worst.

FRB played Caliban, one of his favourite performances. He spent many hours watching monkeys and baboons in the zoo, in order to get the movements and postures in keeping with his make-up. His old nurse saw him one night, dressed in this curious costume, and exclaimed, 'Oh, Mr. Frank, you are the image of your sister in that dress.' FRB delighted in swarming up a tree on the stage and hanging from the branches head downwards, while he jibbered at Trinculo.

Elisabeth Bergner, a German leading actress who settled in Britain, in *The Boy David*, written for her by J. M. Barrie, His Majesty's, December, 1936. Reviewed by Paul Holt.

Bergner makes the boy David, who sang before Saul and slew the Philistine, a cross between Cinderella and Peter Pan. A blonde Peter Pan with pigtails.

Instead of two ugly sisters he has seven hulking brothers, and he is sent to bed without any supper for telling lies about the lion and the bear he slew.

And, instead of a scene with a crocodile, David sees a great big giant in the gloom and he puts a pebble in his sling and 'Ping!' — the giant falls over with an awful clatter . . .

The snag is that Miss Bergner gets no support from her colleagues in this whimsy. Godfrey Tearle behaves like a King of Israel; John Martin Harvey behaves like a Prophet. Which isn't much good to Bergner behaving like Bergner . . .

Sarah Bernhardt (1844-1923). Of her debut in Racine's *Iphigenie* (1862) the critic Sarcey wrote:

Mlle Bernhardt is a tall, pretty girl with a slender figure and a very pleasing expression. The upper part of her face is remarkably beautiful. She holds herself well, and her enunciation is perfectly clear. That is all that can be said for her at present.

This should give encouragement to any young actress who has suffered from a dismissive review for her first part.

and as Magda in *Heimat,* by Hermann Sudermann, Daly's, June, 1895. Reviewed by George Bernard Shaw in the *Saturday Review.*

Madame Bernhardt has the charm of a jolly maturity, rather spoilt and petulant, perhaps, but always ready with a sunshine-through-the-clouds smile if only she is made much of. Her dresses and diamonds, if not exactly splendid, are splendacious; her figure, far too scantily upholstered in the old days, is at its best; her complexion shews that she has not studied modern art in vain . . . She paints her ears crimson and allows them to peep charmingly through a few loose braids of her auburn hair. Every dimple has its dab of pink; and her fingertips are so delicately incarnadined that you fancy they are transparent like her ears, and that the light is shining through their delicate blood-vessels. Her lips are like a newly painted pillar box; her cheeks, right up to the languid lashes, have the bloom and surface of a peach; she is beautiful with the beauty of her school, and entirely inhuman and incredible . . . One feels when the heroine bursts upon the scene, a dazzling vision of beauty, that instead of imposing on you, she adds her own piquancy by looking you straight

Sarah Bernhardt (1881) with John Hollingshead. By Alfred Bryan.
'. . . far too scantily upholstered in the old days . . .'

in the face, and saying, in effect: 'Now who would ever suppose that I am a grandmother?'

Master Betty (William Henry West Betty, 1791-1874), a boy actor who was taken up by the fashionable world. He played Romeo and Hamlet at the age of twelve; he also played Richard III! The craze lasted about two years. Eventually Leigh Hunt, who had campaigned against him, was able to write in the *News*, 1804-5:

The charm of novelty is at length broken . . . and the town is just now somewhat in the position of a husband who, after passing the honeymoon with a beautiful but childish woman, finds his reason once more returning and is content to sit down and ask why he has been pleased.

Thomas Campbell (1774-1844) Mrs Siddons' biographer, wrote:

The popularity of that baby-faced boy, who possessed not even the elements of a good actor, was a hallucination in the public mind, and a disgrace to our theatre history.

Finally, the tide of his popularity having turned, here he is in *Mahomet* at Bath in 1807, reviewed by Mrs Philip Lybbe Powys:

. . . his youth and manner could never make one suppose him the character he represents, and his voice is now quite horrid. The company at Bath did not seem the least sorry at his departure, and the actors, as one might suppose, were much rejoiced.

Claire Bloom as Viola in Shakespeare's *Twelfth Night*, Old Vic, 1953-4. Reviewed in *Time and Tide*.

Claire Bloom played Viola like a wistful little Peter Pan who is worried to death about Tinkerbell.

Madge Brindley in *A Dead Secret* by Rodney Ackland, Piccadilly, 1957. Reviewed by Robert Speaight in the *New Statesman*.

Miss Lummins, as Miss Madge Brindley presents her, is straight out of Rowlandson, and she has a deadly aim with her saliva.

Tony Britton as Lord Illingworth in *A Woman of No Importance* by Oscar Wilde, Duchess, 1968. Reviewed in *Plays and Players*.

Tony Britton's habit of curling his lip villainously and so relentlessly gives one the impression that he has had it permanently waved.

Pamela Brown as Millamant in *The Way of the World* by William Congreve, Lyric, Hammersmith, 1953. Reviewed by Kenneth Tynan.

. . . Millamant must be the empress of her sex, and her words, whether tinkling like a fountain or cascading like Niagara, must always flow from a great height. From Miss Brown's mouth they do not flow at all; they leak . . .

Peter Bull in *Luther* by John Osborne, Paris, 1960.

* When we took *Luther* to Paris the posters quite calmly announced, 'Albert Finney dans *Luther* avec Peter Dull.'

Richard Burton as Caliban in Shakespeare's *The Tempest*, Old Vic, 1954. Reviewed in the *Sunday Express*.

It was in this same production that Robert Hardy also received his worst review, page 29.

As for Richard Burton's Caliban, there is no possible explanation, so I will attempt none. He looked like a miner with a tail coming up from a coal face.

Simon Callow in *Amadeus* by Peter Shaffer, directed by Peter Hall, Olivier, National, 1979. Reviewed by Benedict Nightingale.

* Mozart, played by Simon Callow as a goonish cross between a chimp and a donkey . . .

and of a performance of Shakespeare's sonnets, National, July, 1980.

Simon Callow was wildly applauded at the end — but not by me. If he had spent his time with a ferret down his trousers or stuffing his face with hard-boiled eggs, I might have been more impressed.

Mrs Patrick Campbell (1865-1940) as Juliet in Shakespeare's *Romeo and Juliet*, Lyceum, September, 1895. Reviewed in *Punch*.

. . . As for the final stabbing, she might as well have tickled herself with a straw and died o' laughing.

and in *Fedora*, Herman Merivale's translation of the play by Victorien Sardou, Haymarket, May, 1895. Reviewed again by George Bernard Shaw.

It is greatly to Mrs Patrick Campbell's credit that, bad as the play was, her acting was worse. It was a masterpiece of failure . . .
It cannot, I think, be disputed now that Mrs Campbell's force, which is intense enough, has only one mode, and that one vituperative. This was proved at one stroke in the first act, when Fedora goes to her husband's bedside and discovers him dead, Mrs Campbell uttered a shriek, as any actress would; but it was a shriek that suggested nothing of grief, or mortally wounded tenderness, or even horror . . . In short, it was a scream of rage . . .

Mr Carne in *A Leader of Men* by E. D. Ward, Comedy, February, 1895. Reviewed by George Bernard Shaw in the *Saturday Review*.

Something was supposed to be wrong with Mr Carne's acting as the Archdeacon. The defect was really in his wig, which was a powdered servant's wig, and gave him an irresistible air of being his own coachman.

I don't know who Mr Carne was — Shaw's index doesn't even give him an initial — but how expertly this tiny stone is cast.

Julie Christie in a Birmingham Rep. Revue. She had to sing a blues song alone on stage. The local daily paper said the next day:

* Julie Christie should never, ever, be allowed to sing unaccompanied on stage again.

Diane Cilento in *Naked* by Pirandello, Royal Court, April, 1963. Reviewed by Roger Gellert in the *New Statesman.*

Diane Cilento, an attractive but unreal blend of Nefertiti and Sheila Hancock, wages a losing battle to convince us that we ought to care.

John Cleese in the film of the Amnesty Show, Her Majesty's. Reviewed by Roger Gellert in the *New Statesman.*

* And then John Cleese appears. He walks across the stage, rather stiffly, and the audience collapses. He sits down and opens up an *Evening Standard:* loud barks of merriment fill the auditorium like rifle shots. There is, however, something peculiar about Mr Cleese. He emits an air of overwhelming vanity combined with some unspecific nastiness, like a black widow spider on heat. But nobody seems to notice. He could be reciting Fox's *Book of Martyrs* in Finnish and these people would be rolling out of their seats.

Tom Courtenay as Lord Fancourt Babberley in *Charley's Aunt* by Brandon Thomas, directed by Braham Murray, Apollo, December, 1971. Reviewed by Frank Marcus.

Tom Courtenay as Charley's Aunt reminded me of Whistler's Mother.

Tom Courtenay in Charley's Aunt *as Lord Fancourt Babberley with Wolfe Morris as Stephen Spettigue. Courtesy of* Punch.

William Augustus Conway in Shakespeare's *Romeo and Juliet,* Covent Garden, 1814. Reviewed by Hazlitt.

Of Mr Conway's Romeo we cannot speak with patience . . . There is, we suppose, no reason why this preposterous phenomenon should not be at once discarded from the stage, but for the suppressed titter of secret satisfaction which circulates through the dress-boxes whenever he appears. Why does he not marry?

And we complain that modern critics are rude.

Annette Crosbie as Sarah Davenport in *My Place* by Elaine Dundy, Comedy, February, 1962.

* Annette Crosbie, who is normally an intelligent actress, if nothing else, spent the evening chasing her voice about the stage as if it were an escaped canary . . .

and in Shakespeare's *Twelfth Night*

* Annette Crosbie played Viola like a Shetland pony.

* **Cyril Cusack** once played the leading role of Ernest/John Worthing in *The Importance of Being Earnest* by Oscar Wilde and was the only member of the cast not to get a mention in a review the following morning.

Paul Daneman as Richard in Shakespeare's *Richard III*, Old Vic, March, 1962. Reviewed by Bernard Levin in the *Daily Express.*

Clearly little thought has gone into Mr Paul Daneman's Richard. He seems to think that the more he sends up the lines, the funnier the part will be, which is true.

Frances de la Tour in *Duet for One* by Tom Kempinski, Duke of York's, September, 1980. Reviewed by Michael Billington in the *Guardian.*

* Frances de la Tour, looking astonishingly like James Coburn's twin sister . . .

Judi Dench as Regan in Shakespeare's *King Lear* Stratford-on-Avon, 1976. Reviewed by Irving Wardle in *The Times.*

Judi Dench's Regan compensates for her strong scowl with a nervous speech impediment which, no doubt, is all Lear's fault.

Judi Dench herself felt her Regan was a failure and withdrew from the production before it transferred to the Aldwych. She confessed as much in a Times *interview after the event. Her remarks then show that Wardle at least picked up the psychological reading she had intended: that Regan's nastiness was all Daddy's fault. Here is Dench by Dench.*

'I simply couldn't get it right. I had this theory that she couldn't be all bad . . . I thought maybe it was all to do with her relationship with Lear, so whenever she was with him I gave her a stammer.

Sonia Dresdel (1909-1976) in *Doctor Jo* by Joan Morgan, Aldwych, February, 1956. Reviewed by Kenneth Tynan in the *Observer*.

. . .What catches one's astounded eye is Sonia Dresdel's performance as the marauding sister, replete with gargantuan *oeillades* and a fund of reminiscences ranging from the joys of the garden ('I love it, every green blade of grass') to the problems of fighting the tsetse fly. This is a character-study worthy of Joan Crawford; an antiseptic, over-dressed, malarial virgin who acquired, in one of my more frivolous nightmares, the nickname of Boofy Schweitzer. A definite curiosity value attaches to Miss Dresdel's attempts to convey benevolence and self-sacrifice. Her affectionate scenes with a young nephew are especially sinister, it being apparent that, given the smallest textual encouragement, Miss Dresdel could and would bite her little friend's arm off at the elbow. It is to the Eumenides, and not to the humanities, that this intimidating actress should confine herself.

Eleonora Duse. By C. de Fornaro.

Gerald du Maurier and **Gladys Cooper** in *The Last of Mrs Cheyney* by Frederick Lonsdale, St James's, September, 1925. Reviewed by Hannen Swaffer in the *Sunday Express*.

. . . 'Do you know? Du Maurier moved his face twice!' said a friend. 'He must have remembered he wasn't at Wyndham's now!'
    'Isn't she beautiful?' they said, of course, of Miss Cooper. I am getting a little tired of that remark.

Eleonora Duse (1858-1924). Duse bewitched and disarmed critics to the point where serious criticism, such as Ivor Brown's complaint that he could not hear what she said, was buried in a great hymn of praise for her sensibility etc. For example:

. . . I saw a wraith-like figure, as grey as gracious, move with infinity of beauty through a simple peasant tragedy. Had my Italian been of the soundest I doubt whether I could have understood her. She mumbled her part, but even her mumbling had a beauty denied to many a rare mistress of speech.

Max Beerbohm, however, was immune to her spell. He wrote of her as Hedda in *Hedda Gabler* by Ibsen, May, 1907:

. . . in this, as in every part she plays, she behaved like a guardian angel half-asleep at her post over humanity. Her air of listlessness, in this instance, happened to be apt; but otherwise she showed not a shadow of comprehension of her part.

Paul Eddington in *Komuso,* Arts, 1955. Reviewed in the *Financial Times.*

* Paul Eddington plays a howling cad in a topee who gives his hostess an unaccustomed nip of gin, seduces her during an earthquake and appears in the last act in riding breeches and boots — or did one dream it?

Robert Eddison in Shakespeare's *Twelfth Night,* Old Vic, November, 1950. Reviewed in *Bandwagon,* Jan/Feb, 1951.

* . . . Robert Eddison plays a conventional Sir Andrew Aguecheek, looking like a dripping toffee-apple.

and as Mephistopheles in *Dr Faustus* by Christopher Marlowe, New, 1948. Reviewed by Harold Hobson in the *Sunday Times.*

Mr Eddison's haunted Mephistopheles has a fine melancholy. So had his recent Feste, so had Hamlet. I expect that this rising actor will shortly give us a finely melancholy Charley's Aunt.

Edith Evans (1888-1976) as the Countess in Shakespeare's *All's Well That Ends Well,* Stratford-on-Avon, 1959. Reviewed by Kenneth Tynan.

. . . The role of the Countess, curiously described by Shaw as the most beautiful old woman's part ever written (it is in fact merely the only old woman's part in Shakespeare that is neither a scold nor a murderess), is played by Dame Edith in her characteristic later manner — tranquillized benevolence cascading from a great height, like royalty opening a bazaar.

I was a walk-on in this production and was so deeply in awe of everything and everybody that I cannot comment upon Tynan's notice — except to say that Dame Edith was every bit as majestic off-stage as on.

Mia Farrow as Puck in Shakespeare's *A Midsummer Night's Dream,* Haymarket, Leicester, February, 1976. Reviewed by Irving Wardle in *The Times.*

Visually, Miss Farrow is superbly equipped for parts like Puck and Ariel . . . when she uncoils from a dark corner and spreads her hands, she seems to be heralding something unearthly, but the performance that follows rather brings things down to the level of the Artful Dodger.

Albert Finney in the title role of *Tamburlaine the Great* by Marlowe, Olivier, National, October, 1976. Reviewed by Arthur Thirkell.

With his full mane of curly hair and dressed in a gold-encrusted tightly fitting mini-skirted costume, he struck me as more of an overweight elf than the savage conqueror of Asia.

and by John Peter.

. . . he soon retreats into snarling statuesque balefulness, giving in part one a portrait of the tyrant as a young bull, in part two a portrait of the tyrant as an old bull.

and by the *Wimbledon News.*

Albert Finney playing King of the World much as he played most of his stage successes, as King of the Teds.

Albert Finney as Tamburlaine with Denis Quilley as Bajazeth in Tamburlaine the Great. *Courtesy of* Punch.

David Garrick (1717-1779), leading actor of his day, equally admired in contemporary plays and in Shakespeare. His 'naturalistic' acting drove out the more formal, declamatory style of Quin, his predecessor in popularity. Garrick's greatest part was Lear — played in a scarlet coat.

Dr Johnson talking about him, as recorded in Fanny Burney's *Diary*, 1778.

An epilogue of Mr Garrick's to *Bonduca* was then mentioned, and Dr Johnson said it was a miserable performance, and everybody agreed it was the worst he had ever made . . . 'I don't know', said Dr Johnson, '. . . what is the matter with David; I am afraid he is grown superannuated, for his prologues and epilogues used to be incomparable.

'Nothing is so fatiguing,' said Mrs Thrale, 'as the life of a wit; he and Wilkes are the two oldest men of their ages I know, for they have both worn themselves out by being eternally on the rack to give entertainment to others.'

'David, madam,' said the Doctor, 'looks much older than he is; for his face has had double the business of any other man's; it is never at rest; when he speaks one minute, he has quite a different countenance to what he assumes the next; I don't believe he ever has the same look for half an hour together in the whole course of his life; and such an eternal, restless, fatiguing play of the muscles must certainly wear out a man's face before its real time.'

O Lord, what about a woman's?

John Gielgud as Romeo in Shakespeare's *Romeo and Juliet*, Regent, May, 1924. Reviewed by Ivor Brown.

* Mr Gielgud has the most meaningless legs imaginable.

and in *The Ages of Man,* a solo recital, selected from George Rylands' *Shakespeare Anthology*, 46th Street theatre, New York, 1959. Reviewed by Kenneth Tynan.

* Tynan said it was a pity Gielgud only had two gestures — Gielgud mentioned in passing that he wondered how he could contrive any more without the use of his other members.

and Tynan also wrote of this performance:

I have always felt that Sir John Gielgud is the finest actor on earth from the neck up . . .

Julian Glover as Antony in Shakespeare's *Antony and Cleopatra* Bankside Globe, August, 1973.

* Julian Glover's Antony, who enters red, sweaty and with his bow-tie askew, like some raddled, over-used debs' delight . . .

Dulcie Gray in *Candida* by George Bernard Shaw, Piccadilly, June, 1960. Reviewed by Milton Shulman in the *Evening Standard.*

* As Candida, Miss Dulcie Gray is so worthily earnest that not only can we not imagine that two men would be fighting over her but, worse, we suspect that the winner could be the ultimate loser.

Mrs Guiness, a member of Frank Benson's Company, which toured England in the 1890s, performing the plays of Shakespeare; described by Constance Benson in *Mainly Players.*

Mrs Guiness, I remember, curiously enough, would always get tied

John Gielgud as Hamlet 1934. By Nerman. '. . . the most meaningless legs imaginable . . .'

up in one particular speech in *Twelfth Night,* where Olivia first meets Viola. She would invariably say 'Two chins with lids to it, one black eye, and so forth.' Another time, in the scene with the Friar, her memory failed her, and she made her exit with the following couplet:

Then lead the way, for Father, heaven so shine,
I can't remember another blessed line.

Alec Guinness in *Incident at Vichy* by Arthur Miller, Phoenix, January, 1966. Reviewed in the *New Statesman.*

Guinness has always shown a weakness for saintly parts, for the lofty jaw, the luminous blue stare, the gentle, unnerving answer. Here he indulges his weakness to the full. Mr Miller yearns after living nobility and *Incident at Vichy* envisions it in a form which lures Guinness into playing like a garrulous middle-aged Galahad presenting the Grail on Prize Day at Camelot.

Cedric Hardwicke as Marlowe's *Dr Faustus*, New, September, 1948. Reviewed by Hubert Griffith in the *Sunday Graphic.*

He conducted the soul-selling transaction with the thoughtful dignity of a grocer selling a pound of cheese.

Robert Hardy as Ariel in Shakespeare's *The Tempest,* Old Vic, April, 1954. Directed by Robert Helpmann.

Hardy says: 'My appearance was, I suppose, unusual for that period — it was 1954 — in that I wore next to nothing, except a sort of genital sunburst, little wings on my legs, and an overall colour one might describe as faintly saffron with sparkles.

'Among the killers were these words from a Catholic paper:'

* Mr Hardy was for some unexplained reason painted the colour of an auk's egg, and postured throughout like a stone hatstand in a Second Empire Turkish bath.

Robert Harris in Shakespeare's *Cymbeline,* Stratford-on-Avon, July, 1957. Reviewed by Felix Barker in the *Evening News.*

There seems something a little wooden about Robert Harris's king. Cymbeline is an unrewarding part, but surely he is more than a testy Father Christmas in cricket pads.

Robert Helpmann as Oberon in *The Fairy Queen* by William Purcell, adapted by Constant Lambert, Covent Garden, 1946. Reviewed by Kenneth Tynan.

* Lastly there was Robert Helpmann, who was very desolate. He pads and prowls about the draughty arena in a most sinister fashion (with only a prodigious cloak to comfort him), looking very severely at the pit. Male dancers, said Leigh Hunt, loftily, are commonly *gawkies,* but Mr. Helpmann begs the question by not dancing at all. One

imagines he shot a sidelong glance at Miss Rawlings, concluded (rightly) that she was several stones too heavy for him, and then set out to sulk for the rest of the evening. He speaks a good deal of verse in his thin, ascetic voice, glowering all the time with his aghast little hatchet face; and he occupies his silences by trying to intimidate the audience with his favourite facial expression: that appalled look out of the corner of his eye, as who should say 'My God, there's an owl on my shoulder'.

and as Shylock in Shakespeare's *The Merchant of Venice,* Old Vic, January, 1957. Reviewed in *The Bulletin,* Sydney, Australia.

Robert Helpmann's Shylock, hook-nosed, gesticulating and White-chapel-German in accent, amounts rather to caricature — his voice has all the finesse of a ventriloquist's doll.

Wendy Hiller in the title role of *St Joan* by George Bernard Shaw, Malvern Festival, July, 1936. Criticized in a personal letter from Shaw.

* My dear Wendy,
   I had another look at St Joan and saw you trying your pet stunts for all they were worth. They failed completely, as I told you they would . . .

and as Hermione in Shakespeare's *The Winter's Tale,* Old Vic, 1955-6 a critic wrote:

She treats Shakespeare's words as banisters to slide down, and reaches the end of her speeches with a hearty thump. In one oration . . . she appeared to be suddenly seized by an extraordinary fit of verbal scrupulosity, and pronounced every syllable with the care of a conscientious teacher dictating to a class of backward foreigners.

Mrs Holden a late seventeenth century actress as Lady Capulet in Shakespeare's *Romeo and Juliet.* Performance reviewed in *Roscius Anglicanus,* or *An Historical View of the Stage,* pub. 1708.

There being a fight and scuffle in this play between the House of Capulet and the House of Paris, Mrs Holden acting his wife entered in a hurry crying 'Oh my dear Count.' She inadvertently left out the 'o' in the pronunciation of the word 'count', giving it a vehement accent, put the house into such a laughter that London Bridge at low tide was silence to it.

Ian Holm in *The Wars of the Roses:* Shakespeare's *Richard III* Stratford-on-Avon, July, 1963. Reviewed in *The Times.*

* Mr Holm still presents Gloucester as a likeable juvenile, open-faced and friendly in spite of his hump and surgical boot. Mr Holm's reading . . . fails totally to develop into Satanic magnitude. Instead of the boar, the bottle spider or the hunchbacked toad, Mr Holm remains a high-spirited minor; he exhausts his lung-power in the

later scenes, but finishes up on Bosworth Field, loaded down with an armoury of medieval weapons, crooning to himself like a baby inside his visor.

Morag Hood as Natasha in the BBC2 production of *War and Peace* by Tolstoy, 1972. Reviewed by Clive James in the *Observer.*

* As for Morag Hood's Natasha . . . Miss Hood has been excellent in other things and will be excellent again, once she has got over being told to jump up and down rapidly on the spot, lithp with her sinuses, skip on to the set like Rebecca of Sunnybrook Farm and declare with a jaw well-nigh dislocated by youthful vitality that she is Natasha Rostov. Poor mite, can she help it if she arouses throughout the country an unquenchable desire to throw a tarpaulin over her and nail down the corners?

Anthony Hopkins in the title role in *Coriolanus*, National Theatre at the Old Vic, May, 1971.

[Hopkins was] dressed like a cross between a fisherman and an SS man, evoking doggedly a Welsh rugby captain at odds with his supporters' club.

Michael Hordern as Cassius in Shakespeare's *Julius Caesar,* Old Vic, October, 1958. Reviewed in the *Sunday Times.*

* Michael Hordern's Cassius has an anxious air. This Cassius watches John Phillips' alarmingly tall Brutus like an insurance agent estimating how much life cover he can offer without insisting on a medical examination.

and as Malvolio in Shakespeare's *Twelfth Night,* Old Vic, 1953-4. Reviewed by J. C. Trewin in *The Lady.*

As Malvolio, his smile, when it came, reminds one of a crumpled tin tray after a lorry has ground over it.

Alan Howard in Shakespeare's *Richard II,* Aldwych, November, 1981. Reviewed by Robert Cushman in the *Observer.*

Almost my first impression at Tuesday's premiere of *Richard II* was of Alan Howard in the title role addressing his uncle Gaunt as 'old John of York, time-honoured Lancaster', a dynastic confusion that if spotted in time might have prevented the Wars of the Roses.

Gayle Hunnicutt as Viola in Shakespeare's *Twelfth Night* at Greenwich. Reviewed by Bernard Levin.

* Miss Hunnicutt's Viola was not Patience on a Monument — it was a monument of patience!

and as *Peter Pan* by J. M. Barrie, Shaftesbury, December, 1979. Reviewed by Irving Wardle in *The Times.*

Gayle Hunnicutt, this year's Peter, supplies an advertising industry view of the role . . . This Peter is clearly not going to spend his future camping out in an obscure tree house.

Wilfrid Hyde-White in *Not in the Book* by Arthur Watkyn, Criterion, April, 1958.

Alas, in researching, important details sometimes get lost. I cannot find the critic in this case, but his sketch of the actor is as effective as a cartoon.

Precise, half-desiccated and very wary, Wilfred Hyde White prowls around the stage in search of laughs with all the blank single-mindedness of a tortoise on a lettuce hunt.

Henry Irving (1838-1905), actor-manager who dominated the London stage for the last thirty years of Queen Victoria's reign. Discussed by George Bernard Shaw in the *Saturday Review,* September, 1896.

Sir Henry Irving as Hamlet. By Blackburn.

A prodigious deal of nonsense has been written about Sir Henry Irving's conception of this, that, or the other Shakespeare character. The truth is that he has never in his life conceived or interpreted the characters of any author except himself. He is really as incapable of acting another man's play as Wagner was of setting another man's libretto.

Henry James, who was far from polite about the English theatre in general, had this to say about Irving (1877):

To a stranger desiring to know how the London stage stands, I should say, 'Go and see this gentleman; then tell me what you think of him.' And I should expect the stranger to come back and say, 'I see what you mean. The London stage has reached that pitch of mediocrity at which Mr Henry Irving overtops his fellows.'

Glenda Jackson as Gudrun in *Woman in Love,* the film of D. H. Lawrence's novel. Reviewed by Jack de Manio, BBC Radio.

* Glenda Jackson has a face to launch a thousand dredgers.

Glenda Jackson. Courtesy of Punch.

Barbara Jefford as Beatrice in Shakespeare's *Much Ado About Nothing,* Old Vic, October, 1956. Reviewed by Derek Granger in the *Financial Times.*

Miss Barbara Jefford's Beatrice delivers herself of her vaunted raillery with brisk competence and dispatch, rather in the manner of a stalwart school captain bossing the hockey team to victory.

Celia Johnson in *St Joan* by George Bernard Shaw, Old Vic, December, 1947. Reviewed in the *Daily Graphic.*

Celia Johnson, in the title role, might I feel have played Jim Hawkins in *Treasure Island.*

Freddie Jones remembers the following about himself which he thinks was in the *Daily Express*.

* When I go to see a whodunnit, I find myself trying to discover who did it. I begin by looking amongst the more improbable red herrings. Freddie Jones playing a gum-chewing, provincial aspiring journalist was not only improbable as a red herring and a journalist — he even contrived to be improbable as a human being.

and as Pompey in an epic film of *Antony and Cleopatra* with Charlton Heston directing and playing the lead, which enjoyed a notice headed:

* THE BIGGEST ASP DISASTER IN THE WORLD

Edmund Kean (1787-1833) ranks as one of the geniuses of the English stage. He once played opposite the great Siddons, who thought he played well but was too small a man to amount to much. In 1814 he was given his chance at Drury Lane and chose Shylock as his first role there: his success was immediate. The freshness of Kean's interpretations, his energy and violence of emotion, were in direct contrast to the postures and recitations of John Philip Kemble, whom he supplanted.

In Shakespeare's *Romeo and Juliet* Drury Lane, 1815. Reviewed by Hazlitt.

His Romeo has nothing of the lover in it. We never saw anything less ardent or less voluptuous. In the Balcony scene in particular, he was cold, tame, and unimpressive. It was said of Garrick and [James] Barry in this scene, that the one acted it as if he would jump up to the lady, and the other as if he would make the lady jump down to him. Mr Kean produced neither of these effects. He stood like a statue of lead . . . The only time in this scene when he attempted to give anything like an effect, was when he smiled on over-hearing Juliet's confession of her passion. But the smile was less like that of a fortunate lover who unexpectedly hears his happiness confirmed, than of a discarded lover who hears of the disappointment of a rival . . .

Penelope Keith in *The Apple Cart* by George Bernard Shaw, Chichester, 1977.

* Miss Keith plays Orinthia as though she has lost the last race at Goodwood.

Penelope Keith added that she couldn't make up her mind whether she was supposed to have been riding, or betting on the horse.

John Philip Kemble (1757-1823), brother of Sarah Siddons, was assessed as a cold, clinical and correct actor who took punctilious care in 'the disposition of his mantle'. He played leading Shakespearean roles, of which his Coriolanus was considered to be the greatest. He was the first actor to introduce historically authentic costuming on the stage.

Here he is discussed by Charles Lamb in the *London Magazine,* April, 1822.

He flagged sometimes in the intervals of tragic passion. He would slumber over the level parts of an heroic character. His Macbeth has been known to nod . . . The story of his swallowing opium pills to keep him lively upon the first night of a certain tragedy, we may assume to be a piece of retaliatory pleasantry on the part of the suffering author. But, indeed, John had the art of diffusing a complacent equable dullness (which you could not quarrel with) over a piece which he did not like . . .

Fanny Kemble (1809-93) was the daughter of Charles Kemble, and Sarah Siddons' niece. With that genealogy, everybody expected a great deal of her. Her initial appearance as Juliet created a flurry of enthusiasm, but when the novelty wore off she was found wanting.

Leigh Hunt on her first performance as Juliet in 1829.

The moment she gave us the first burst of feeling, our expectations fell many degrees, and they never rose again . . .

Stephen Kemble (1758-1822), the younger brother of John Kemble, was a much less successful actor. In later life his girth was so huge that he played Falstaff without padding.

In Shakespeare's *Henry IV,* Part I and *The Merry Wives of Windsor* Drury Lane, 1816. Reviewed by Hazlitt.

The town has been entertained this week by seeing Mr Stephen Kemble in the part of Sir John Falstaff . . . We see no more reason why Mr Stephen Kemble should play Falstaff, than why Louis XVIII is qualified to fill a throne, because he is fat, and belongs to a particular family.

Rachel Kempson in *Jacobowsky and the Colonel* by Franz Werfel, adapted by S. N. Behrman, Piccadilly, June, 1945. Reviewed by James Agate.

Miss Rachel Kempson as Marianne drenched the southwest corner of France with the authentic perfume of Wimbledon.

Catherine Lacey in *Electra* by Sophocles, Old Vic, 1951. Reviewed by Cecil Wilson in the *Daily Mail.*

Catherine Lacey's Clytemnestra needs only a well-twirled handlebar moustache to complete the caricature of villainy.

Dinsdale Landen in Shakespeare's *The Winter's Tale,* Stratford-on-Avon. Reviewed by Bernard Levin.

* Last night Mr Dinsdale Landen as Florizel managed to destroy the magic of Bohemia in minutes nay seconds.

I was a walk-on in this production too, and remember having to do a particularly exhausting dance in demonstration of Bohemia. Clearly it was to no avail.

and as Beethoven in *The Copyist* by Stephen Deutsch, BBC, May, 1978. Reviewed by Nancy Banks Smith.

* Let's face it, Mr Dinsdale Landen was not born to play Beethoven. However last night he took a running jump at it and landed up as Lon Chaney.

Charles Laughton as Bottom in Shakespeare's *A Midsummer Night's Dream,* Stratford-on-Avon, 1959. Reviewed by Kenneth Tynan.

. . . Finally, we have Charles Laughton, a ginger-wigged, ginger-bearded Bottom. I confess I do not know what Mr. Laughton is up to, but I am sure I would hate to share a stage with it. He certainly takes the audience into his confidence, but the process seems to exclude from his confidence everyone else in the cast. Fidgeting with a lightness that reminds one (even as one forgets what the other actors are talking about) how expertly bulky men dance, he blinks at the pit his moist, reproachful eyes, softly cajoles and suddenly roars, and behaves throughout in a manner that has nothing to do with acting, although it perfectly hits off the demeanour of a rapscallion uncle dressed up to entertain the children at a Christmas party.

I had a walk-on part in this one too. Could there be a connection between my walk-on presence and bad notices?

and in Shakespeare's *Henry VIII,* Sadlers Wells, November, 1933. Reviewed by James Agate.

Mr Laughton came to Sadlers Wells with all his blushing film vulgarities thick upon him.

Gertrude Lawrence (1898-1952) in *Moonlight is Silver* by Clemence Dane, Queen's, September, 1934.

Miss Lawrence's second act frock of black velvet has a *chevaux de frise* of black tulle around the shoulders so exorbitant and breathtaking that, looking at it, play and player vanish. Also, one knows perfectly well that any woman wearing such a frock for the first time would not notice if her husband throttled her. Her self-approbation would be proof against Othello himself.

Margaret Leighton (1922-1976) as Rosalind in Shakespeare's *As You Like It* Stratford-on-Avon, 1952. Reviewed by Kenneth Tynan.

. . . This Rosalind was a gay and giddy creature — loads of fun, game for any jape, rather like a popular head girl — but a tiring companion, I felt, after a long day.

35

Moira Lister in *The Gazebo* by Alec Coppel, Savoy, March, 1960. Reviewed by Bernard Levin.

Miss Moira Lister speaks all her lines as if they are written in very faint ink on a tele-prompter slightly too far away to be read with comfort.

Ralph Lynn in *Wild Horses* by Ben Travers, Aldwych, November, 1957. Reviewed by Harold Hobson in the *Sunday Times.*

Ralph Lynn is an extraordinary actor. His performance in this Ben Travers farce, for example, seems to be entirely independent of the part he is called on to play.

Charles Macready (1793-1873). As Edmund Kean faded from the scene, Macready took over his position as leading tragedian of the English stage. Between 1837 and 1839 he managed a company at Covent Garden, where he did much to clear the theatre of rowdyism and make it a respectable place of entertainment. Restraint came into his acting too, and his style influenced the conversion of theatre from its earlier passions to the gentility of drawing-room realism.

Macready discussed by William Hazlitt.

Mr Macready, sometimes, to express uneasiness and agitation, composes his cravat, as he would in a drawing-room. This is, we think, neither graceful nor natural in extraordinary situations.

and by an unknown critic, whom Macready quoted in his *Diaries:*

* The critic observed that my performance of Beverley in *The Gamester* would have been altogether excellent, if not perfect, but for the unaccommodating disposition of Nature in the formation of my face.

Alec McCowen in *Luther* by John Osborne, BBC1, October, 1965, directed by Alan Cooke. Reviewed by Maurice Richardson.

* . . . an inspired piece of miscasting . . . a frail schizoid pixie in a robust cycloid role . . . it helped if you shut your eyes.

and as Satan in a recital of *Paradise Lost* by John Milton. Reviewed by Allan Massie.

* Worst of all was Alec McCowen as Satan . . . This Satan oscillated between being a peevish housemaster, a coy old lady, and the Demon King of pantomime.

Siobhan McKenna in *Sons of Oedipus,* Greenwich, February, 1977.

Miss McKenna's normal stage voice is exactly halfway between a goosegirl and a whole company of keening mourners.

Virginia McKenna as Rosalind in Shakespeare's *As You Like It,* Old Vic, 1954-5. Reviewed by Milton Shulman in the *Evening Standard.*

In an attempt to be boyish she raises her voice so loudly that at times I had the impression she was a desperate auctioneer trying to sell the lines.

Geraldine McEwan as Queen in *Edward II* by Brecht, National Theatre at the Old Vic, 1968. Reviewed by Milton Shulman.

* Geraldine McEwan, powdered white like a clownish, whey-faced doll, simpered, whined and groaned to such effect as the Queen, that Edward's homosexuality became both understandable and forgivable.

Keith Michell as Benedict in Shakespeare's *Much Ado About Nothing*, Old Vic, October, 1956. Reviewed by Ramsden Greig in the *Evening Standard.*

* It is like watching Marlon Brando, whom Mr Michell strongly resembles, leap about completely uninhibited after a successful session with his psychiatrist.

and in *Dear Love* by Jerome Kilty, Comedy, May, 1973. Reviewed by the *Catholic Herald.*

Mr Keith Michell has much talent handicapped by charm . . . He moves with excessive grace. Portraying Robert Browning the poet in *Dear Love* he jockeys on the balls of his feet as if about to dissolve in a waltz and, at the character's more exalted movements, takes flight like a Davis Cup finalist standing in as Peter Pan.

Bernard Miles in *John Gabriel Borkman* by Henrik Ibsen, Mermaid, 1961. Reviewed by Alan Brien in the *Sunday Telegraph.*

Bernard Miles played him like an effigy of Charles Dickens attacked by a fit of the mange.

John Mills in *The Uninvited Guest,* St James's, 1953.

* . . . and Mr John Mills wanders around the stage at the St James' theatre looking like a bewildered carrot.

John Mills says he was wearing what he thought was the best red wig that Wig Creations had ever made.

Ernest Milton in *The Strong are Lonely* by Fritz Hochwalder, Haymarket, January, 1956. Reviewed by Kenneth Tynan in the *Observer.*

. . . Ernest Milton, with his sickened scowl, hieratic voice and arachnoid bearing, makes a highly implausible spy, though his general aspect supports the view that man is nothing but a reed which thinks . . .

Roger Moore in his first starring role with Lana Turner in the film *Diane,* 1955.

* Lana Turner came on as Diane de Poitiers to the clicking of high heels (and) fluttering of false eyelashes, followed by a lump of English roast beef.

Kenneth More in *Rookery Nook* by Ben Travers, Wolverhampton Grand, 1939.

* He went so fast, he disappeared in his own dust.

John Neville in Shakespeare's *Henry V,* Bristol Old Vic at the Old Vic, 1953. Reviewed by Kenneth Tynan in the *Evening Standard.*

For the first quarter hour of the Bristol Old Vic's production in the Waterloo Road I was fascinated by the performance of the leading player, John Neville. Here at last, I felt, was the authentic Richard II: a lithe, sneering fellow, who curdled the milk of human kindness even as he dispensed it, but at whose heart there was abject insecurity. My excitement was marred, however, by the fact that the play being presented was *Henry V.* Mr Neville's nervous introspection, well suited for one speech — the soliloquy before Agincourt — was elsewhere quite useless . . .

John Neville as King Henry with Maureen Quinney as Katherine, David Bird as Fluellen and James Cairncross as Pistol in Henry V. *Courtesy of* Punch.

David Niven in *Dodsworth,* a film directed by William Wyler, MGM, 1935. Reviewed by the *Detroit Free Press.*

* In this picture we are privileged to see Mr Samuel Goldwyn's latest 'discovery'. All we can say about this actor is that he is tall, dark and not the slightest bit handsome.

Framed and on his lavatory wall.

Laurence Olivier as Shylock in ATV's production of Shakespeare's *The Merchant of Venice,* 1974. Reviewed by Clive James in the *Observer.*

. . . any fan of Walt Disney comics could turn on the set and see that he had modelled his appearance on Scrooge McDuck.

Whatever Olivier had done to his front teeth left his long top lip curving downwards in a fulsome volute on each side, producing a ducky look to go with his quacky sound, since for reasons unknown he had chosen to use a speeded-up version of his Duke of Wellington voice. When he put a top hat on over all this, the results were Disney's canard zillionaire to the life.

Michael Penrington as Angelo in Shakespeare's *Measure for Measure,* Stratford-on-Avon, 1974. Reviewed by Michael Billington.

* [He] seems less a self-deceiving Puritan facing the truth about himself than a soiled Prince Charming from the Actors' Studio.

John Penrose in a Peter Bull production at Perranporth. Reviewed by the *West Cornwall Advertiser.*

Mr John Penrose gave a sharp twist to both his parts.

Mr Penrose is now a theatrical agent — presumably finding acting too painful.

Stephen Phillips, a member of Frank Benson's Company in 1886. Described by Constance Benson.

He became more and more uninterested in his parts. When playing Prospero in *The Tempest,* he would sometimes use his wand as a fishing rod, suspending it over the orchestra, and through the beautiful words of Act I he would tell me (then playing Miranda), in a stage whisper, various kinds of fish he had caught and from which particular musical instrument.

Thank heavens the audience doesn't hear the alternative dialogue that sometimes goes on. I remember once in a performance of King Lear, *playing Cordelia to Paul Scofield, in that very tender scene towards the end of the play, when they are reunited, the dialogue went as follows:*

Cordelia: Had you not been their father, these white flakes did challenge pity of them.
Lear (under breath): Are you suggesting I've got dandruff?

Ronald Pickup as Cassius in Shakespeare's *Julius Caesar,* directed by John Schlesinger, National, March, 1977. Reviewed by Michael Billington.

* Ronald Pickup plays Cassius like a malignant ferret snapping at the air.

Donald Pleasance in Shakespeare's *The Merchant of Venice,* Stratford-on-Avon, 1953. Reviewed by Kenneth Tynan.

* . . . I cannot imagine what Donald Pleasance was trying to make of Launcelot Gobbo, who is not, I suggest, an organ-grinder's monkey . . .

Alexander Pope (not the poet, but an early nineteenth century actor of the same name) discussed by Leigh Hunt in his *Dramatic Essays,* published 1807.

There is . . . an infallible method of obtaining a clap from the galleries, and there is an art known at the theatre by the name of *clap-trapping,* which Mr Pope has shown great wisdom in studying. It consists of nothing more than in gradually raising the voice as the speech draws to a conclusion, making an alarming outcry on the last four or five lines, or suddenly dropping them into a tremulous but energetic undertone, and with a vigorous jerk of the right arm rushing off the stage. All this astonishes the galleries; they are persuaded it must be something very fine, because it is so important and so unintelligible, and they clap for the sake of their own reputation.

This still goes on. Keep an eye open for it — it can be fun spotting a clap-trapper.

Anthony Quayle in *Incident at Vichy* by Arthur Miller, Phoenix, January, 1966. Reviewed by Ronald Bryden in the *Observer.*

There is also a doctor who is a Good Chap, Anthony Quayle, who has the jaw-clenching movements around invisible pipe stems that indicate integrity in pretentious plays.

Anthony Quayle as Leduc with Sir Alec Guinness as Von Berg in Incident at Vichy. *Courtesy of* Punch.

Denis Quilley as Charles Condamine in *High Spirits* (musical version of *Blithe Spirit*, by Noel Coward), Savoy, 1965. Reviewed by Bernard Levin.

* Denis Quilley played the role with all the charm and animation of the leg of a billiard table.

James Quin (1693-1766), a leading Shakespearean actor, very popular as Falstaff. He was de-throned by Garrick. Discussed by Richard Cumberland.

With a deep, full tone, accompanied by a sawing kind of gesture, which had more of the senate than of the stage in it, he rolled out his heroics with an air of dignified indifference.

Basil Radford in *The Innocent Party* by H. M. Harwood and Lawrence Kirk, St James's, January, 1938. Reviewed by James Agate, in the *Sunday Times.*

Mr Basil Radford imitates an American so inadequately that I arranged to take the next boat to New York to lay my apologies at the feet of that continent.

Charlotte Rampling in the film, *Orca the Killer Whale.* Reviewed by Alexander Walker in the *Evening Standard.*

* At the end, when the whale has lured Harris north with a come-hither flick of its tail, Miss Rampling is caught on the icefloes, leaping from one to t'other and clad in thigh boots, homespun poncho *and a turban,* as if she expected David Bailey to surface and photograph her for *Vogue*'s Arctic number.

Michael Redgrave in *Hobson's Choice* by Harold Brighouse, January, 1964.

Some have seen overtones of Lear in his portrayal. I would have thought that a somewhat bad-tempered Father Christmas would have been nearer the mark.

and discussed by Kenneth Tynan.

The difficulty about judging this actor is that I have to abandon all my standards of great acting (which include relaxation and effortless command) and start all over again. There is, you see, a gulf fixed between good and great performances; but a bridge spans it, over which you may stroll if your visa is in order. Mr Redgrave ignoring this, always chooses the hard way. He dives into the torrent and tries to swim across, usually sinking within sight of the shore. Olivier pole-vaults over in a single animal leap; Gielgud, seizing a parasol, crosses by tightrope; Redgrave alone must battle it out with the current. The ensuing spectacle is never dull, but it can be very painful to watch . . .

Ralph Richardson in *An Inspector Calls* by J. B. Priestley, Old Vic, 1947.

Mr Richardson, looking for something to act in a nebulous part, paraded like some dummy in the Tailoring Section of a 'Britain Used to Make It' exhibition.

and in an American touring production of *Uncle Vanya* by Chekhov, 1946. Reviewed by George Jean Nathan.

Ralph Richardson's Uncle Vanya is just his Falstaff with a hangover.

Diana Rigg in *Abelard and Heloise* by Ronald Millar, Wyndham's, May, 1970. Reviewed by John Simon in *New York Magazine.* Apropos the nude scene:

Diana Rigg is built like a brick mausoleum with insufficient flying buttresses.

I remember making my way to the theatre the following day, darting from doorway to doorway and praying I wouldn't meet anyone I knew. The cast behaved with supreme tact and pretended they hadn't read the review.

Norman Rodway in *The Patrick Pearce Motel,* 1972. This play is a farce in which Norman Rodway says he had to play an Eamonn Andrews figure. This review in the *Slough Evening Mail* was headed 'This Blarney is Baloney'.

* . . . as the TV man, Norman Rodway loses his trousers and his acting reputation.

Flora Robson in *Ghosts* by Ibsen, Old Vic, 1958. Reviewed by Alan Brien.

Flora Robson as Mrs Alving — she accepts the news of her son's syphilis with an air of a district nurse facing an epidemic of sniffles.

Prunella Scales, playing all six female parts in *Anatol.*

* Vocally Prunella Scales distinguished nicely between the six roles; but she cannot change her face, which is that of a worried hamster.

Paul Scofield as Sir Thomas More in *A Man For All Seasons* by Robert Bolt, Globe, July, 1960. Reviewed by Bernard Levin in the *Daily Express.*

Unfortunately, Mr Scofield's performance for over half the evening is so bad that it obscures the play's merits.

His face frozen, his voice dull and level except at the end of a sentence, when the pitch falls like a bad violinist's 'glides', he makes every line sound like a platitude and extinguishes every spark of fire that Mr Bolt manages to blow into brightness.

Towards the end, when he is bowed and grey but unbroken, Mr

Scofield comes into his own, for greyness is then needed. But until then, his playing bores the doublet and hose off me.

Paul Scofield as Sir Thomas More with Leo McKern as The Common Man in A Man for All Seasons. *Courtesy of* Punch.

Sarah Siddons (1755-1831) was one of the twelve children of a provincial strolling player (one of her brothers was John Kemble), and as a child appeared on the stage with other members of her family. At twenty, her success in the provinces persuaded Garrick to bring her to London. She made her debut as Portia in *The Merchant of Venice* at Drury Lane in 1775 and was a dismal failure. She spent the next six years touring the provinces and her second London appearance in the title role of Southerne's *Isabella, or The Fatal Marriage* gained her immediate recognition as the greatest tragic actress of her day.

In the tragedy *Cleone* by Dodsley, reviewed in *The Devil's Pocket-Book* in 1786.

Mrs Siddons is manifestly the child of Art; her best positions convey strongly the idea of having been previously studied; they do not seem to rise out of the circumstance of the moment. The most confirmed ideot (sic) of the Theatre, who has seen her exhibit but three different characters, can tell, by the extension of one arm, when to expect an *Ah!* and by the brandishing of the other, when to expect an *Oh!* The same gestures accompany her exertions in all parts; and it does not signify a rush whether the heroine of the piece is an Eastern Princess, or a private gentlewoman.

and, as a private person, in Fanny Burney's *Diary*, 1787.

I expected her to have been all that is interesting; the delicacy and sweetness with which she seizes every opportunity to strike and to captivate upon the stage had persuaded me that her mind was formed with that peculiar susceptibility which, in different modes, 43 must give equal powers to attract and to delight in common life. But I was very much mistaken. As a stranger, I must have admired her noble appearance and beautiful countenance, and have regretted that nothing in her conversation kept pace with their promise; and as a celebrated actress, I had still only to do the same.

I've included this as an example of the sort of reaction an actor or actress is in danger of meeting. We are generally expected to be as scintillating off-stage as on!

Alastair Sim (1900-1976) in Shakespeare's *The Tempest,* Old Vic, 1962. Reviewed by Kenneth Tynan in the *Observer.*

Hesitantly directed by Oliver Neville, *The Tempest* is remarkable mainly because of its Prospero. Rather than play the part Alastair Sim chooses to reconnoitre it, you might think him a tentative pantomime dame standing in for Tommy Cooper, the music-hall magician whose tricks never work . . .

Sarah Siddons as Cleone.

Maggie Smith in *Virginia* by Edna O'Brien, Haymarket, February 1981. Reviewed by Victoria Radin in the *Observer.*

What [Maggie Smith] cannot do, what she will not do, is let the words speak for themselves. In her bouts of wit, she drawls the key word as if the sentence could not otherwise, in Virginia's lovely phrase, fall on its feet; in bouts of gloom, terror and despond . . . there are the closed eyes, the stifled sob, the insistent quaver . . . and we never for a moment forget this is a performance.

Tommy Steele as Tony Lumpkin in She Stoops to Conquer. *Courtesy of Punch.*

Terence Stamp in *Dracula,* by Hamilton Deane and John L. Balderstone, based on the novel by Bram Stoker, Shaftesbury, September, 1978. Reviewed by Irving Wardle in *The Times.*

Terence Stamp's Dracula has nothing to offer apart from a noble profile. His entrances are insignificant, his voice without menace or mystery and his physical tricks consist largely of flapping his cloak, like a bat failing to take off.

Tommy Steele in *She Stoops to Conquer* by Oliver Goldsmith, Old Vic, 1960. Reviewed by Bernard Levin in the *Daily Express.*

Matters are not helped by Mr Tommy Steele's attempt to make the party go by shouting the house down as Tony Lumpkin. (Audiences later in the run will be spared the worst, as Mr Steele is headed for laryngitis within the week, at this rate.)

Dudley Sutton as Jacko in *Incident at Vichy* by Arthur Miller, Phoenix, 1966. Reviewed by Alan Brien in the *Sunday Telegraph.*

Peter Woods' efficient production has some odd lapses, such as casting Dudley Sutton as the one Jew who was identified by the size of his nose, though everyone knows Mr Sutton's nose, which gives his face that fascinating look of a squashed car-seat, is non-existent.

Elizabeth Taylor played a walk-on part at the Oxford Playhouse in February 1966 — an event so unlikely, it had the critics turning up in droves. The part was Helen of Troy, appearing in a brief vision in Christopher Marlowe's *Dr Faustus*. Richard Burton, her husband at the time, was playing Faustus. Reviewed in *The Times*:

Those who visit the production to see Miss Taylor as a speechless apparition of Helen of Troy will not be out of the theatre before 10.45.

and by Alan Brien in the *Sunday Telegraph*:

If Mr Burton seemed determined to avoid being typed as his screen image, Elizabeth Taylor, looking impossibly pretty in a filmy nighty on a carpet of smoke, was everybody's dream of a film star. But this was a Hollywood. or rather a television commercial, version of Helen like a cunning soft sell for lingerie.

and in *The Little Foxes* by Lillian Hellman, Victoria Palace, March, 1982. Reviewed by Robert Cushman in the *Observer*.

. . . The audience come to see a star: not to see her act but just to see her. Elizabeth Taylor's performance hardly carries into the auditorium.

Ambrose Hammer — a critic who loves to heave the old harpoon into actors — might carry on from there. I merely say that the first night . . . is as grisly as an undertaker's picnic and may be grislier.

Ellen Terry (1847-1928). She came to prominence after 1878 when she was engaged by Henry Irving to play Ophelia to his Hamlet. Until 1896 she was the leading lady in all Irving's Shakespearean productions at the Lyceum theatre. After leaving Irving she performed the plays of her contemporaries, Shaw and Barrie.

In Shakespeare's *The Merchant of Venice,* January, 1881. Reviewed by Henry James in *Scribner's Monthly*.

Her manner of dealing with the delightful speeches of Portia, with all their play of irony, of wit and temper, savours, to put it harshly, of the schoolgirlish. We have ventured to say that her comprehension of a character is sometimes weak, and we may illustrate it by a reference to her whole handling of this same opportunity. Miss Terry's mistress of Belmont giggles too much, plays too much with her fingers, is too free and familiar, too osculatory, in her relations with Bassanio. The mistress of Belmont was a great lady, as well as a tender and clever woman; but this side of the part quite eludes the actress, whose deportment is not such as we should expect in the splendid spinster who has princes for wooers. When Bassanio has chosen the casket which contains the key of her heart, she approaches him, and begins to pat and stroke him. This seems to us an appallingly false note. 'Good heavens, she's touching him!' a person sitting next to us exclaimed — a person whose judgement in such matters is always unerring.

Daniel Thorndike in Shakespeare's *Hamlet,* Old Vic, 1957. Reviewed by Ivor Brown in *Time and Tide.*

Daniel Thorndike's Ghost is the most stentorian of my acquaintance. There must have been some intended point in his roaring, but I missed it. At any rate, he proved that to be poisoned first and coffined after can be quite a lung tonic.

Sybil Thorndike (1882-1976) in *Oedipus Rex* by Sophocles, New theatre, 1945. Reviewed by Kenneth Tynan.

. . . Sybil Thorndike played Jocasta in an entirely different convention which I found jarring. The *prima donna* tragedienne (an oracular Sybil), with plump arms and a bellowing contralto, given to sudden hawk-like sweeps up and down the stage, she played with that traditional blazing intensity which, so far from illuminating the personality, strangles it into a sort of red-hot anonymity. She treated every line as if it were the crucial line of the play: it was all so ponderously weighted that when the big hurdles approached, the horse couldn't jump.

Christopher Timothy appeared in, and by his own admission was dreadful in, a thriller called *By Whose Hand* at Worthing in 1963. The local paper hammered the show, and showed its estimate of his performance by saying:

* Christopher Timothy (appears by kind permission of the National Theatre ???) . . .

Herbert Beerbohm Tree (1852-1917) as Falstaff in Shakespeare's *Henry IV* Part I, Haymarket, May, 1896. Reviewed by George Bernard Shaw in the *Saturday Review.*

Mr Tree wants one thing to make him an excellent Falstaff, and that is to get born over again as unlike himself as possible . . . The basket-work figure, as expressionless as that of a Jack-in-the-Green; the face, with the pathetic wandering eye . . . belying such suggestion of character as the lifeless mask of paint and hair can give . . . the hopeless efforts of the romantic imaginative actor, touching only in unhappy parts, to play the comedian by dint of mechanical horseplay: all that is hopeless, irremediable. Mr Tree might as well try to play Juliet.

There was a genuine difficulty about disguising Tree on stage, which Shaw explained clearly and beautifully in an essay he contributed to a memorial volume published after the actor's death.

. . . his handicap was not a light one. Instead of that neutral figure which an actor can turn into anything he pleases, he was tall, and built like nobody else on earth.

Dorothy Tutin as Madame Dubarry in *Reflections* by John Peacock, Haymarket, March, 1980. Reviewed by Alan Drury in the *Listener.*

Her performance trundles on, firing on all pistons, like a combine harvester reaping an empty field.

and in *St Joan* by George Bernard Shaw.

* Dorothy played St Joan like a beatnik in a coffee-bar.

Irene Vanbrugh (1872-1949) as Gertrude in Shakespeare's *Hamlet,* Haymarket, 1931. Reviewed by James Agate in the *Sunday Times.*

. . . the Queen of that delicious comedienne, Miss Irene Vanbrugh, is one of the least convincing. The cockneyism of her 'Good Hamlet, cast thy nighted colour *orf*!' settles that.

James Villiers in Shakespeare's *The Winter's Tale,* Old Vic, 1955. Reviewed by Harold Hobson in the *Sunday Times.*

Mr James Villiers' Bear must be seen to be believed, or not to be believed.

Gwen Watford in *Mary Stuart* by Schiller, Old Vic, October, 1960. Reviewed by Mervyn Jones in the *Tribune.*

As sane and kindly as an enlightened headmistress, Gwen Watford was billed to play Mary but did nothing of the sort.

and as Titania in Shakespeare's *A Midsummer Night's Dream,* Old Vic, 1961. Reviewed by Caryl Brahms in *John o'London.*

Gwen Watford was a thoroughly nice fairy from Kensington Gardens.

Orson Welles as Captain Ahab in Moby Dick. *Courtesy of* Punch.

Orson Welles as Captain Ahab in *Moby Dick,* based on the novel by Herman Melville, Duke of York's, 1955. (Adapted and directed by Orson Welles.) Reviewed by Kenneth Tynan in the *Observer.* It is only fair to say that, in this review, though Tynan criticized Welles in this part, he went on to compliment him as a director.

He has a voice of bottled thunder, so deeply encasked that one thinks of those liquor advertisements which boast that not a drop is sold till it's seven years old. The trouble is that everything he does is on such a vast scale that it quickly becomes monotonous. He is too big for the boots of any part. He reminds one of Macaulay's conversation, as Carlyle described it: 'Very well for a while, but one wouldn't *live* under Niagara.' Emotion of any kind he expresses by thrusting out his chin and knitting his eyebrows. Between these twin promontories there juts out a false and quite unnecessary nose. Sir Laurence Olivier began his film of *Hamlet* with the statement that it was "the tragedy of a man who could not make up his mind." At one point Mr Welles's new appendage started to leave its moorings, and *Moby Dick* nearly became the tragedy of a man who could not make up his nose.

Timothy West in *Ring Round the Moon* by Jean Anouilh. The leading parts are of the twins, Hugo and Frederick, and playing them both is a massive job.

47

* The local paper gave paragraph after paragraph to every other performance in the production, and at the end said: Timothy West as the twins showed no fatigue from running round behind the scenes.

and in Shakespeare's *The Merchant of Venice.* Reviewed by James Fenton, 1980.

The Jew, played by Timothy West, is that familiar figure on the Rialto, the bad-tempered Hungarian economic adviser.

Billie Whitelaw in *The Dutch Courtesan* by Marston, National Theatre at the Old Vic, October, 1964. She spent many weeks with records and at the Dutch Embassy to perfect her accent. The result was this from Milton Shulman.

* Billie Whitelaw's Dutch accent sounded like a Welsh au pair girl by way of Calcutta.

Kenneth Williams in *Signed and Sealed* by Georges Feydeau and Maurice Desvallieres, directed by Patrick Garland, Comedy, June, 1976. Reviewed by Michael Billington in the *Guardian.*

So what have we here? Kenneth Williams of the flared nostrils, funny voices and camp outrage playing a respectable, lecherous suburbanite who finds himself involved in a bigamous triangle. It doesn't make any sense, and because it doesn't make sense it is not remotely funny. There is no point in seeing a man reduced to hysterical panic if hysterical panic is his forte . . .

Simon Williams in *The Last of Mrs Cheyney* by Frederick Lonsdale, Cambridge, October, 1980. Reviewed by Ned Chaillet in *The Times.*

What Mr Williams could use as a performer is a voice that did not always sound strangulated by black ties . . .

Diana Wynyard as Charlotte Bronte in *Wild Decembers* by Clemence Dane, Apollo, May, 1933. Reviewed by James Agate in the *Sunday Times.*

. . . There is hardly a moment at which, despite laudable efforts to the contrary, Miss Wynyard does not gloriously and triumphantly and radiantly wreck the play.

Donald Wolfit (1903-1968) discussed by James Agate in the *Sunday Times,* February, 1944.

He can summon up all the expressions there are except the tragic one, the lack of which, in a tragic actor, must be a shortcoming.

Edward Woodward in *Cyrano* adapted by Patrick Garland from Rostand, 1970. Reviewed by Kenneth Hurren in the *Spectator.*

As swashbuckling Cyrano, Mr Woodward's performance buckles more often than it swashes.

CHAPTER TWO

A Critic's Device

This section is given over to a device that most critics employ at one time or another, and which often produces high comedy. It is usually brought into play when the critic is exasperated beyond the point at which straightforward, intelligent comment is appropriate, or even possible.

It consists of relating the plot, usually in quite simple terms and without comment, and then standing back to let the thing hang itself. Sometimes a critic will enter more deeply into the spirit of the exercise by adopting the voice and style of the author. (See Nicholas de Jongh on *Wild Orchids*.)

Bernard Levin used the critic's device assiduously in his campaign against drawing-room comedy in the late 1950s, developing it to a point where he could devote a whole review to itemizing the details of a typical set. (See his review of *The Geese are Getting Fat*.)

The device is capable of abuse: if you think about it, some of the best plays in the world can be made to sound silly by a deadpan rendering of their plots. But the examples in this chapter struck me as having a certain weight of intent (if not always of justice) behind them.

For those readers who get as much enjoyment from recognizing the device as I do, further examples may be found in the section on Musicals and in the American section.

We start with Shaw's all-time classic in the genre.

True Blue, a new and original drama of the Royal Navy in five acts by Leonard Outram and Stewart Gordon, Lt. R. N., Olympic theatre, March, 1896. Reviewed by George Bernard Shaw in the *Saturday Review.*

Headline: BOILED HEROINE

First, there is the lady matador who loves the captain and hates the heroine, whom the captain loves. Then there is the heroine who also loves the captain. And there is the heroine's maid who loves the comic sailor, who loves the bottle. Suddenly the cruiser is ordered to up anchors and sweep England's enemies from the sea. The women resolve not to desert the men they love in the hour of danger. The matadoress, a comparatively experienced and sensible woman, slips quietly down into the pantry adjoining the captain's cabin. The maid gets into one of those settee music boxes which are, it appears, common objects on the decks of cruisers, and is presently carried into the captain's cabin. The heroine, taught by love to devise a surer hiding-place, gets into one of the ship's boilers. Here the hand of the idiot is apparent, striking out a situation which would never have occurred to Shakespeare. Once fairly at sea, the matadoress gives way to an inveterate habit of smoking and is smelt out by the captain. She throws her arms boldly about him, and declares he is hers forever. Enter, inopportunely, the navigating officer. He is scandalized, but retires. When he thinks it is safe to return, it is only to find the maid emerging from the settee to dispute possession of the captain, on behalf of the heroine, with the matadoress. Hereupon he describes the ship as the captain's harem, and is placed under

arrest. Then comes the great dramatic opportunity of the matadoress. Becoming acquainted, heaven knows how, with the hiding place of the heroine, she takes the stage alone, and draws a thrilling picture of her rival's impending doom. She describes her in the clammy darkness of that boiler, listening to the wild beats of her own heart. Then the sensation of wet feet, the water rising to her ankles, her knees, her waist, her neck and only by standing on tip toe, with frantic upturned face, can she breathe. One mercy alone seems vouchsafed to her: the water has lost its deadly chill. Nay, it is getting distinctly warm, even hot — hotter — scalding! Immortal powers, it is BOILING; and what was a moment ago a beautiful English girl in the exquisite budding of her beautiful womanhood, is now but a boilerful of soup, and in a moment will be but a condenser full of low-pressure steam. I must congratulate Mrs Raleigh on the courage with which she hurled this terrible word-picture at a house half white with its purgation by pity and terror, and half red with a voiceless, apoplectic laughter. Need I describe the following scene in the stoke-hold — how the order comes to fill the boiler; how the comic sailor, in shutting the manhole thereof, catches sight of the white finger of the captain's young lady; how the matadoress in disguise comes in, and has all but turned on the boiling water when the comic sailor disables the tap, by a mighty blow from the sledge-hammer; how he rushes away to tell the captain of his discovery; how in his absence the fires are lighted and the cold water turned on; and how at the last moment the captain dashes in shouting 'Draw the fires from No 7' (the heroine is in No 7), rushes up the ladder to the manhole and drags out the heroine safe and sound, without a smudge on her face or a crumple in her pretty white frock, amid delirious cheers from the audience.

The Bird of Time *with Gladys Cooper as Mrs Gantry and Clive Morton as Wilfred Gantry. Courtesy of* Punch.

The Bird of Time by Peter Mayne, Savoy, June, 1961. Reviewed by Kenneth Tynan in the *Observer*.

All serious plays whose titles are quotations from poems have a tendency to be second-rate; and Peter Mayne's *The Bird of Time* (Savoy) — acknowledgments to Edward FitzGerald — is no exception. The setting, a remarkably cluttered affair, represents two houseboats on a river in contemporary Kashmir. The one on the right is occupied by Gladys Cooper, a crumbling pillar of the Raj, while aboard the other we have the astonishing spectacle of Diana Wynyard as a Eurasian dressmaker, smoking hashish to forget a long departed English lover. 'I was like a flower,' she murmurs to herself, reminiscing. She has Annigoni's portrait of the Queen tacked in reproduction to the wall and uses such phrases as 'What care I?' and 'Come back, heedless girl!' (addressed to her daughter not to Her Majesty).

Miss Cooper, once her defeated rival in love, affects to despise her because she pretends to be English. A Chinese invasion of Kashmir, conveniently instigated by the author, brings the two women together, but their truce is short-lived. Miss Cooper catches Miss Wynyard at the hubble-bubble. 'Your eyes are *shagged* with Hashish!'

she cries, wresting the apparatus from its slave and flinging it into the river. . . .

The Birthday Party by Harold Pinter, Lyric, Hammersmith, May, 1958. Reviewed by W. A. Darlington in the *Daily Telegraph*.

The author never got down to earth long enough to explain what his play was about, so I can't tell you. But I can give you some sketch of what happens, and to whom.

To begin with there is Meg (Beatrix Lehmann) who lets lodgings in a seaside town. She is mad. Thwarted maternity is (I think) her trouble and it makes her go soppy over her unsavoury lodger, Stanley (Richard Pearson).

He is mad too. He strangles people. And I think he must have strangled one person too many, because a couple of very sinister (and quite mad) characters arrive (John Slater and John Stratton) bent on — I suppose — vengeance.

There is also a mad girl (Wendy Hutchinson), nymphomania being her fancy.

The one sane character is Meg's husband (Willoughby Gray) but sanity does him no good. He is a deeply depressed little man, a deckchair attendant by profession.

Oh, well, I can give him one word of cheer. He might have been a dramatic critic, condemned to sit through plays like this.

The Cocktail Party by T. S. Eliot, Edinburgh Festival, August, 1949. Reviewed by Ivor Brown in the *Observer*.

What was it all about? Well, there at a party is Alec Guinness as a Mystery Guest, who might be devil or saint and turns out to be a psychotherapist remarkable for taking no fees and keeping Lady Sneerwell (Cathleen Nesbitt) as an eavesdropper in his anteroom. His business seems to be mending other people's marriages or lack of them. He tells a quarrelsome couple some stinging home truths, which apparently reconciles them, and sends a sad young woman to a death worse than fate in a way which struck me as purely sadistic. I have rarely disliked anybody so much as this icy healer of Mr Eliot's.

Don Quixote by Thomas D'Urfey (1653-1723). D'Urfey's plays were famous for their scurrility. Reviewed by Jeremy Collier, 1698.

He diverts the ladies with the charming rhetoric of *snotty-nose, filthy vermin in the beard, nitty jerkin, louse-snapper, and letter in the chamber pot;* and with an abusive description of a countess, and a rude story of a certain lady with some other varieties of this kind too coarse to mention . . . There is more of physic than comedy in such sentences as these. *Crocus metallorum* will scarce turn the stomach more effectively.

Flare Path by Terence Rattigan, New York, December 1942. Reviewed by George Jean Nathan.

Flight Lieutenant Teddy Graham's wife, Patricia, a former actress, has, unknown to him, enjoyed protracted premarital sexual experience with a moving-picture idol, Peter Kyle by name. Peter, now at forty-seven passé for screen purposes, pursues her to a provincial hotel where she is staying to be near her husband and tells her that he needs her more than ever. Patricia, it is at once apparent, still is amorously fetched by him but, interrupted only by the periodic rushing in and out of RAF fliers and gunnery noises off stage, for the subsequent hour and a half indulges in the elaborate repertoire of facial contortions commonly employed under such circumstances to indicate, *seriatim,* doubt, hesitation, gradual process of decision, and, finally, resolve. At ten-thirty she accordingly decides that not only her heart but the rest of her anatomy and physiology belong to Peter and is about to give him her all when the door opens and in staggers Teddy just returned from a bombing raid.

Teddy is broken. He senses what is up and confesses to Patricia that he needs her even more than Peter does, since he has lost his nerve and can no longer do his flying duty unless he can lean on her love, rest on her faith, and know when away that she will be waiting for him with receptive arms. Taking a cue from Candida, Patricia concludes that it is the weaker of the two who needs her most, sends Peter packing, and reinspires Teddy to new feats of derring-do against the enemy.

The playwright's brilliant imagination does not, however, end here. Appreciating that there must be some humorous relief, he brings in a Polish flier who has enlisted in the RAF and permits him to induce ten or twelve minutes of wild hilarity in the English characters by pronouncing *peasants* as *pheasants . . .*

The Geese are Getting Fat by Arthur Watkyn, Phoenix, December, 1960. Reviewed by Bernard Levin in the *Daily Express* (the entire review).

When the curtain rises on Mr Watkyns' new play, we are in the drawing-room. The walls are covered with canvas-coloured wallpaper, with a paler, cream paper for the stairs. On the extreme left is a window-seat, upholstered in pale blue to match the curtains. On the window-seat there are three rust cushions and one pink one, the pink one having a fringe of bobbles. On the window sill is a photograph in an imitation gilt frame, heavily chased. In front of the window seat there is a round occasional table bearing a pot-plant and a heavy, red glass ashtray. Moving round the back of the stage to the left, the next thing is an alcove divided into four shelves (the shelves are white, the back of the alcove blue). The curved top section of the alcove is decorated to look like the inside of a shell. On the shelves of the alcove are two green urns, three plates, a fruit dish, a vase, some figurines and nine books. To the right of the alcove are two miniatures on red velvet mounts. In front of it is a desk, with a white telephone and a heavy stemmed lamp with a pleated silk shade. Behind the desk is a chair. At the back of the room, to the left of the staircase (which is in the middle, and has a left-hand bend in it), is a tall plant-stand carrying some more pot-plants. On the back wall, by the foot of the stairs, are three pictures in imitation gilt frames. Half way up the stairs there is the bottom half (all that can be seen) of another, larger, oval picture. On the right hand side of the foot of the stairs is another occasional table, with a vase of white flowers and a heavy, plain glass ash tray. Further round is another alcove, twin to the first, including the two red-velvet-mounted miniatures on the wall by its side. In place of the green urn, the fruit dish and the books, however, this one has a bronze bust (possibly of Shakespeare), a decanter and some glasses and a row of bottles, including whisky, brandy, Grand Marnier, Crème de Menthe and orange squash. On the right-hand wall are six oblong pictures, two big and four small. One of the big ones looks like an imitation Tintoretto. (Further round is another oval one which, my favourite redhead asserted, was an imitation Goya. I myself express no opinion on this.) Beneath the imitation Tintoretto is a fireplace, with a brass fender, and a mantelpiece bearing an ormolu clock, two blue Lalique figures, a pair of brass candlesticks and a photograph. To the right of the fireplace is a serving-trolley on which stands a lamp with a blue silk shade. On the right of the fireplace is another occasional table with a cigarette box in imitation malachite and another photograph. On the extreme right is a cocktail cabinet. In the middle is a three-piece suite with russet sofa, and one pink and one blue armchair. On the sofa are two imitation petit-point cushions and one pink one, the last with a bobbled border. Behind the sofa is another occasional table. Hanging from the ceiling is a light, made as an imitation lantern. On either side of the alcoves is a bracket containing two lights with pink shades. And a very merry Christmas to all my readers. And a happy New Year.

The Man with Expensive Tastes by Edward Percy and Lilian Denham, Vaudeville. Reviewed by Kenneth Tynan in the *Evening Standard*, July, 1953.

Only a year ago the patrons of the Vaudeville theatre were briefly privileged to see a play in which Donald Wolfit was visited with a plague of frogs. Last night, under the same roof, something equally bizarre occurred — *The Man with Expensive Tastes*, the theme of which is forgery by hypnosis.

It happens in Mill Hill, where lives Sylvester Ord, bland epicurean, played with shatteringly dated jollity by George Curzon. His line is graphology, the study of handwriting, out of which he has made enough money to furnish his house like an antique shop on the eve of a fire sale; he also, for reasons which may have been excised at the third rewrite, has green fingers. His principal lark, however, is forgery, as we learn from his house-guest, an inexpressibly sinister clergyman who is readily identifiable as an international crook. The actor here is Peter Bull, fooling nobody with a silver-grey wig. A self-confessed ex-president of the Oxford Union, he commands what must be the least secretive band of outlaws in the annals of crime. At Mr. Bull's request, Ord explains his technique of forgery. First, you divide your victim's calligraphy into two sections, the capital letters and the rest ('I live with these two alphabets. I saturate myself in them'); you then hypnotize yourself and forge ahead. This satisfies Mr. Bull, who is known in the trade as Monsieur Onyx.

The main action is precipitated by the presence in the neighbourhood of two other graphologists — Ord's daughter, whom he is raising to be a forger, and her American boy-friend, a private eye who has been engaged to investigate the forthcoming forgery coup. Onyx, ignoring Ord's helpless protests ('Self-hypnosis twice in one day!') urges haste; and, fully in the public and private eye, preparations for the coup go forward. The scheme is wrecked by the Corsican girl who smashes Ord's forging fingers in the door of a safe.

I forgot to mention the Corsican girl. She is a fiery creature named Yrena, highly yrresponsible, whom Ord has adopted and calls his little sparrow. She carries a stiletto, which later proves to be the only rational excuse for her existence on stage. The private eye has meanwhile concluded that he is among thieves; rather than call the police, however, he observes with characteristic obtuseness: 'There's one piece of this jigsaw puzzle that doesn't quite fit.' The final fitting takes place when Ord agrees to hypnotise his daughter into forging a cheque for £80,000. His alcoholic brother, who collects typewriters, points a torch at the girl; Ord himself intones some Svengali-esque sleepy-talk; in the garden a coloured chauffeur called Spike Munch keeps guard; and upstairs, listening in on the house telephone, is the private eye — or is it the young journalist?

I forgot to mention the young journalist. He came to interview Ord in the first scene and stayed to fall in love with his daughter. I will not reveal, because I can barely recall, the third-act resolution. I remember that Mr. Bull sprang across the stage with, as they say, an agility surprising in one of his bulk; that he ended up with a Corsican stiletto through his jugular; and that Mr. Curzon escaped with a compassionate caution. At all events, those who care about the problems of hypnotic forgery had their pet subject well aired. Others, less intimately concerned, may echo my opinion that *The Man with Expensive Tastes* is the crassest crime play since *The Inn-keeper's Button,* which disfigured the theatrical season of 1897-8. Peter Bull, a trout among minnows, is magnificently assured; and Philip Stainton bumbles sibilantly through the role of the drunken brother — though even he is unable to save the scenes he shares with the comic Irish housekeeper.

I forgot to mention the comic Irish housekeeper . . .

Critics often have their favourite monsters — plays or productions which in their awfulness rise above the common run and become enshrined as archetypes of all that a play or production should not be. *The Manxman* came to occupy this position in the dramatic criticism of George Bernard Shaw. Here is his original review.

The Manxman by Wilson Barrett, a play in four acts, adapted from Hall Caine's celebrated novel, Shaftesbury, November, 1895. Reviewed by George Bernard Shaw.

In the bill *The Manxman* is described as 'adapted from Hall Caine's celebrated novel.' Who is Hall Caine? How did he become celebrated? At what period did he flourish? Are there any other Manx authors of his calibre? If there are, the matter will soon become serious; for if that gift of intolerably copious and intolerably common imagination is a national characteristic in the Isle of Man, it will swamp the stage with Manx melodrama the moment the islanders pick up the trick of writing for the stage.

Whether the speeches in *The Manxman* are interpolated Wilson Barrett or aboriginal Hall Caine I cannot say, as I have not read the celebrated novel, and am prepared to go to the stake rather than face the least chapter of it. But if they correctly represent the colloquial habits of the island, the Manx race are without a vernacular . . . In the Isle of Man you do not use the word 'always': you say 'Come weal come woe, come life come death'. The most useful phrases for the tourist are, 'Dust and ashes, dust and ashes', 'Dead sea fruit', 'The lone watches of the night', 'What a hell is conscience', 'The storm clouds are descending and the tempest is at hand' and so on. The Manx do not speak of a little baby, but of a baby 'fresh from God'. Their philosophy is that 'love is best — is everything — is the cream of life — better than worldly success'; and they conceive woman — or, as they probably call her, 'the fair sex' — as a creature 'giving herself body and soul, never thinking what she gets by it. That's the glory of a Woman!' And the Manx woman rather deserves this. Her idea of pleasantry is to sit on a plank over a stream dangling her legs; to call her swain's attention to her reflection in the water; and then, lest he should miss the coquetry of the exhibition, to cut off the reflected view of her knees by wrapping her skirt round her ankles in a paroxysm of reflected bashfulness. And when she sprains her ankle, and the gentleman tenders some surgical aid, she requests him to turn his head the other way. In short, the keynote of your perfect Manxman is tawdry vulgarity aping the heroic, the hearty, the primevally passionate, and sometimes, though here the show of vigour in the affectation tumbles into lame ineptitude, the gallant and humorous . . .

As to the acting, most of the sixteen parts are so indefinite in spite of their portentous names — Black Tom, Ross Christian, Jemmy Lord and so on — that there is nothing to act in them . . . Professional methods were . . . illustrated by Mr Hamilton Knight as the Manxsome governor. He, having to leave the stage with the innocent words 'Come and see us as soon as you can', shewed us how the experienced hand can manufacture an effective exit. He went to the door with the words 'Come and see us soon.' Then he nerved himself; opened the door; turned dauntlessly; and with raised voice and sparkling eyes hurled the significant words 'as you can' in the teeth of the gallery . . .

Mr Lewis Waller managed to get a moment of real acting into the end of the first act, and then relapsed into nonsensical solemnity for the rest of the evening. I do not know what he was thinking of; but it can hardly have been of the play. He delivered his lines with the automatic gravity of a Brompton Cemetery clergyman repeating the burial service for the thousandth time. He uttered endless strings of syllables; but he did not divide them into words, much less phrases. 'Icannotwillnotlistentothis Iwon'thearofit,' was the sort of thing he inflicted on us for three mortal acts. As to Miss Florence West, if she persists in using her privilege as the manager's wife to play melodramatic heroines, she will ruin the enterprise . . .

The Old Folks at Home by H. M. Harwood, Queen's, December, 1933. Reviewed by James Agate in the *Sunday Times.*

I have decided to become mellow, in other words to enter the third of every dramatic critic's four periods. In the first he is boundless in confidence, crying lo here and lo there, as world geniuses swim into his ken . . . In the second period he wearisomely reiterates that there were great players before Alexander . . . The third is the critic's mellow period in which, finding nobody to hold up his arms, he tires of maintaining the standard and desists from giving battle . . . He murmurs that today's everything and everybody are magnoperative and pre-eminent, and will somebody pass the port, please! In the fourth period . . . he is gaga, and then only is that which he writes believed!

Entering, as I say, upon my third period, I must declare Mr Harwood's play to outshine anything this brilliant writer has done before . . . and everybody in the cast to contribute to the greatest first night since Genesis.

Professor and Lady Jane Kingdom are the parents of one Liza Kingdom, a beauty-ninny who is never out of the gossip columns. They also have a daughter-in-law, one Sybil, a vapourish young woman always expecting to find a soul-mate in good-looking young men who are looking for something else. In the opinion of these daft creatures Lady Jane has long been relegated to the mutch and crutch status, with just enough eyesight to reach to her tambour. Then comes a summer night *à la* Goring Thomas, which in the theatre means moonlight and nightingales, balcony and adjoining bedrooms. So purblind Lady Jane puts Sybil and her would-be seducer next to one another and calls attention to the amorous state of the weather. Whereby about two in the morning there is a terrible shindy in which Sybil and her now victorious lover, Liza and her dope-riddled, pistol-mongering admirer all collide on the balcony like motor-cars jammed in a fog. In the third act Sybil is going to make a mess of everything by taking her seduction seriously, whereupon Lady Jane intervenes, saying in effect: 'Why, because you want to be happy, must you make your husband miserable? I have lied to the Professor and deceived him, in the best French sense, for thirty years during which I have been a faithless and capable wife. When you get a man worth deceiving your husband for, I advise you to do the same. But not until!' It would be unfair to describe the play's charming last-minute twist, which comes between this exposition of the Whole Duty of Married Women and Miss Tempest's good-night curtsey.

Were I still in my second period I should point out that the play is too long by ten of its earlier minutes. In the embittered years I might also have drawn attention to the fact that the effulgently Saxon and concave Professor and his lady could not by any possible race-theory have produced anything so rapturously raven and convex as their daughter Liza. Heretofore, I might have suggested that Lady Jane's sense and breeding would have long ago turned such a daughter out of the house or dry-bread-and-watered her into some kind of decency. Time was, perhaps, when I might have opined that so boring a character as Sybil called for an actress with the power to make pretentiousness amusing, and that Miss Nora Swinburne is too faithful to tedium to make us at any time laugh at it. But the morbid years are over, and therefore I shall simply say that everything in connection with this piece is of a sparkle to make cyphers of Congreve and Wilde, Maugham and Coward.

The Passing of the Third Floor Back by Jerome K. Jerome, St James's, September, 1908. Reviewed by Max Beerbohm in the *Saturday Review.*

The reformation of a bad person by a supernatural visitor is a theme that has often been used. Mr Jerome . . . was struck by the bright idea that the effect would be a dozen times as great as if there were a dozen converts. So he has turned a supernatural visitor loose in a boarding-house inhabited by a round dozen of variously bad people — 'A Satyr', 'A Snob', 'A Shrew', 'A Painted Lady', 'A Cheat' and so on. Now, supposing that these characters were lifelike, or were amusing figments of the brain, and supposing that we saw them falling, little by little, under the visitor's spell, till gradually we became aware that they had been changed for the better, the play might be quite a passable affair. But to compass that effect is very far beyond Mr Jerome's power . . . Mr Jerome shows no sign of having ever observed a fellow-creature . . . Take Major Tompkins and his wife and daughter, for example. Major and Mrs Tompkins are anxious to sell their daughter for gold to an elderly man. 'His very touch,' says the daughter, according to custom, 'is loathsome.' The Major persists and says — what else could a stage-major say? — 'Damn your infernal impudence!' The unnatural mother tries to persuade the unwilling daughter to wear a more decolleté dress. The daughter, of course, loves a young painter in a brown velveteen jacket; but she is weak and worldly, and she is like to yield to the importunities of the elderly man. The young painter — but no, I won't bore you by describing the other characters . . . Mr Jerome's humour, however, is his own, and he plasters it about with a liberal hand. What could be more screamingly funny than the doings at the outset? The landlady pours tea into the decanter which is supposed to hold whisky, on the chance that the drunken boarder won't notice the difference. Then she goes out, and the servant drinks milk out of the jug and replenishes the jug with water. Then *she* goes out, and the 'Painted Lady' comes in and steals a couple of fresh candles from the sconces on the piano and substitutes a couple of candle ends. Then *she* goes out, and the Major comes in and grabs the biscuits off the plate and drops them in his hat. Then *he* goes out, and the 'Cad' and the 'Rogue' come in and unlock the spiritcase with an illicit key and help themselves to what they presently find is tea. He's inexhaustibly fertile in these sequences is Mr Jerome K. Jerome. When the 'Passer-by' knocks at the front door, and is admitted with a lime-light full on his (alas, Mr Forbes-Robertson's) classic countenance, the sequences set in with awful severity. The benificent stranger has one method for all evil-doers, and he works it on every one in turn, with precisely the same result. He praises the landlady for her honesty; then the landlady is ashamed of her dishonesty and becomes honest. He praises the Major for his sweet temper; then the Major is ashamed of his bad temper, and becomes sweet-tempered. He praises the 'Painted Lady' for her modesty in not thinking herself beautiful without paint; then the 'Painted Lady' is ashamed of her paint, and reappears paintless ... Steadily (the visitor) works his way through the list, distributing full measure of devastating platitudes all the way. The last person on the list, the Major's daughter, says suddenly, 'Who are you?' The visitor spreads his arms, in the attitude of 'The Light of the World'. The Major's daughter falls on her knees in awe. When the visitor passes through the front door a supernatural radiance bursts through the fanlight, flooding the stage; and then the curtain comes slowly down. Well, I suppose blasphemy pays.

Out of this World by Giuseppe Marotti, translated by William Weaver, Phoenix, November, 1960. Reviewed by Bernard Levin in the *Daily Express.*

Strictly speaking, I cannot swear that being kicked in the stomach by a horse would be an experience preferable to seeing this play by Signor Giuseppe Marotti ... (translated by William Weaver) because I have never been kicked in the stomach by a horse.

But I have seen this play, and I can certainly say that if a kick in the stomach by a horse would be worse, I do not wish to be kicked in the stomach by a horse.

And I can certainly add that, unpleasant though the prospect of being kicked in the stomach by a horse may be, I would certainly rather be kicked in the stomach by a horse than see the play again.

The first two acts are about nothing at all; the third is largely about impotence.

A business man with a plan to uproot a Paris cemetery and build a block of flats is visited by a posse of ghosts, indignant at the prospect of being disturbed.

The youngest and handsomest falls in love with the business man's wife, a kind of amateur trollop, but before he can consummate his feelings, he is given an other-worldly injection which renders him entirely unable to do so. Some years later, the curtain falls.

The plot runs out not more than twenty minutes after the play begins and a slow and horrible congealing takes place among the audience from then on, beside which the corpse-like make-up affected by the ghosts appears a positive flush of good health.

Indeed, such is the state of catalepsy which sets in that the old stage effects from *Blithe Spirit* are actually awarded a round of applause, and when the sofa begins to revolve it nearly stops the show.

The lines consist alternately of Gallicisms (such expressive people, these French) like, 'You've been entirely taken in by the complexes of that little minx', and rapier-like exchanges along the lines of this:— 'We're holding our breath.' 'But we haven't got any breath.' 'It's a figure of speech.'

It is also, of course, one of those plays in which the cast spend much of their time explaining the plot to one another, but I respectfully suggest that in the next one they do it off-stage, and save us the pain of involuntary eavesdropping.

The Saxon's Dust, an episode of *Churchill's People,* BBC1, January, 1975. Reviewed by Clive James.

The Saxon's Dust starred John Wood as Edward the Confessor. Wood is one of the best, most treasurable actors we possess — a high stylist. Turn an actor like him, when you can find one, loose on good material, when you can find that, and lyricism will ensue. Give him rubbish to act and he will destroy himself like a Bugatti lubricated with hair-oil.

The script being almost entirely exposition, the characters were mainly engaged in telling one another what they knew already. Since Edward was the centre of the action, he was occupied full time not only with telling people what they knew, but with being told what *he* knew in return. A certain air of boredom was therefore legitimate, which Wood amply conveyed. I myself have never heard dialogue like it, but Edward made it clear that he had been hearing it for years.

'He's making Robert of Whatnot Bishop of London, did you know?' 'A Frenchman to be Bishop of London?' 'He's trying to make us a French colony.' 'But if I leave my nephew as heir . . .' 'Sire, Bishop Beefbroth has come back: the news is good from Rome.' 'That is good, good.' 'On one condition.' 'What condition, pray?' 'News from Dover, Sire!' 'Dover shall pay dear for this!' 'Your uncle Toxic, Queen of the Welsh, proclaims the Bastard heir!' 'This is the last straw. Where do *you* stand, Bostic?' 'Your half-brother Norman the Exhibitionist's son, Cyril . . .'

And so on, world without end. Straining to convey information the writing reveals nothing about the past of the English people, but much about the present state of the English language. 'While we wait here for the Assembly to assemble . . .' one poor sod found himself saying, and straight away his silly hat looked even sillier, since how can an actor go back through time if given lines mired so inextricably in the present? It was The Turkey in Winter. A two-line exchange of dialogue between a pair of shaggy nobles said it all.

'Why do you not give it up?' 'Because I need the money.'

Rosie by Harold Mueller, Bush, July, 1977. Reviewed by Irving Wardle in *The Times.*

... It is evidently beyond even Mr Mueller to translate the alcoholic hard-luck story into a dramatic form.

Everything happens to Rosie. She starts (wouldn't you know) as a would-be violinist, groped by her teacher and thwarted by her father who reroutes her into the hotel business, only to be fired after a night of love with one of the guests.

Thence it is a swift decline through dead-end jobs as switchboard operator, factory worker, barmaid, and prostitute, while she passes through the hands of a succession of steadily less presentable but indistinguishably pig-like males who put her through every sexual outrage from the knitting-needle abortion to gang rape (she is, of course unwell at the time).

Wild Orchids by Frank White (with June Brown as 'Marge'), New End, March, 1976. Reviewed by Nicholas de Jongh in the *Guardian.*

By golly they're hot stuff, country folk, aren't they? And I'll never forget what they all did down there at Goat Spring Farm — not my kind of folk, I can tell you straight. Sex crazy, that's what I call them. I suppose you know old farmer Ben Carver, well he was having his fancy woman, Jenny, that hussy with red hair if you please, canoodling with her, while his wife Marge, we all loved Marge, hasn't she suffered enough after the operation, was on holiday in France with her daughter Lucy. You remember Lucy, the fat one who went off to university and came back little Miss Knowall, not that pride didn't come before a fall, hankering after her brother-in-law.

And talking of fall, reminds me of Bess, her half sister, Ben's first wife's daughter. Now there was a fancy woman if ever I saw one, slouching about the farmhouse in a mini-skirt and wearing one of those see-through blouses. The one I felt sorry for was her husband Geoff — Geoff whom Lucy loved and worked on the farm as well.

Now he loved his wife, really loved her, though folks couldn't see why, seeing that everyone knew that she was making a whorehouse of herself with that young Ronnie, the farm labourer in the caravan. Of course, I blame her father, there's folks who say, and I'm one of them, that he was a little too partial to his daughter. Though after Jenny killed herself driving into the wall, there's some who say it wasn't an accident, he didn't have any fancy goods left.

But then Geoff got a new job and was nearly killed, though it wasn't as awful as the night when they found Bess doing it in the farmhouse with young Ronnie. I think it was Marge who found them — she was never the same after the hysterectomy. Theatre? Oh no, love, it wasn't theatre at all; it was real, true life, heart ... By golly, it did me good. But the one I felt sorry for was lovely June Brown, I just kept hoping that lovely old Colonel who kept calling would take her away from it all ...

Will Shakespeare by Clemence Dane, Shaftesbury, November, 1921. Reviewed by St John Ervine in the *Observer*.

Miss Clemence Dane, whose new play, *Will Shakespeare,* was done at the Shaftesbury Theatre on Thursday night, admits in advance that her case is a trumped-up one or as she prefers to call it, an 'invention', but she defends herself from our dispraise by pleading a worthy purpose: to show by what strange and moving experiences a poet grows. Shakespeare would hardly, I imagine, thank her for her singular advocacy, but might, on the contrary, be confirmed in his belief that women are queer ones; for Miss Dane bases her assertions on the very feminine assumption that a thing must have happened because there is nothing to prove that it didn't. Kit Marlowe was killed in a tavern by someone, and since there is no evidence to show that Shakespeare did not kill him (chiefly because no one has hitherto thought of charging him with the crime), it is permissible, in Miss Dane's opinion, to assume that he did. No one can prove that Shakespeare was not tricked into marrying Anne Hathaway by a pretence that she was pregnant through him. Therefore, he was tricked. Was Jude the Obscure not similarly humbugged, and if he could be deceived, why not Shakespeare? . . . It is just as likely that Mary Fitton was the Dark Lady of the Sonnets as that she was not. Therefore she was. And if Keats could completely lost his head over Miss Fanny Brawne, may not Miss Dane assume that Shakespeare, with as much abandon, lost his over Mary? We cannot believe that Shakespeare killed Marlowe without a strong motive, and so, although her name has not before been mentioned in connection with Kit, we are entitled to assume that Mary Fitton and he had been playing fast and loose with each other, and that Shakespeare killed his friend, accidentally or deliberately, out of jealousy. We can even trace the origin of *Othello* in this misadventure, with Shakespeare as the original Moor, Marlowe as the original Iago and Mary Fitton as the original Desdemona. And is not the fact that none of the State records show that Queen Elizabeth had locked Shakespeare in her palace until he had finished *As You Like It* the clearest possible evidence that she did imprison him, especially when we remember that Sheridan was locked in his room until he had completed a play for Drury Lane? . . . If Sir Arthur Conan Doyle sees visions, may we not conclude that Anne Hathaway saw some too, to the extent of imagining Hamlet, Shylock, Lear, Macbeth, and the whole Shakespearean gallery long before her husband had a hint of them?

Will Shakespeare *by Clemence Dane. Courtesy of* Punch.

Shaw, who perfected the 'critic's device' as a weapon for shooting down plays, also applied it to the business of undermining the actor's art. He loved to have a go at Sir Henry Irving, and it is with huge relish that he brings the device to bear on Irving's tear-jerking performance as an old veteran of Waterloo . . .

A Story of Waterloo by A. Conan Doyle, Lyceum, May, 1895.
Reviewed by George Bernard Shaw in the *Saturday Review.*

Headline: MR IRVING TAKES PAREGORIC

Anyone who consults recent visitors to the Lyceum . . . as to the
merits of Mr Conan Doyle's *Story of Waterloo,* will in nineteen cases
out of twenty learn that the piece is a trifle raised into importance by
the marvellous acting of Mr Irving as Corporal Gregory Brewster.
As a matter of fact, the entire effect is contrived by the author, and is
due to him alone. There is absolutely no acting in it . . .

Before the curtain rises, you read the playbill; and the process
commences at once with the suggestive effect on your imagination
of 'Corporal Gregory Brewster, age eighty-six, a Waterloo veteran,'
of 'Nora Brewster, the corporal's grandniece,' and of 'Scene —
Brewster's lodgings.' By the time that you have read that your own
imagination, with the author pulling the strings, has done half the
work you afterwards give Mr Irving credit for. Up goes the curtain;
and the lodgings are before you, with the humble breakfast table, the
cheery fire, the old man's spectacles, and Bible. Lest you should be
unobservant enough to miss the significance of all this, Miss Annie
Hughes comes in with a basket of butter and bacon, ostensibly to
impersonate the grandniece, really to carefully point all these things
out to you, and to lead up to the entry of the hero by preparing
breakfast for him. When the background is sufficiently laid in by this
artifice, the drawing of the figure commences. Mr Fuller Mellish
enters in the uniform of a modern military sergeant, with a breech-
loading carbine. You are touched: here is the young soldier come to
see the old — two figures from the Seven Ages of Man. Miss
Hughes tells Mr Mellish all about Corporal Gregory. She takes down
the medal, and makes him read aloud to her the press-cutting pasted
beside it which describes the feat for which the medal was given. In
short, the pair work at the picture of the old warrior until the very
dullest dog in the audience knows what he is to see, or imagine he
sees, when the great moment comes. Thus is Brewster already
created, though Mr Irving has not yet left his dressing room. At last,
everything being ready, Mr Fuller Mellish is packed off so as not to
divide the interest.

A squeak is heard behind the scenes: it is the childish treble that
once rang like a trumpet on the powder-waggon at Waterloo. Enter
Mr Irving in a dirty white wig, toothless, blear-eyed, palsied, shaky at
the knees, stooping at the shoulders, incredibly aged and very poor,
but respectable. He makes his way to his chair, and can only sit
down, so stiff are his aged limbs, very slowly and creakily. This
sitting down business is not acting: the callboy could do it; but we
are so thoroughly primed by the playbill, the scene-painter, the stage-
manager, Miss Hughes and Mr Mellish, that we go off in enthusiastic
whispers, 'What superb acting! How wonderfully he does it!' The
corporal cannot recognize his grandniece at first. When he does, he
asks her questions about children — children who have long gone to
their graves at ripe ages. She prepares his tea: he sups it noisily and
ineptly, like an infant. More whispers: 'How masterly a touch of

second childhood!' He gets a bronchial attack and gasps for paregoric, which Miss Hughes administers with a spoon, whilst our faces glisten with tearful smiles. 'Is there another living actor who could take paregoric like that?' The sun shines through the window: the old man would fain sit there and peacefully enjoy the fragrant air and life-giving warmth of the world's summer . . . Hark! a band in the street without, Soldiers pass: the old warhorse snorts feebly, but complains that bands don't play as loud as they used to . . . Mr Fuller Mellish comes back with the breech-loading carbine. The old man handles it; calls it a firelock; and goes crazily through his manual with it. Finally, he unlocks the breech, and as the barrel drops believes that he has broken the weapon in two. Matters being explained, he expresses his unalterable conviction that England will have to fall back on Brown Bess when the moment for action arrives again . . . Mr Fuller Mellish, becoming again superfluous is again got rid of. Enter a haughty gentleman. It is the Colonel of the Royal Scots Guards, the corporal's old regiment. According to the well-known custom of colonels, he has called on the old pensioner to give him a five-pound note. The old man, as if electrically shocked, staggers up and desperately tries to stand for a moment at 'attention' and salute his officer. He collapses, almost slain by the effort, into his chair, mumbling pathetically that he 'were a'most gone that time, Colonel.' 'A masterstroke! Who but a great actor could have executed this heart-searching movement?'

The veteran returns to the fireside: once more he depicts with convincing art the state of an old man's joints. The Colonel goes; Mr Fuller Mellish comes; the old man dozes. Suddenly he springs up. 'The Guards want powder; and, by God, the Guards shall have it.' With these words he falls back to his chair. Mr Fuller Mellish, lest there should be any mistake about it (it is never safe to trust the intelligence of the British public), delicately informs Miss Hughes that her granduncle is dead. The curtain falls amid thunders of applause.

Every old actor into whose hands this article falls will understand perfectly from my description how the whole thing is done . . . The whole performance does not involve one gesture, one line, one thought outside the commonest routine of automatic stage illusion. What, I wonder, must Mr Irving, who knows this better than anyone, feel when he finds this pitiful little handful of hackneyed stage tricks received exactly as if it were a crowning instance of his most difficult and finest art?

Sir Henry Irving. By Harry Furniss.

CHAPTER THREE

Plays in Britain

Plays (and playwrights) come in for as much flak as those who act in them. Here, however, the critic is on more dangerous ground: a bad notice of a play can backfire if the play goes on to become a landmark in theatre history. In these circumstances, a review which was not particularly interesting at the time it was written may have the weight of irony as you read it today.

Thus we have contemporary reviews of Ibsen, Shaw and Oscar Wilde and, from our own time, of John Osborne and Arnold Wesker, Harold Pinter and T. S. Eliot. In the same spirit, I have included Samuel Pepys' views on some of the most popular classics of Shakespeare.

In reading this section you will find that good plays have received treatment as scathing as others which undoubtedly deserved it. (Much the same can, of course, be said of the actors and actresses.)

Shakespeare's major tragedies have not been exempt from the fray. They are not to be found here, but in a separate section devoted to the Classic Roles.

The Amorous Prawn by Anthony Kimmins, Saville, December, 1959. Reviewed by Bernard Levin in the *Daily Express.*

I think *The Amorous Prawn* is perhaps the most grisly, glassy-eyed thing I have encountered in the theatre for a very long time, and even outside the theatre its like is rarely met with except on a fishmonger's slab, and now I feel very ill indeed, and would like to lie down.

Before doing so, I should say that *The Amorous Prawn* is a farce made out of cobwebs and mothballs, my old socks, empty beer bottles, copies of *The Strand Magazine,* dust, holes, mildew, and Mr Ben Travers's discarded typewriter ribbons . . .

And now I really *must* go and lie down, and I hope I shall feel better in the morning.

Arms and the Man by George Bernard Shaw, Avenue theatre, April, 1894. Reviewed by William Archer in the *World.*

I begin positively to believe that (Shaw) may one day write a serious and even an artistic play, if he will only repress his irreverent whimsicality, try to clothe his character-conceptions in flesh and blood, and realize the difference between knowingness and knowledge.

Becket by Jean Anouilh, Aldwych, 1961. Reviewed by Kenneth Tynan.

Becket, in short, is just what one would expect of an author who can write, as M. Anouilh does in his preface: 'I suppose I am not very serious; after all, I work in the theatre . . .'

By such wry disclaimers as this does the second-rater declare himself . . .

Belles without Beaux, a play with an all-women cast of seven, Lyceum, 1819. Reviewed by Charles Lamb in the *Examiner.*

The effect was enchanting. We mean, for once. We do not want to encourage these Amazonian vanities.

The Bells by Leopold Lewis — revival at Greenwich in the 1970s. The play was based on Erckmann-Chatrian's *Le Juif Polonais,* and made famous by Henry Irving's performance in 1871. Headline to review by Milton Shulman in the *Evening Standard:*

CLANG!

(Contributed by Freddie Jones, who appeared in the production.)

The Birthday Party by Harold Pinter, Lyric, Hammersmith, May, 1958. Reviewed in the *Manchester Guardian.*

What all this means, only Mr Pinter knows, for as his characters speak in non sequiturs, half-gibberish and lunatic ravings, they are unable to explain their actions, thoughts or feelings. If the author can forget Beckett, Ionesco and Simpson he may do much better next time.

Blow Your Own Trumpet by Peter Ustinov, Playhouse, 1943. Reviewed in *The Times.*

Mr Ustinov is like a painter with an overloaded palette painting to music . . .

Boeing Boeing by Marc Camoletti, Apollo, February, 1962. Reviewed by Bernard Levin in the *Daily Express.*

I think I'll go by boat.

Il Campiello by Carlo Goldoni, directed by Bill Bryden, performed at the official opening of the National Theatre by H. M. Queen Elizabeth, October, 1976. Reviewed by Sheridan Morley in *Punch.*

There is a number of possible explanations for the presence of *Il Campiello* in the repertoire of the National Theatre at the Olivier. The one I like best is that it represents a complete and never-to-be-repeated mental, physical and theatrical breakdown on the part of all concerned.

and

Il Campiello was what the Queen got — and were she not made of sterner stuff than most of us and considerably more experienced at surviving mind-bendingly boring occasions without falling asleep, I suspect the experience would have cured her of theatregoing for good.

and by Milton Shulman in the *Evening Standard.*

The Italian playwright Carlo Goldoni wrote more than 200 plays and no fewer than sixteen in the single year of 1749. If *Il Campiello* at the National Theatre, very surprisingly selected as the offering for the Queen on this official opening represents one of his best efforts, one shudders to contemplate what most of them must be like.

Il Campiello with Patti Love as Lucietta, Peggy Mount as Donna Pasqua and Stephen Rea as Anzoletto. Courtesy of Punch.

The Cenci by Percy Bysshe Shelley — revival at the Old Vic, May, 1959, directed by Michael Benthall. Reviewed in the *Kentish Independent.*

Shelley's *The Cenci* is in fact one of the most horrifying, gruesome, morbid and frankly repulsive pieces of theatre I have ever seen. Its heavy overtones of lust, violence and perversion make *Cat On A Hot Tin Roof* look like a Disney cartoon, and the infamy of Count Cenci makes Lucretia Borgia look like Mrs Dale.

Most plays, however good, manage to get a touch, if not a sprinkling, of adverse criticism. But now and again comes a real blockbuster, a play — or a production — universally hailed as an out-and-out disaster. One such was William Douglas Home's play **The Cigarette Girl** . . . Duke of York's, June, 1962. Reviewed by Arthur Thirkell in the *Daily Mirror.*
Headline: AWFUL

The bird, loud and clear, last night greeted one of the worst plays I have ever seen. *The Cigarette Girl* certainly made me gasp in amazement, it is so unbelievably bad. The action, such as it is, mainly takes place before the last war in a cellar club where posh young chappies go to meet cheerful cockney hard-working hostesses with hearts of gold. The dialogue is putrid, the acting early marionette, the evening disastrous.

and in the *Daily Sketch.*

At the end, the gallery booed and the polite chap in the stalls said 'Can't see this lot lasting till Saturday.' Said his companion, 'Don't tell me today is Friday.'

Cleomenes by John Dryden, first performed 1675. (Slain, in this instance, by sarcasm.) Discussed by Jeremy Collier in *A Short View of the Immorality and Profaneness of the English Stage,* 1698.

. . . to lodge divinity and scandal together; to make the gods throw starts, like snow-balls, at one another, but especially to court in smut, and rally in blasphemy, is most admirably entertaining! This is much better than all the niceties of decorum . . .

The Cocktail Party by T. S. Eliot, Edinburgh Festival, August, 1949. Reviewed by Alan Dent in the *News Chronicle.*

The week after — as well as the morning after — I take it to be nothing but a finely acted piece of flapdoodle.

Coventry Mystery Plays, Coventry Cathedral, August, 1980. Reviewed by Ned Chaillet in *The Times.*

Eve was just yielding to the Devil in the bombed-out ruins of old Coventry Cathedral when the heavens opened, forcing the third revival of the Coventry Mystery Plays into the shelter of the new Cathedral.
    More torrential criticism like that and we might still have Paradise.

A turn stoned by the most powerful Critic of all.

Charles Charming's Challenges on the Pathway to the Throne by Clive James, published in 1981 and performed for a limited season at the Apollo theatre by the author, supported by Russell Davies and Pamela Stephenson. Reviewed by Paul Theroux in the *Sunday Times.*

This is not satire, but name-dropping . . . He writes like a man who wishes he was invited to more parties.

Colonel Satan by Booth Tarkington, Haymarket, 1930s. Reviewed by Hannen Swaffer.

Henry Ainley was originally cast to play the lead, but withdrew during rehearsals on grounds of ill-health.
    I think if I had been Henry Ainley I should have broken down during the rehearsals, just as he did.

Counting the Ways by Edward Albee, 1976. Reviewed by Benedict Nightingale.

It lasts one hour only, but that hour left me feeling I had spent an evening fidgeting in an expensive and pretentious restaurant while a peculiarly snooty waiter insisted on serving me, with impeccable sloth, elaborate objects that turned out to be British Rail buns in disguise.

and in *Newsweek,* February, 1977.

Albee seems to be trying for Auden's marvellous vein of domestic metaphysics . . . but the play sounds like George Burns and Grace Allen trying to keep up a dinner conversation with Wittgenstein . . . I have never seen such desperately ingratiating smiles on the faces of actors.

Cymbeline by Shakespeare, Lyceum, September, 1896. Reviewed by George Bernard Shaw in the *Saturday Review.*

I confess to a difficulty in feeling civilized just at present. Flying from the country, where the gentlemen of England are in an ecstasy of chicken-butchering, I return to town to find the higher wits assembled at a play 300 years old, in which the sensation scene exhibits a woman waking up to find her husband reposing gorily in her arms with his head cut off . . .
  Cymbeline . . . is for the most part stagey trash of the lowest melodramatic order, in parts abominably written, throughout intellectually vulgar and, judged in point of thought by modern intellectual standards, vulgar, foolish, offensive, indecent, and exasperating beyond all tolerance.

Cyrano de Bergerac by Edmond Rostand, Old Vic, November, 1946. Reviewed in the *New Statesman.*

The actors deserved sympathy: like kittens, they took a long, long time to drown.

Here is an instance of a critic celebrating the non-performance of a play.

La Dame aux Camellias by Dumas *fils* (in which Sarah Bernhardt achieved one of her greatest successes in Paris). Discussed by G. H. Lewes in the *Leader,* April, 1853.

At Drury Lane we were threatened with a version of *La Dame aux Camellias,* but the Lord Chamberlain refused a licence to this unhealthy idealization of one of the worst evils of our social life. Paris may delight in such pictures, but London, thank God!, has still enough instinctive repulsion against pruriency not to tolerate them.

Dazzling Prospect by M. J. Farrell and John Perry, Globe, June, 1961. Reviewed by Bernard Levin in the *Daily Express.*

The pitiful little thing has to do with horse-racing, and you might perhaps say that it is by Imbecility out of Staggering Incompetence.

A Doll's House by Henrik Ibsen, first London production by Charles Carrington, Novelty Theatre, 1889. Reviewed by Clement Scott in *Sporting and Dramatic News.*

It is as though someone had dramatized the cooking of a Sunday dinner (no bad subject for a play, one might think nowadays).

and a more recent judgement by James Agate in the *Sunday Times,* 1930:

A Doll's House has no modern application because the modern Nora would simply tell Helmer to stop being daft.

The Elephant Man by Bernard Pomerance, Lyttelton (National), July, 1980. Reviewed by Michael Billington in the *Guardian.*

I wish I could like *The Elephant Man* more . . .

For Ever by Noel Langley, Shaftesbury, November, 1934. Reviewed in the *Daily Express.*

The immortal Dante, that singular ornament of Italy, becomes, as presented to us last night in this costume play with modern dialogue, an insufferable, pettish prig.
But the costumes, designed by the author, are beautiful.
So modern is the first act, both in mincing mannerism and mincing dialogue — for example, 'I could have passed completely away!' and (spoken by Giotto to Dante) 'There are times when I could hit you!' — that the atmosphere of an unfashionable Mayfair muse vanquishes the muse of Dante.
But the settings, designed by E. E. Stern, are delightful.
Miss Margaretta Scott is lovely as Beatrice. Mr Eric Portman makes a feverishly enthusiastic attack on the author's Dante. Miss Lola Duncan is excitingly real as Dante's step-mother.
And — this is the story of Dante's tortured soul, his passion for Beatrice, and his divine talent as seen by the author.
But, as I have said, the costumes and the settings . . .

The Fourth Wall by A. A. Milne, Haymarket, March, 1928. Reviewed by Hannen Swaffer.

How to stifle interest in a play with that most subtly barbed of English compliments, 'How nice!'

The Haymarket did its very best last evening to fall into line with modern tradition. It produced a crook play!
The scene, it is true, was a nicely furnished study in a country

mansion in Sussex, nearly all the characters were ladies and gentlemen and nobody used an improper word.

Still, it was a crook play.

We saw a carefully-arranged murder, plotted as vengeance by two former convicts, and carefully covered up, in view of the audience, as a simple case of suicide.

The ex-convicts, however, were fashionably dressed and the plot was exposed, not by a mere policeman, but by a charming young woman with the nicest of manners, the ward of the victim, and the very presentable man who was in love with her . . . If there had been less chatter, *The Fourth Wall* would have been a perfect example of the English crook play, written for the nicest of audiences.

Fresh Fields by Ivor Novello, Criterion, 1933.

The frocks were charming.

The Gazebo by Alec Coppel, Savoy, March, 1960. Reviewed by Bernard Levin in the *Daily Express.*

A gazebo is a kind of summer house, to anticipate your first question.

The etymology of the word is not certain, but the Oxford Dictionary hazards a guess that it may be facetious coinage on the lines of 'placebo'.

A placebo, to anticipate your *second* question, is a pill which looks impressive but is, in fact, quite inefficacious.

It is given by doctors to hypochondriacs, who need nothing more than reassurance. Its etymology is from the Latin: placebo means 'I will please.'

The Gazebo is a placebo and it doesn't.

The Homecoming by Harold Pinter, RSC at the Aldwych, June, 1965. Reviewed by Anthony Seymour in the *Yorkshire Post.*

Mr Pinter guides us into his strange wasteland of 20th-century loneliness and then deserts us. We are soon lost in his labyrinth of dead ends, unmade roads and confusing signposts.

He is more cruel, gruesome and deliberately offensive in this two-act horror than in his previous plays. On its face value, it is callous and empty enough: what lies in its Freudian depths one dreads to think.

Home Chat by Noel Coward, Duke of York's, October, 1927. Reviewed in the *Westminster Gazette.*

'We expected better.'

'So did I.'

This conversation piece between a voice in a gallery and Noel Coward when he came forward to take a call at the end of his new

Noel Coward.

play *Home Chat* last night was a succinct criticism of the piece. As it is endorsed by the author, it can confidently be put on record.

Ghosts by Ibsen, Royalty, March, 1891. The *Daily Telegraph* attacked the play in a leading article.

Ay! The play performed last night is 'simple' enough in plan and purpose, but simple only in the sense of an open drain; of a loathsome sore unbandaged; of a dirty act done publicly; or of a lazar-house with all its doors and windows open.

and by Clement Scott in the *Illustrated London News*.

. . . in all my experience of the stage . . . I have seldom known a 'cheekier' move than the opening of the Royalty Theatre . . . with a play that has not passed the censorship, and that play none other than the revolting *Ghosts* of the Scandinavian Ibsen. But the 'cheek' does not end there, by any means. It goes on to imply that our poor, neglected and degraded stage, having no literature of its own, and fettered up with the shackles of what the revolutionaries call 'conventionality', is to be taught what literature is with the aid of a dull, verbose preacher, and to learn what freedom is by means of a play that may be obnoxious to many men, and that cannot possibly be discussed in all its morbid details in any mixed assembly of men and women.

An Ideal Husband by Oscar Wilde, Haymarket, January, 1895. Reviewed by H. G. Wells (anonymously) in the *Pall Mall Gazette*.

. . . the play is unquestionably very poor.

and by Clement Scott in the *Illustrated London News*.

Cleverness nowadays is nothing but elaborate contradiction, and the man or woman who can say that black is white or white is black in a fanciful fashion is considered a genius. There is scarcely one Oscar Wildeism uttered in the new Haymarket play that will bear one minute's analysis, but for all that they tickle the ears of the groundlings, and are accepted as stage cleverness.

and discussed in a letter by Henry James.

The thing seemed to me so helpless, so crude, so bad, so clumsy, feeble and vulgar, that as I walked away across St James's Square to learn my own fate, the prosperity of what I had seen seemed to me to constitute a dreadful presumption of the shipwreck of *G.D.,* and I stopped in the middle of the Square, paralysed by the terror of this probability — afraid to go on and learn more. 'How *can* my piece do anything with a public with whom *that* is a success?'

The Importance of Being Earnest by Oscar Wilde, St James's, February, 1895. Unsigned review in *Truth.*

Whether we should have heard as much as we have about it, had anybody else written it, is doubtful; but that only shows the

Oscar Wilde. By Alfred Bryan.

importance of being — Oscar . . . There is no attempt at characterisation, but all the *dramatis personae,* from the heroes down to the butlers, talk pure and undiluted Wildese.

Inadmissible Evidence by John Osborne, Royal Court, September, 1964. Reviewed by Philip Hope-Wallace in the *Guardian.*

Before the end a feeling obtrudes that a bulldozer is being used where a trowel would have done.

and the same production, when it came to the Theatre Royal, Brighton, reviewed by the *Brighton and Hove Herald.*

Mr (Nicol) Williamson has a prodigious memory and a shining talent, but even he cannot counteract the boredom engendered by this incredibly wordy sermon on sex.

Julius Caesar by Shakespeare, Her Majesty's. Discussed by George Bernard Shaw in the *Saturday Review,* January, 1898.

It is impossible for even the most judiciously minded critic to look without a revulsion of indignant contempt at this travestying of a great man as a silly braggart, whilst the pitiful gang of mischief-makers who destroy him are lauded as statesmen and patriots. There is not a single sentence uttered by Shakespeare's Julius Caesar that is, I will not say worthy of him, but worthy of an average Tammany boss. Brutus is nothing but a familiar type of English preacher: politically he would hardly impress the Thames Conservancy Board . . .

Ladies Without, Garrick, March, 1946. Reviewed by James Agate in the *Sunday Times.*

'Sorrow and silence are strong and patient, endurance is Godlike' — from Longfellow's *Evangeline.*

Lady Chatterley's Lover, adapted from D. H. Lawrence by John Hart, Arts, August, 1961. Reviewed by Kenneth Tynan in the *Observer.*

The core of *Lady Chatterley's Lover* is the sexual act, which cannot be shown on the stage. Hence the failure of *Lady Chatterley* (Arts), a dramatisation by John Hart that perfectly illustrates what Lawrence meant by 'sex in the head.' It is all talk and teasing, all hints and evasion, and though it makes theatrical history by using (just before the second-act curtain) the most basic of the four-letter words, it comes no nearer to the act itself than a few tweed-clutching embraces, followed by blackouts and a morning scene in Mellors's bed, which was ruined for me when I perceived that Connie, so far from being naked, was wearing beneath the sheets a flesh-tinted corselette of bullet-proof impregnability . . .

Little Eyolf by Ibsen, Arts, October, 1930. Reviewed by James Agate in the *Sunday Times.*

. . . nowhere else throughout the great works is dullness so rampant as it is in the last half of this play, the chasm between its two tortured souls finding its image in the spectator's yawn.

Lock Up Your Daughters, Rattle of a Simple Man and **Revudeville** all came under attack in the Annual Report of the Public Morality Council in May, 1963. As reported in the *Daily Express.*

The Council claims there are still too many plays with sordid and unhealthy themes. The Rev. Donald Strudwick, Chairman of the Stage Plays, Radio and Television Sub-Committee, writes, 'Why we should continue to be afflicted with plays presenting abnormalities and degradation in an infinity of different forms is something of a puzzle.'

Look Back in Anger by John Osborne, Royal Court, May 1956. Reviewed by Milton Shulman in the *Evening Standard.*

Nothing is so comfortable to the young as the opportunity to feel sorry for themselves. Every generation automatically assumes that it has the exclusive, authentic, gilt-edged, divine right to be described as 'lost'.
   Look Back in Anger . . . sets up a wailing wall for the latest post-war generation of under-thirties. It aims at being a despairing cry but achieves only the stature of a self-pitying snivel.

and by J. C. Trewin in *The Illustrated London News.*

The dramatist of *Look Back in Anger,* we are told, feels that 'as a representative of the younger generation he has every right to be very angry.' Some of his audience may be angrier still, but not for the same reason. The play grated on me like the sustained whine of an ancient tramcar coming down a steep hill. Mr Osborne will have other plays in him, and perhaps he will settle down, now that he has got this off his mind.

Love and Laughter by David Piper, Lyric, Hammersmith, June, 1957. Reviewed by W. A. Darlington in the *Daily Telegraph.*

I am not going to say that *Love and Laughter* is the worst play I have ever seen — I have seen many as bad or worse, whenever I act as judge in a play competition — but these never reach the stage. To see one of this class actually produced had therefore a fearful fascination for me. The author, David Piper, achieved feats of implausibility in plot, incident and character expressed in such a facile flow of undistinguished verse that I sat spellbound. There was a certain morbid interest in waiting to see whether the play had any particular theme or purpose, but this petered out.

Love in a Tub by Sir George Etherege, Duke's theatre, Lincoln's Inn Fields, 1664-5. Reviewed by Samuel Pepys in his *Diary*.

. . . very merry, but only so by gesture, no wit at all.

Major Barbara by George Bernard Shaw, Court theatre, November, 1905. Reviewed by William Archer in the *World*.

There are no human beings in *Major Barbara*: only animated points of view.

Man and Superman by George Bernard Shaw, Royal Court, May, 1905. Discussed by Bertrand Russell in a letter to Goldsworthy Lowes Dickinson, 20 July, 1904, reprinted in Russell's *Autobiography,* Vol. I, 1967.

I think Shaw, on the whole, is more bounder than genius; and though of course I admit him to be 'forcible', I don't admit him to be 'moral' . . . I couldn't get on with *Man and Superman*: it disgusted me.

A Man's Job by Ferdinand Brückner, adapted and translated by Richard Duschinsky, Arts, November, 1959. Reviewed by Bernard Levin in the *Daily Express*.

The awfulness of *A Man's Job* beggars my powers of description, which I flatter myself are considerable. It contains remarks like 'Our shares will rise — in fact they will rocket into the financial stratosphere' and 'In spite of our incompatible attitudes, due to the vicissitudes of our characters, we are all indestructible entities.'

It tells a tale so lurid and ridiculous, so full of mad fragments about a wicked woman who loves her stepson, and a wicked man who loves his stepmother, that even if it had not been couched in language that few actors living could speak without giggling it would still have driven me to wonder whether it was not in fact some wild practical joke that had gone wrong.

But that is not all. Oh, my paws and whiskers, it is not all. The whole appalling thing seemed to have got stuck in some kink in the space-time continuum. Hours and hours went by during which the same thing happened over and over again.

Each member of the cast would explain the plot, in exhaustive detail, to every other member — separately, — whereupon the others would repeat it back, presumably in order to see if they had got it right.

A festive atmosphere spread through the audience; baskets of provisions were produced and shared among the sufferers. Some went out for a few hours and had a meal; nothing had happened when they came back.

Midnight came and went, the sky began to lighten, the milk bottles could be heard clinking in the streets. I began to fear that we were all bewitched, that when we finally awoke we would find ourselves in some strange world of the twenty-first century.

I could bear it no longer; I tiptoed up the aisle and out into the bright, brave day. For all I know, it is going on still.

The Persecution and Assassination of Marat as performed by the Inmates of the Asylum of Charenton under the direction of the Marquis de Sade by Peter Weiss, RSC at the Aldwych, August, 1964. Reviewed by Ronald Bryden in the *New Statesman*.

Weiss has written a brilliant play; not what I'd call an intelligent one.

and discussed by Emile Littler in an interview with the *Daily Telegraph*.

As a governor of the Royal Shakespeare Company and a member of the executive I have dissociated myself from this programme of dirt plays at the Aldwych.

These plays do not belong, or should not, to the Royal Shakespeare. They are entirely out of keeping with our public image, and with having the Queen as our Patron.

Marat/Sade *with Ian Richardson as Herald, Patrick Magee as the Marquis de Sade and Glenda Jackson as Charlotte Corday. Courtesy of* Punch.

Marching Song by John Whiting, St Martin's, April, 1954. Reviewed by David Lewin in the *Daily Express*.

The general dies at dawn in John Whiting's new play — but oh, the talk that goes on through the night before the death.

Talk about hope, talk about defeat, talk about love — and just talk.

Measure for Measure by Shakespeare. Discussed by James Agate in the *Sunday Times*, December, 1933.

My own objections to the play are simple. The first is that the Duke in the long speech 'Be absolute for death' talks the most absolute bosh that ever fell from human lips. 'Thy best of rest is sleep, And that thou oft provokest; yet grossly fear'st Thy death, which is no more,' is on the intellectual level of Miss Seward's: 'Annihilation is only a pleasing sleep without a dream.'

The Merchant of Venice by Shakespeare. Discussed by Kenneth Tynan.

Whenever I see *The Merchant of Venice,* I while away the blanker bits of verse by trying to pull the play together in my mind. Does Shylock stand for the Old Testament (an eye for an eye, etc) and Portia for the New (mercy, etc)? And if so, what does that make Antonio, the shipping magnate whose bond unites the two plots? Does he represent the spirit of Protestantism? These metaphysical hares chase each other round and round; and when I have done, the play remains the curate's egg it always was. Or, rather, the rabbi's egg, because so much depends on Shylock . . .

A Midsummer Night's Dream by Shakespeare, King's Theatre, September, 1662. Reviewed by Samuel Pepys in his *Diary*.

To the King's Theatre, where we saw *Midsummer Night's Dream,* which I have never seen before, nor shall ever again, for it is the most insipid, ridiculous play that ever I saw in my life.

Mourning Becomes Electra by Eugene O'Neill, Old Vic, November, 1961. Reviewed by Bernard Levin in the *Daily Express.*

Mourning Becomes Electra is hollow.

Mrs Warren's Profession by George Bernard Shaw. Reviewed by Max Beerbohm in the *Saturday Review,* May, 1898 after *reading* the play. Public performance was banned by the Censor up to the 1920s.

Of Mr Shaw's philosophy I need merely say that it rests, like Plato's *Republic,* on a profound ignorance of human nature.

Murder on Account by Hayden Talbot and Kathleen Hayden, Wintergarden, Drury Lane, September, 1936. Reviewed by James Agate.

In a novel about ancient Rome, written by a maiden lady residing at Putney, I came across this sentence. 'The lion sprang with eclat upon the Christian martyr, who expired with aplomb.' *Murder on Account* has the same effect on one's critical faculty.

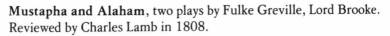

Alice Delysia 1919. By Nerman.

Mustapha and Alaham, two plays by Fulke Greville, Lord Brooke. Reviewed by Charles Lamb in 1808.

Whether we look into his plays, or his most passionate love-poems, we find all frozen and made rigid with intellect.

The Other House by Henry James (1896), performed at the Mermaid, August, 1969. Reviewed by Herbert Kretzmer.

The play is a ponderous plodding Victorian melodrama about the dark and destructive passions a woman is capable of when suffering the pangs of unrequited love.

Having seen this almost unendurable play, I can only salute the sagacity of the long-dead impresario who returned Mr James' play to him by return of post.

Here you see a critic desperately trying to find something to be nice about in what was obviously a terrible play, and all because he was sweet on Miss Delysia.

A Pair of Trousers by Frederick Jackson, Criterion, December, 1930. Reviewed by Hannen Swaffer in the *Daily Express.*

Alice Delysia stood in the centre of the stage last night in one of the most fascinating long coats I have seen upon a woman for months.

She need not have worn it in the drawing-room, as she did. I think a woman would have left it, normally, outside somewhere: but there she stood, anyway, in what Mabel Russell told me was a caramel-coloured chiffon-velvet coat trimmed with red fox.

The fine line of this garment made a most pleasing picture, and Delysia, knowing that it would look like that, turned round and stood with her back to the audience, so that all could see it.

Delysia knows all the tricks of that kind. We saw a lot of them last night — her feline charm, her mild protests, her indignations.

And, once, we heard her sing. She is interesting enough to watch, whatever she does.

A Pair of Trousers concerns a strange artist, of some kind of another, who tore his trousers in a lady's boudoir and while they mended them, was discovered by the lady's friends . . . I did not understand why half the things that were done were done . . .

Still, it shows off Delysia, which is saying a lot.

Besides, although the play will not stand examination, it is played with her accustomed verve by Delysia herself . . .

Here's another blockbuster, one of those plays the critics made a meal of.

The Pastime of Monsieur Robert by Howard Sackler, Hampstead Theatre Club, February, 1966. Reviewed by David Nathan in the *Sun.*

Unfortunately, there is little to distinguish the play itself from the playlets within, and they are described as trash. This shows confidence on the part of the author, if nothing else.

and by Milton Shulman in the *Evening Standard.*

There was a time about a decade ago when lush, steamy writing was all the rage. There was Christopher Fry, Giraudoux, early Anouilh, Enid Bagnold and a host of imitators. *The Pastime of Monsieur Robert . . .* not only seems to have missed the bus, but is walking home in the rain.

Peer Gynt by Ibsen. Reviewed by Clemens Petersen in *Faedralant,* 1867.

. . . it is not poetry, because in the transmutation of reality into art it fails to meet the demands of either art or reality.

and by Hans Andersen in 1870.

Read *Peer Gynt,* which is written by a mad poet. One goes crazy oneself reading this book.

The Princess and the Butterfly by Arthur Wing Pinero, St James's, March, 1897. Reviewed by George Bernard Shaw in the *Saturday Review.*

And now . . . we have Mr Pinero, who was born . . . in 1895, quite unable to get away from . . . the horrors of middle age. He has launched at us a play in five acts — two and a half of them hideously superfluous — all about being over forty. The heroine is forty, and can talk of nothing else. The hero is over forty, and is blind to every other fact in the universe. Having this topic of conversation in common, they get engaged in order that they may save one another from being seduced by the attraction of youth into foolish marriages. They then fall in love, she with a fiery youth of twenty-eight, he with a meteoric girl of eighteen. Up to the last moment I confess I had sufficient confidence in Mr Pinero's saving sense of humour to believe that he would give the verdict against himself, and admit that the meteoric girl was too young for the hero (twenty-seven years' discrepancy) and the heroine too old for the fiery youth (thirteen years' discrepancy). But no: he gravely decided that the heart that loves never ages; and now perhaps he will write us another drama, limited strictly to three acts with, as heroine, the meteoric girl at forty and her husband at sixty-seven, and, as hero, the fiery youth at forty-nine with his wife at sixty-two.

Rain on the Roof by Dennis Potter, television play on LWT, November, 1980. Reviewed by Clive James in the *Observer*.

. . . Billy was either mentally defective or holy. Perhaps he was both. Seducing Janet under a quilt, he murdered John with a knife of glass. Yes, he had certainly transformed their middle-class lives.

It is a cardinal principle with Dennis Potter that all middle class people except certain playwrights need to have their lives shaken up.

A River Breeze by Roland Culver, Phoenix, September, 1956. Reviewed by Kenneth Tynan in the *Observer*.

A River Breeze (Phoenix), by Roland Culver, is a theatrical coelacanth; a thing we had long thought extinct, now surfacing unexpectedly in semi-fossilised form. It is a Loamshire comedy. The heroine's head, shaved because of ringworm, reveals a birthmark (the nine of diamonds) which proves that she was switched in the cradle with another tot. This is lucky, since she has fallen in love with the boy she thought to be her brother. Incest and vermin keep the plot spinning, and there is a long and irrelevant pause in which a kitchen accessory known as 'the Kenwood Chef' is interminably demonstrated . . .

Romeo and Juliet by Shakespeare, March, 1662. Reviewed by Samuel Pepys in his *Diary*.

Romeo and Juliet . . . is a play, of itself, the worst that ever I heard in my life.

Roots by Arnold Wesker, Royal Court, July, 1959. Reviewed by Dick Richards in the *Daily Mail*.

A well-observed play, but what about a little glamour instead of these peeks through everyday keyholes?

and by Alan Dent in the *News Chronicle*.

If Arnold Wesker's play is true to life, then the agricultural labourers of Norfolk suffer aches and pains and paralysis nearly all the time and talk of little else, and their womenfolk must all be deplorable housewives.

Rosencrantz and Guildenstern are Dead by Tom Stoppard, National Theatre at the Old Vic, April, 1967. Reviewed by W. A. Darlington in the *Daily Telegraph*.

It is the kind of play . . . that one might enjoy more at a second hearing, if only the first time through hadn't left such a strong feeling that once is enough.

and by Robert Brustein in *The Third Theatre* (Cape, 1970).

In outline, the idea is extremely ingenious; in execution, it is derivative and familiar, even prosaic. As an artist, Stoppard does not fight hard enough for his insights — they all seem to come to him, prefabricated, from other plays — with the result that his air of pessimism seems affected, and his philosophical meditations, while witty and urbane, never obtain the thickness of *felt* knowledge. Whenever the play turns metaphysical, which is frequently, it turns spurious, particularly in the author's recurrent discourses upon death: 'Death is not romantic . . . and death is not a game which will soon be over . . . death is anything . . . death is not. It's an absence of presence, nothing more . . . the endless time of never coming back.' This sort of thing is squeezed out like toothpaste throughout the play, the gravity of the subject never quite overcoming the banality of its expression . . .

There is, in short, something disturbingly voguish and available about this play, as well as a prevailing strain of cuteness which shakes one's faith in the author's serious intentions.

Rosencrantz and Guildenstern are Dead *with John Stride as Rosencrantz and Edward Petherbridge as Guildenstern. Courtesy of* Punch.

Rosmersholm by Ibsen, first performed in England at the Vaudeville, 1891. Reviewed in the *Gentlewoman.*

These Ibsen creatures are 'neither men nor women, they are ghouls', vile, unlovable, unnatural, morbid monsters, and it were well indeed for society if all such went and drowned themselves at once.

and in *Topical Times.*

There are certain dishes composed of such things as frogs and snails, stews in which oil and garlic reek, and dreadful compounds which we taste out of sheer curiosity and which, if we expressed our honest, candid opinion, we should pronounce to be nasty and unpleasant . . . *Rosmersholm* is beyond me.

The Rover by Mrs Aphra Behn, Covent Garden, February, 1757. Reviewed in the *London Chronicle*. Aphra Behn (c. 1640-1680), was a prolific woman writer who ushered in an era of female playwrights which has never been equalled in the theatre subsequently. Dr Doran wrote of her: 'With Dryden she vied in indecency and was not overcome.' Virginia Woolf recalled her achievement in these words: 'Here begins the freedom of the mind . . . For now that Aphra Behn had done it girls could say . . . I can make money by my pen.'

. . . One of the Personages of the Drama takes off his Breeches in the Sight of the Audience, whose Diversion is of a complicated Nature on the Occasion. The Ladies are first alarmed; then the Men stare: the Women put up their Fans . . . It is a Matter of Wonder that the Upper Gallery don't call for an Hornpipe, or, 'Down with the Drawers', according to their usual custom of insisting upon as much as they can get for their money. But to be a little serious, it should be remembered by all Managers that this Play was written in the dissolute Days of Charles the Second; and that Decency at least is, or ought to be, demanded at present.

Saved by Edward Bond, Royal Court, November, 1965. Reviewed by W. A. Darlington in the *Daily Telegraph*.

The key scene in this piece is one in which a gang of young South London roughs work themselves up into a savage frenzy in which they stone a baby to death, as delinquent children might stone a puppy or a kitten.

The effect of this scene on me is precisely the opposite of what the author intended me to feel. I had no sense of horror, no dramatic illusion.

I knew there was no baby in the pram, just as I could see there were no stones in the actors' hands. My only emotion was cold disgust at being asked to sit through such a scene.

Saved *with Tony Selby as Fred and John Castle as Len. Courtesy of* Punch.

The Second Mrs Tanqueray by Pinero, St James's, 1893. Reviewed by George Bernard Shaw.

This play provided one of the major roles in which actresses at the turn of the century, notably Mrs Patrick Campbell, swayed their audiences. Pinero was hailed on its appearance as a prophet of social change and a new Ibsen.

Mr Pinero, in fact, invented a new sort of play by taking the ordinary article and giving it an air of novel, profound, original thought. This he was able to do because he was an inveterate 'character actor' (a technical term denoting a clever stage performer who cannot act, and who therefore makes an elaborate study of the disguises and stage tricks by which acting can be grotesquely simulated) as well as a competent dramatist on customary lines. His performance as a thinker and a social philosopher is simply character acting in the domain of authorship, and can impose only on those who are taken in by character acting on stage.

and a revival at the Haymarket, August, 1950. Reviewed by John Barber in the *Daily Express*.

The plot is somewhat musty, and Cecil Beaton's ponderous brocades and tapestries drape it like a museum piece.

Shakespeare's Sister performed in Monstrous Regiment's feminist season, ICA, December, 1980. Reviewed by Irving Wardle in *The Times*.

The point about Shakespeare's sister, as Virginia Woolf imagined her, is that there was no escape from conventional womanhood even for a girl who had it in her to write *Hamlet*.
  Nobody in this piece seems up to writing anything more than a line to the milkman.

Sirocco, by Noel Coward, Daly's, November, 1927. Reviewed by St John Ervine, in the *Observer*.

This play was a famous disaster, consistently booed by audiences.

We must not allow ourselves to be dazzled by (Mr Coward's) youth — after all, Marlowe wrote *Tamburlaine the Great* before he had left Cambridge; Shakespeare was doing decent stuff before he was the age Mr Coward now is . . . What Mr Coward now has to do is not to make us realize how young he is, but that he is growing up. Is he? This play in my opinion proves that he is. It proves, too, that the process is painful . . .
  Young Mrs Griffin, married to a beefy oaf and obliged to spend too much time in Italy in the society of elderly, frowsty and mentally bankrupt persons, finds herself in the state of danger to which young, beautiful and romantic women are prone when they discover themselves to be unsuitably married. She seeks relief from her boring life in the tempestuous but tawdry passion of Syrio Marson, son of an English father and an Italian mother, and allows herself to

Sirocco *with Ivor Novello as Syrio Marson, Frances Doble as Lucy Griffin* (below) *and Ada King as Miss Johnson. From* The Illustrated Sporting and Dramatic News.

be seduced by him in a low-class dining saloon. Thereafter she lives with him in his slovenly studio for a week. At the end of that time she has no illusions left about the glory of romantic passion. The whole business has become unutterably disgusting to her and Syrio, with his Elinor Glyn emotions, is discovered to be a nasty little dago with the spiritual and mental outlook of an enlarged newt. Mr Coward has, in short, written a tract. This, he says in effect, is what all this cinema romance amounts to — something foul and sluttish and finally impossible. Routine affection may be and no doubt is devastatingly dull, but vamp love, movie passion, these are duller still and those who mistake Hollywood for Heaven are likely to land in hell . . .

When Mr Coward took the stage at the end of this play in the face of a hostile audience, I thought he displayed a courage that was wholly admirable. His indignation — as indignation in excess nearly always does — robs him of his sense of humour. There are situations and lines in this play of a banality which is unbelievable. The flippant Mr Coward would not have invented them. But the deadly earnest Mr Coward naturally does because his earnestness is greater than his experience . . .

The Sleeping Prince by Terence Rattigan, Phoenix, November, 1953. Reviewed by Kenneth Tynan in the *Daily Sketch.*

Once upon a time there was an actor called gruff Laurence Olivier, whose wife was an actress called pert Vivien Leigh, and a playwright called clever Terence Rattigan wrote a play for them called *The Sleeping Prince,* with a gruff part for him and a pert part for her, and to nobody's surprise it ran happily ever after, with twice-weekly matinées.

There was also a villainess called wicked Martita Hunt, who stole the play from under everyone's nose, which was a very great sin indeed; and if you, children, ever do that to ladies and gentlemen who are stars, you will very likely get your little rib-cages crushed for you.

In terms such as these, history may record the arrival of Mr. Rattigan's new 'occasional fairy-tale' at the Phoenix Theatre last night.

Among the select group of plays written for eminent husband-and-wife teams in coronation years, it ranks very high . . .

The Sleeping Prince *with Vivien Leigh as Mary, Laurence Olivier as The Grand Duke and Jeremy Spenser as The King. Courtesy of* Punch.

Sons of Light by David Rudkin; RSC at the Aldwych, 1977. Reviewed by Bernard Levin in the *Sunday Times*.

It is said that the original version of David Rudkin's *Sons of Light* would have lasted for eight hours. The R S C, no doubt mindful of their great patron's opinion that the quality of mercy is not strained, are giving a performance that takes only three . . . the play is certainly obscure enough to satisfy the most tenacious holder of the belief that being bored in a theatre is good for you . . .

The Sound of Murder by William Fairchild, Aldwych, August, 1959. Reviewed by Bernard Levin in the *Daily Express*.

As I left, clutching my spinning head, I swear I heard people in the theatre shout 'Bravo!'

I assume they were applauding the bare-faced impudence of the author for writing stuff like this, and of the management for hiring a theatre in the West End of London and putting it on.

Critics are often told they must not give away the plots of murder plays. Mr William Fairchild need not fear that I will reveal his secrets.

The plot is of such titanic and recondite imbecility that I couldn't reveal it if I wanted to. It concerns a kind of male Enid Blyton whose wife and supplanter decide to murder him, not for the excellent reasons provided by the stories he writes (most of which are read to the audience in the course of the action) but simply in order to get married.

There is a tape-recorder which faithfully repeats great slices of the dialogue — an entirely unnecessary proceeding, since most of the play is in any case repeated by the actors in ten-minute stretches, like some mad Bach fugue.

There is a gun, and a vicar, and chrysanthemums, and thunder and lightning, and whisky and champagne (the champagne gets a credit in the programme, though the whisky does not — why?) and a telephone which is the only thing in the play, from beginning to end, that rings true.

Most of the dialogue consists of the members of the cast explaining the plot to one another, a service I can well imagine they need.

But I cannot see that they need the explanations to be couched in language of such shattering banality.

The Spanish Friar by John Dryden. Reviewed by Jeremy Collier, 1698.

. . . This litter of epithets make the poem look like a bitch over-stocked with puppies, and sucks the sense almost to skin and bone.

A Streetcar Named Desire by Tennessee Williams, Aldwych, October, 1949. Reviewed by J. C. Trewin in the *Observer.*

. . . when the night's tumult and shouting — much of it for Vivien Leigh — had died, at least one playgoer emerged puzzled by the reputation of a tedious and squalid anecdote . . . Now and then good writing glimmers, but little to explain the Broadway reputation and run.

The Tempest by Shakespeare, discussed by Charles Lamb.

. . . to have the conjuror brought before us in his conjuring-gown, with his spirits about him . . . involves such a quantity of the hateful-incredible, that all our reverence for the author cannot hinder us from perceiving such gross attempts upon the senses to be in the highest degree childish and inefficient.

Tell Tale Murder by Philip Weathers, Q Theatre, 1952. Reviewed by J. C. Trewin in the *Observer.*

Cornwall will never reveal itself to the casual visitor. Most plays set west of Tamar are by up-country men, either cottage-pie writers who chat about the climate and the food, or ghoulie-and-ghostie specialists who raise a House of Usher in every village. At any Cornish drama festival *Tell-Tale Murder,* by Philip Weathers (Q Theatre) would get a whoop of joy; it is in the winding-sheet class, with Freda Jackson to gloom, D. A. Clarke-Smith to boom, and Thomas Heathcote to loom. Other words chime naturally: doom and tomb. This is a night of clean sepulchral fun, a warning to visitors to avoid unfenced mine-shafts. Stoically, Miss Jackson carries the burden of her past as a not-too-merry widow. Her housekeeper jabs pins into waxen images. Iss, us can be proper primitive.

The Tenth Man by Paddy Chayefsky, Comedy, April, 1961. Reviewed by Bernard Levin in the *Daily Express.*

There is a certain kind of bad play to which critics are supposed to be kind because it is what is known as 'well-meaning'.

Plays about religion, plays about Jews, plays about mental illness — all come into this category.

So I suppose I must say of this play by Mr Paddy Chayefsky, the author of *Marty,* that it is well-meaning. For it is about religion, Jews AND mental illness.

Toys in the Attic by Lillian Hellman, Piccadilly, November, 1960. Reviewed by Richard Findlater in *Time and Tide.*

It is curious how incest, impotence, nymphomania, religious mania and real estate speculation can be so dull.

and by Harold Hobson in the *Sunday Times.*

Lillian Hellman has chosen to write on a Tennessee Williams theme in an Agatha Christie style.

Treasure Hunt by M. J. Farrell and John Parry, Apollo, September, 1949. Reviewed by Leonard Mosley.

(This) is supposed to be an up-to-date play about what happens when the hungry English arrive for relaxation (and ham and eggs) in modern day Ireland. But don't be deceived by the modern setting and the 1949 slang. It is a story that was wearing moth around the collar when Queen Victoria was alive . . .

There were moments when I positively smiled at the antics of the dear old Irish. But there were more when I wished they would go and jump in a dear old Irish bog.

Twelfth Night by Shakespeare, Duke's House, January, 1663. Reviewed by Samuel Pepys in his *Diary.*

After dinner to the Duke's House, and there saw *Twelfth Night* acted well, though it be but a silly play . . .

Tyger, a celebration of William Blake by Adrian Mitchell, music by Mike Westbrook, National Theatre Company at the New, July, 1971.

. . . the cast includes about three dozen of the National Theatre Company who, assuming they are able to read, seem remarkably acquiescent.

Vincennes, a drama cited as an example of the kind of play which 'plumb(s) depths of tedium which not even your magnetic player can relieve.' Recalled by James Agate in the *Sunday Times,* March, 1932.

I once saw a drama called *Vincennes*. This was about Marie-Antoinette, and all that Sarah Bernhardt could do to lighten the dreary orgy was to wear a puce going-away, or better, getting-away, dress and, when she couldn't succeed, lay that puce bodice and the tousled auburn mop which was her hair upon a violet tablecloth in a mauve boudoir, the whole fusing into a sea of raspberry-sauce about which I still have nightmares.

What's Got Into You? by Elaine Morgan, Tricycle Theatre, April, 1981. Reviewed by Irving Wardle in *The Times*.

Possibly it sounds closer to life in Wales where this Bag and Baggage production has toured with alleged success. As for me, I left the show feeling very keen to get home to the washing up.

When we are Married by J. B. Priestley, Lyttelton, December, 1979.

It would make an ideal treat as a night out for your despicable in-laws. Send them a couple of tickets, then meet afterwards at the theatre restaurant for a blazing row.

Who Killed Agatha Christie? by Tudor Gates, October, 1978, Ambassadors. Reviewed by Bernard Levin in the *Sunday Times*.

Tudor Gates has insured against an adverse reception by writing a play about an actor author who murders a drama critic; unsympathetic notices can thus be attributed to hostility among reviewers resentful at seeing one of their number suffer so undignified a fate . . .

As it happens, I have more cause for complaint than any of my colleagues; the victim is told by the murderer that there is nothing personal involved, and that he is to have his throat cut in a purely representative capacity, but instead of embracing with selfless heroism the role of scapegoat, he responds (with what I, at any rate, cannot help feeling is a singular lack of professional solidarity) 'Why not Bernard Levin?' The shocked silence that fell upon the house at this deplorable suggestion was eloquent testimony to the abilities of the British theatre-going public to recognize a cad when they see one.

Unfortunately, the play is the most dreadful tosh, and fully half of it seems to be simply padding, designed to keep the curtain up for an hour or so after the author's invention runs out. Among the unkinder passages from the critic-victim's notices that the murderer reads to him is one which runs: 'The plot has as many holes as a sieve and is far less entertaining.' I rather think I said that myself, and even if I didn't I have now.

Wild Horses by Ben Travers, Aldwych, November 1952, with Ralph Lynn and Robertson Hare appearing together for the first time in twenty years. Reviewed by Beverley Baxter in the *Sunday Express*.

There are moments when the plot runs down and has to be wound up like an aged gramophone . . . For those who can afford it I strongly recommend a dozen oysters and a glass of champagne as an appetizer.

Woman of the Year, Embassy, September, 1954. Reviewed by Kenneth Tynan in the *Observer.*

Woman of the Year (Embassy) unpleasantly exploits the surgical transformation of a transvestite into a 'woman'. The androgyne is gruffly played by Miss Rojina Manclark, whose name obsessed me during the second act, discovering itself finally to be an anagram of Major Ian Lack, R.N.

The World of Suzie Wong by Paul Osborn based on a novel by Richard Mason, November, 1959. Reviewed by Bernard Levin in the *Daily Express.*

It is . . . a lot of Chinese junk. And the reason is not hard to seek.

You can hang your stage with silver and dress your cast in cloth of gold.

You can hire an assorted dozen mandarins to give the thing tone.

You can dangle paper lanterns all over the place, cunningly lit up from within.

You can bang gongs and tinkle cymbals and burn joss-sticks and make the stage revolve at the speed of lightning and several times.

But if the play is empty, it will still only give off a hollow booming sound when you hit it. And *The World of Suzie Wong* IS empty . . .

The World of Suzie Wong *with Tsai Chin as Suzie Wong. Courtesy of* Punch.

In wise old Lee Vin's opinion, if you want more of China than wide sleeves and more of a play than romantic twaddle, to pay it a visit would be to enter the world of choosy wrong.

Young England by Walter Reynolds, directed by Lyn Perring, Victoria Palace, September, 1934.

This was a straight patriotic melodrama which looked forward to an England aglow with the ideals of the Scout movement. As such it was a failure, but audiences and critics found its unintended humour so hilarious that it ran on. It acquired a following of young people who knew the lines by heart from going night after night and would chant them along with the actors — and the author, initially rather hurt by the turn of events, seemed to enter into the spirit of things in the end . . .

Reviewed by W. A. Darlington in the *Daily Telegraph*.

Any sophisticated playgoers who chanced to be present at the first performance of *Young England* at the Victoria Palace got one of the best laughs of their lives.

Walter Reynolds, at the age of 83, has written the play in a direct attempt to bring back to the stage the quality of melodramatic downrightness which it has lost. He expresses himself in a forgotten idiom; and consequently his play has that surest of all laughter-making qualities — that it says and does in complete seriousness all the things which the writer of burlesques does with his tongue in his cheek.

Here we have once again the villain at whom all must hiss, and his counterpart the incredibly noble hero who scorns to disprove or even deny false charges against his honour. The villain makes plain his villainy in the time-honoured way by consistently wearing a top-hat in the depths of the country. His son, the Second Robber, has been brought up to date. He is some sort of officer in the Boy Scouts, and brings shame on that highly respected body by committing his major crime while dressed in its uniform. But he has at least the grace to get into the immaculate evening dress proper to his kind when he wants to get drunk.

There is also a dissolute young Earl, very much in the old tradition, who spouts fine sentiments about the nobility of his race, and the impossibility of anybody in the play being allowed to marry his sister, immediately after having forged a cheque to pay his gambling debts.

The hero himself, a noble Scoutmaster, knows about the forged cheque, but his good deed for that particular day is to buy it with the money intended for his own legal defence, and to suppress it.

This is all gorgeously funny stuff, and the play may be a huge success for that reason . . .

And here is the kind of press the play was getting by the time it moved to the Piccadilly theatre in March, 1935. Report in the *News Chronicle*.

The first night of *Young England* — patriotic melodrama and

Stormy Petrel of the stage — in its new home at the Piccadilly theatre passed off with the usual uproarious fun.

The 'old gang' who had cheered and ragged it to success turned up in force to shout their welcome . . .

Girls who obviously knew the play by heart had come determined to enjoy themselves. During the second act streamers from the gallery fell in the orchestra stall.

With the last act enthusiasm grew rather out of hand. The interruptions were so continuous that the speeches of the actors could hardly be heard.

Commissionaires stepped into the middle rows to warn the rowdiest. There were cries of 'Quiet!' 'We can't hear the jokes.' 'There is still some more good stuff to come.' 'Speak up.' And more streamers from the gallery worked up to a riotous finale.

and in the *Sunday Express.*

The audience spotted Mr Walter Reynolds, who was overwhelmed with handshakes, slaps on the back and good wishes.

'The end of the run is not even in sight,' he said.

A classic case of disaster turning into triumph.

CHAPTER FOUR

Musicals, Revues, Variety and their Stars

Musicals particularly lend themselves to bad reviews. Part of the trouble is that people expect to leave the theatre in a state of exhilaration, having feasted their eyes and ears, and anything short of this is a huge disappointment. Secondly, because the whole undertaking is so complicated with its various components, there is a great deal that can go wrong. This I learnt to my cost recently, when I rashly decided to enter the musical field in America. The experience was a nightmare of crossed lines, withheld information, megalomania, misinterpretation and certifiable madness. And even when the musical is a success, playing to packed houses, the whole of London transported by it, you have to reckon with the still, small voice of the critic who insists on keeping both eyes open and both feet on the ground.

Alongside musicals in this section I have included revues and single star performances by such as Marlene Dietrich and Johnny Ray, which are in effect one man/one woman musicals.

James Agate, scourge of the musicals of his day, wrote of them in the *Sunday Times*, August, 1928,

There flows through this form of entertainment a stream of mindlessness . . .

and in the same newspaper, December, 1926,

Happy is the country which has no history, and happier still is that musical comedy about which one can find nothing to say.

The Arcadians, in the third year at the Shaftesbury, June, 1911. Reviewed in *Play Pictorial.*

Play Pictorial, an illustrated periodical which started up just after the turn of the century, developed a style all its own in the coverage it gave to Edwardian musical comedy. Its reviews of current productions were always anonymous and purported to give a straightforward account of what was to be seen on stage. However, the plots of these productions were often so absurd and far-fetched that any straightforward account of them in plain words invariably ended up funny, an outcome to which the reviewers themselves could often not resist adding an extra tweak of mockery. The tone, very often, is disarmingly bland, but the content takes over.

Joseph Smith makes his appearance in Arcadia by falling off an aeroplane. In explaining his presence to the beautiful Arcadian ladies he tells a lie and is immersed in a well, the Well of Truth. He comes up clothed as an Arcadian. Sombra takes possession of him and decides that he, now called Simplicitas, shall accompany her and Chrysea to Earth, there to establish truth and banish lies.

Choosing a racecourse as a starting point, the three arrive at Askwood. Still dressed in their Arcadian costumes, they find themselves the centre of considerable interest. Then follows one of the funniest scenes ever witnessed on the stage. Simplicitas makes love to his own wife who does not recognize him in his Arcadian costume. Peter Doody, a jockey, has been attacked by the horse he was to ride and Jack Meadows fears that, owing to there being nobody to ride the beast for him, he must lose his fortune and his future bride Eileen Cavanagh. The Arcadians understand the language of animals and Simplicitas steps into the breach, rides the horse and wins the race.

The third act takes place in the Arcadian restaurant, London, where Peter Doody has become a waiter and Simplicitas is having a really good time. Truthfulness is still far from Simplicitas, however, and on his telling another lie he is dipped once more, which turns him again into plain Joseph Smith.

Biarritz, a musical farce by Jerome K. Jerome, music by F. Osmond Carr, Prince of Wales, April, 1896. Reviewed by George Bernard Shaw in the *Saturday Review*.

Some of the . . . ladies on the stage have no artistic business there at all. Why are there so many mannerless girls, graceless girls, silly girls, impudent girls, and girls condemned to hopeless ugliness by having to wear trousers with jackets cut to fit waists like corset advertisements — a stupidity that would make Psyche herself unpresentable? . . . Two minutes of *Biarritz* would reconcile a Trappist to his monastry for life.

Hal Bryan in the pantomime **Robinson Crusoe**, King's, Hammersmith, Jan-Feb, 1937. Report in the *Daily Express*. Headline: HE 'GAGGED' HITLER.

Here's an actor stoned by the Lord Chamberlain of his day. Reading it, I felt like giving some belated applause. Also, it's ironic, when you think of the satirical jibes we go in for today!

A 'gag' about Hitler led to the appearance of pantomime comedian Hal Bryan with the proprietors and manager of the King's Theatre, Hammersmith, at West London Police Court yesterday.

Mr Lawson-Walton, for the Director of Public Prosecutions, said that the Lord Chamberlain sent his assistant secretary to see the performance of the pantomime *Robinson Crusoe* at the theatre. He reported that in one scene Hal Bryan, made up to represent Herr Hitler, ran on the stage giving the Nazi salute and asked 'Wass ist this all about?'

Mr Lawson-Walton said that the Lord Chamberlain did not permit gags about foreign rulers or foreign personages. 'It is only fair to say,' he added, 'that the performance was otherwise clean and excellent.'

Hal Bryan was fined £10, Thomas Piggott, the manager, £15.

Ian Carmichael in the Globe Revue, 1952. Reviewed by Milton Shulman.

* The new revue arrived on that stage of the Globe Theatre last night with all the chic of an elegant Parisian bandbox tied up with ribbon.

As the bow was untied and the lid removed, however, out fluttered a collection of aged moths.

This prompted Noel Coward who had a song in the show to telegram the company with:

DEAR AGED MOTHS CONGRATULATIONS BUT WATCH OUT OR I SHALL BE AFTER YOU WITH SOME BALLS LOVE NOEL.

Cats, based on T. S. Eliot's *Old Possum's Book of Practical Cats*, music by Andrew Lloyd-Webber, New London, May, 1981. Reviewed by Robert Cushman in the *Observer.*

Here is a hot flash. A musical called *Cats* . . . opened last week at the New London. That is the end of the mews . . .

Marlene Dietrich, BBC2, January, 1973. Reviewed by Clive James in the *Observer.*

While a Burt Bacharach arrangement of 'Falling in Love Again' (complete with sour mutes on the trumpets) sounded longingly from the pit, the house lights went down and the discs of two limes randomly searched the fore-stage . . . Finally she emerged, and the fans did their collective nut. So ecstatic was her reception that it was obvious the performance she was about to deliver had already been taken as read, so there was no real reason why she shouldn't have turned round and gone home again — especially considering that the tail end of her coat, composed of the pelts of innumerable small animals, had undoubtedly not yet left the dressing room. But she had much to give, and proceeded to give it, making it obvious from the first bar that forty years away from Germany had done nothing to re-jig the vowels which first intrigued the world in the English language version of *The Blue Angel.*

'I get no kick in a plen,' she announced. 'Flying too highee with some guyee in the skyee/ is my idea of nothing to do.' Equally, mere alcahall didn't thrill her at ol. Any lingering doubts that such sedulously furbished idiosyncrasy is an acceptable substitute for singing were annihilated by the tumult which greeted each successive rendition, the brouhaha being reinforced at key points by a lissom shedding of pelts and a line of patter marked by those interminable coy pauses which in the world of schlock theatre are known as 'timing', although they have little to do with skill and everything to do with a celebrity using prestige as leverage.

As the great lady went on recounting the story of her life in song and anecdote, the sceptical viewer was torturing himself with the premonition that there might never be an end. There was, though — although the final number was only the beginning of it, there being a convention in this branch of theatre that the star takes twice as long to get off as she does to get on. It was at this point that the floral tributes started hitting the stage, to the lady's overmastering astonishment: perhaps she had expected them to throw book-tokens. The show threatened to fade on the spectacle of these epicene

Marlene Dietrich (with William Blezard). Courtesy of Punch.

maniacs bombarding her with shrubbery, but as the curtains closed and the applause dipped she paged the tabs with a practised sweep of the arm and emerged to milk dry the audience's last resources of pious energy. If she'd been holding a loaded Luger they couldn't have responded more enthusiastically. They had no choice.

Drake's Dream, Shaftesbury, December, 1977. Reviewed by Irving Wardle in *The Times.*

With this out of the way, I feel I have nothing to fear from the other Christmas shows.

Evita with Joss Ackland as Peron, Elaine Page as Eva and David Essex as Che. Courtesy of Punch.

Evita by Tim Rice and Andrew Lloyd-Webber, Prince Edward, July, 1978. Reviewed by Bernard Levin in the *Sunday Times.*

The (music) has been generally hailed in terms which would have been extravagant if applied to *Cosi Fan Tutte* or the Eroica Symphony, and the composer (Andrew Lloyd-Webber) has been particularly applauded for the eclecticism of its idiom, as if drawing on six varieties of rubbish was more praiseworthy, or for that matter more difficult, than employing one . . . I shall content myself with saying that its best tune, the already famous 'Don't cry for me, Argentina,' is inferior as a melody to the ones I used when a boy to hear improvised on a saxophone outside the Albert Hall by a busker with only three fingers on his left hand.

Fanny, from the book by Marcel Pagnol. Drury Lane, November, 1956.

What can I possibly find to praise in this dreadful musical? . . . The second act is an improvement on the first, being shorter.

Fire Angel, by Paul Bentley and Roger Haines, based on Shakespeare's *Merchant of Venice* directed by Braham Murray, Her Majesty's, March, 1977. One of the most expensive shows ever presented in the West End, it cost £16,000 a week to run and lost thousands. Reviewed by Bernard Levin.

With Fire Angel, yet another doomed attempt at a British musical galumphs on to the stage, topples slowly over, and lies in a heap breathing stertorously. Resuscitation is attempted by shouting in its ear (music by Roger Haines) but little hope can be held out other than reverend burial.

Flower Drum Song, Palace, March, 1960. Reviewed by Bernard Levin in the *Daily Express*.

. . . an American musical, so bad that at times I longed for the boy-meets-tractor themes of Soviet drama.

Flower Drum Song *with Yama Saki as Linda Low and Tim Herbert as Sammy Fong. Courtesy of* Punch.

Gay Divorce, Palace, November, 1933. Reviewed by James Agate in the *Sunday Times.*

A very distinguished colleague began his criticism of this show by asking what is Mr Astaire's secret. Mr Astaire's secret is that of the late Rudolf Valentino and of Mr Maurice Chevalier . . . sex. But sex so bejewelled and be-glamoured and be-pixied that the weaker vessels who fall for it can pretend that it isn't sex at all but a sublimated,

Barriesque projection of the Little Fellow with the Knuckles in his Eyes.

You would have thought by the look of the first-night foyer that it was Mothering Thursday, since every woman in the place was urgent to take to her chinchilla'd bosom this waif with the sad eyes and twinkling feet . . . But what of those of us who are not mothers? To the dull, dotish, impercipient male eye it would appear that Mr Astaire is neither a stage-shaking dancer nor a world-shaking dancer. As a dancer he is not in the Nijinsky class . . . nor the Dolin. When he mounts into the air it is by means of a chair and table, and his descents are similarly accomplished.

You say that Mr Astaire does not attempt these things . . . Then in heaven's name what does he attempt? I take it to be that hybrid known as ballroom dancing, an art which is compounded equally of the lithe, sinuous panther, the lissom, supple gigolo, and the light-shod, look-slippy waiter who can steer a tray and twenty-four glasses through a crowd without spilling. Even so, there was ballroom dancing before Astaire, and so we get back to the little word with which we started, 'only quite nicely, of course!' This charming actor wears the ineffably sad expression . . . that choir-boys put on with their surplices and leave in the vestry.

Godspell (a revival), Young Vic, 1981. Reviewed by Michael Billington in the *Guardian*.

Heralded by a sprinkling of glitter-dust and much laying on of microphones, *Godspell* is back in London at the Young Vic. For those who missed it the first time, this is your golden opportunity: you can miss it again.

Guys and Dolls, Coliseum, May, 1953. Reviewed by Harold Hobson in the *Sunday Times*.

The aim of art is to produce desirable states of mind, and the state of mind from which *Guys and Dolls* proceeds can, if it is typical of America, cause only disquiet. Is America really peopled with brutalized half-wits, as this picturization of Damon Runyon's story implies? Is it really witty to bring a Salvation Army girl to the edge of fornication by the not very original trick of putting intoxicants into her milk shake? Is it clever to quote words of Jesus in the melancholy hope of raising a laugh? Let us make clear that I am not protesting against either irreverence or impropriety as such. I only ask that they should attain a certain level of intelligence. I see no reason why religion should not be attacked or even traduced in the theatre. It is, I am sure, quite strong enough to defend itself. But let the attack have some rational intellectual basis. Otherwise it becomes a bore. That, alas, is what *Guys and Dolls* is, despite its striking, incidental merits; an interminable, an overwhelming, and in the end intolerable bore.

The following is the only performance I've heard of which failed because the STAGE didn't arrive on time!

Heidi. A musical with which Elizabeth Short and Deborah Johnson opened and closed their 'Mask Theatre' at Tring. Once it got going, *Heidi* took £1,359 in five weeks — at which point the theatre in a converted cinema went bust, with costs grossly exceeding income. The directors, aged twenty-one and twenty respectively, blamed its failure on lack of capital and 'inexperience'. Report in *The Times,* November, 1965.

The premiere of the musical show *Heidi* at Tring, Hertfordshire, ended in fiasco last night. Show business personalities were in the invited audience of 300 for the opening of the Mask Theatre but the stage arrived only a few hours before the show was due to start and the cast had no time to rehearse. They sang six of the show's fourteen numbers and in half an hour the audience was leaving the theatre.

Jesus Christ Superstar by Tim Rice and Andrew Lloyd Webber, Palace, August, 1972. Reviewed by Jeremy Kingston.

It is kitsch and vulgar, idiotic and amusing in details — rather like, in fact, the Baroque interiors of those Bavarian churches with the unpronounceable names.

Jesus Christ Superstar *with Dana Gillespie as Mary, Paul Nicholas as Jesus and Stephen Tate as Judas. Courtesy of* Punch.

Joie de Vivre, a musical from *French without Tears* by Terence Rattigan, Queen's, July, 1960. Reviewed by Kenneth Tynan in the *Observer.*

. . . [The set] is designed by Peter Rice, who somehow reminds me of Oliver Messel *frappé.* The director, William Chappell, might be described as Michael Benthall *en cocotte*; and how shall I sum up Mr Rattigan himself? On this showing, perhaps, as André Roussin *sur* toast; although when his intentions are more sombre, an apter phrase might be Pinero *en gelée.* I should add that I quitted the theatre when the first act ended and was well into my *ris de veau financière* (sweetbreads à la H. M. Tennent) before I remembered that the curtain was due to rise again on the second half, which may well have been a triumph of wit, audacity, colour and movement. I doubt it, though.

The King's Proxy, a new opera by S. J. Arnold, Lyceum, 1815. Reviewed by Hazlitt.

A new Opera was brought out at the Lyceum, last week, called *The King's Proxy* or *Judge for Yourself.* If we were to judge for ourselves, we should conceive that Mr Arnold must have dreamt this opera. It might be called the Manager's Opera. It is just what might be supposed to occur to him, nodding and half asleep in his arm-chair after dinner, having fatigued himself all morning with ransacking the refuse of the theatre for the last ten years. In this dozing state, it seems that from the wretched fragments strewed on the floor, the essence of four hundred rejected pieces flew up and took possession in his brain, with all that is threadbare in plot, lifeless in wit, and sickly in sentiment. Plato, in one of his immortal dialogues, supposes a man to be shut up in a cave with his back to the light, so that he sees nothing but the shadows of men passing and repassing on the wall of his prison. The manager of the Lyceum Theatre appears to be in much the same situation.

Frankie Laine, London Palladium, 1952. Reviewed by Kenneth Tynan.

. . . [Mr Laine] is a beefy man with a strangler's hands and a smile like the beam of a lighthouse, but he sings almost exclusively about tears and regrets. You form a mental picture of him sobbing into his pillow, hammering it with his fists until the bed collapses under him. His approach to the microphone is that of an accused man pleading with a hostile jury. He complains of betrayals, and shouts his defiance of faithlessness. It is like the day one's elder brother was dropped from the first eleven . . .

Liberace, in *The Music Box Show,* Palladium, April, 1960. Reviewed by Bernard Levin in the *Daily Express.*

The new variety bill at the Palladium includes Mr Liberace, the Beverley Sisters, Miss Janet Medlin, some acrobats and a ventriloquist.
The deepest lake in the British Isles is Loch Moar. The new variety bill at the Palladium includes Mr Liberace, the Beverley Sisters, Miss Janet Medlin, some acrobats and a ventriloquist.
The lethal dose of *clostridium botulinum* type D is 0.00006 milligrams for an adult male by a peritoneal injection. The new variety bill at the Palladium includes Mr Liberace, the Beverley Sisters, Miss Janet Medlin, some acrobats and a ventriloquist.
The average daily net sale of the *Daily Express* during March was 4,132,000. The new variety bill at the Palladium includes Mr Liberace, the Beverley Sisters, Miss Janet Medlin, some acrobats and a ventriloquist.

Bogata is a city in Colombia. The new variety bill at the Palladium includes Mr Liberace, the Beverley Sisters, Miss Janet Medlin, some acrobats and a ventriloquist.

The postal rate for reply-paid cards sent to a foreign country is eightpence. The new variety bill at the Palladium includes Mr Liberace, the Beverley Sisters, Miss Janet Medlin, some acrobats and a ventriloquist.

The distance by road from Leeds to Gloucester is approximately 159 miles. The new variety bill at the Palladium includes Mr Liberace, the Beverley Sisters, Miss Janet Medlin, some acrobats and a ventriloquist.

Melbourne time is 10 hours later than Greenwich Mean Time. The new variety bill at the Palladium includes Mr Liberace, the Beverley Sisters, Miss Janet Medlin, some acrobats and a ventriloquist.

One pound of avoirdupois is the equivalent of 4.536 hecto-grammes. The new variety bill at the Palladium includes Mr Liberace, the Beverley Sisters, Miss Janet Medlin, some acrobats and a ventriloquist.

The charge for a journey in the Paris Metro is the same, no matter how many stations are passed. The new variety bill at the Palladium includes Mr Liberace, the Beverley Sisters, Miss Janet Medlin, some acrobats and a ventriloquist.

The telephone number of the main London offices of the Board of Trade is Trafalgar 8855. The new variety bill at the Palladium includes Mr Liberace, the Beverley Sisters, Miss Janet Medlin, some acrobats and a ventriloquist.

Nystagmus is an eye disease common among miners, of which the chief symptom is the continual oscillation of the eyeballs. The new variety bill at the Palladium includes Mr Liberace, the Beverley Sisters, Miss Janet Medlin, some acrobats and a ventriloquist.

Editor's Note: Shortly after writing the above, Mr Levin was found wandering in an exhausted condition in the Old Kent Road. He refuses to answer to his name, maintaining he is Julius Caesar.

Lucky Girl, a musical comedy, Shaftesbury, 1928. Reviewed by Hannen Swaffer in the *Daily Express.*

Lucky Girl contains more machine-made jokes than any musical comedy I have seen for years.

Lumber Love by Leslie Stiles, music by Bert and Emmett Adams, Lyceum. Reviewed by James Agate.

The plot was of a fatuity which one would call incredible but for the fact that one is asked to believe in it about five times in any musical comedy season. A young woman buys a lumber forest for 250,000 dollars and, because of a hitch in the deal, must marry the only man in the Canadian Rockies she cannot abide.

A previous lyric had run,
    'Some day perhaps you'll
    change your mind
    and see my point
    of view.'

And now we had a long, dramatic recitative which went something as follows. 'What's this I hear? The cheque with which you were to have paid for twenty-five thousand acres of lumber at a dollar an acre has not materialized? Then my previous option holds good. What have you to say to that?'

What I have to say is that the composers of *Jephtha, Don Giovanni* and Saint Paul, putting their heads together, could not have coped with these words. Nor could Rubini, Garcia and Lablache, singing as one man, have delivered them satisfactorily.

The piece abounded in gems of unconscious humour, as when the hero turned to a number of guests at a Montreal evening party and bade them,
    'Prate not to me
    of the open sea!'

There was another delicious moment when the heroine entered, veiled in elephant-breath tulle, and the sun was so shocked that it at once set behind the Rockies to harps and clarinets.

On one other occasion was the spirit unexpectedly refreshed, and that was when Mr Basil Howes, blanketing his loins and elfing his hair in knots, gave a very reasonable imitation of Poor Tom and said wistfully, 'I'm just a story that didn't come true.'

No, this was certainly not an entertainment for the sophisticated.

The Mitford Girls, Globe, October, 1981. Reviewed by Robert Cushman in the *Observer*.

The Mitford Girls is bursting with calculated high spirits, not one of which managed to raise mine.

As might be expected, the subjects of this musical have the wittiest comment on it: in the Mitford family, it is known as 'La Triviata'.

Not to Worry, Garrick, February, 1962. Reviewed by Milton Shulman.

Positively the worst revue I have ever seen . . . let me not weary you with details, but I cannot recall a moment when I was not yearning to be released from my seat.

and by another unknown critic (the entire notice).

In the 1930s there was a revue that was so bad that on the first night the management did not raise the curtain after the interval. They showed no such leniency last night.

Off the Record, Victoria Palace, November, 1954. Reviewed by Milton Shulman in the *Evening Standard*.

It must have been a very bad summer in Blackpool this year. Not only was there all that rain, but they had twenty-two weeks of a revue called *Off the Record,* now to be seen at the Victoria Palace. One is torn between wonder at the long-suffering qualities of Lancashire and awe at weather that could drive so many indoors to see this as an alternative to sitting out in the hail and sleet . . .

Oh! Calcutta! a musical devised by Kenneth Tynan, Round House, July, 1970. Reviewed by Peter Lewis in the *Daily Mail*.

. . . *Oh! Calcutta!* is five years too late to be the great liberating sensation it was obviously intended to be . . .
 . . . a so-called erotic revue which is anti-erotic and in which nearly every sketch is embarrassing — not because it is rude, but because it isn't funny with it.

and by Philip Hope-Wallace in the *Guardian*.

. . . though I, in my depraved way, felt a bit let down after all the fuss, I certainly would not think *Calcutta* corrupting or even depraving . . . Generally, there were stretches which seemed more like a long, dirty schoolboy joke than 'elegant eroticism'. But *chacun à son gout*.

O Kay, by Guy Bolton and P. G. Wodehouse, music by George Gershwin, His Majesty's, September, 1927. Reviewed by James Agate.

Insofar as I can make out any of the imbroglio of this piece, it concerns a cretinous earl, so harassed by supertax that he is reduced to rum-running in his last remaining possession, his yacht. With him is his sister, who is apparently called Kay. Kay, clothed in a mackintosh, makes a burglarious midnight entry into the house of oné Irving Winter, whom she has previously saved from drowning. Jimmy, who is arranging to marry a second wife before completely divorcing the first, now falls in love with Kay. It also happens that another rum-runner, one Shorty McGee, has also chosen Winter's house in which to store, without permission, his stock of illicit liquor.
    The establishment possesses forty unexplained housemaids and a baker's dozen of inexplicable footmen, who from time to time interrupt such action as there is.
    This is the entire story and I can frankly say that I have known nothing in the musical comedy line of greater melancholy.

Pal Joey, book by John O'Hara, music by Rodgers and Hart, Princes, 1954. Reviewed by Eric Keown in *Punch*.

Far from being a love philtre, *Pal Joey* is an emetic. With one exception, a nit wit girl, none of the other characters is even momentarily attractive . . .

A rich woman buys a nauseating gigolo, sets him up in a flat and night club and throws him out on the street again when he palls. We could easily have been persuaded to like him and to believe the woman was in love, but as it is the whole thing is utterly cynical. Wit might have saved it, but for that we are given grubby little bedroom jokes; for a story, a rambling series of night club scenes in which half-clad girls demonstrate yet again the infinite boredoms of anatomy.

Paris in London, by Mary and Donovan Parsons, Comedy, August, 1932. Reviewed by L. L. H. in the *Daily Express.*

The kind of musical show I have often laughed at in the Hippodromes and Palaces of the industrial north appeared in London last night.

The West End, sitting in the stalls, watched it in shocked silence, very amusing to the irreverent.

The only possible reason for producing it is the praiseworthy one of earning a little London money before sending the show to its spiritual home, the Potteries . . .

And now, I hope we shall not see anything like this again outside the Wigan Empire.

Phyllis Dixie in **Peekaboo,** Whitehall, May, 1944. Reviewed in the *Observer.*

Miss Phyllis Dixie is again stationed at the Whitehall Theatre. She calls herself 'England's popular pin-up girl', but her share of the entertainment seems largely to be unpinning, an operation performed with sustained archness.

Peggy, Gaiety, April, 1911. Reviewed by *Play Pictorial.*

Peggy Barrison was a manicurist at the new Hotel London. The management evidently found it necessary for Peggy to have some help, for she had eight assistants. Everybody loved Peggy but she was engaged to Albert Umbles, the hotel hairdresser. They were an ill-assorted couple, but it was all for the best as it turned out. Among Peggy's admirers was one James Bendoyle, the honourable James Bendoyle, a very wealthy and not unattractive young man. Peggy did not love him so he hatched a little plot. His friend Auberon Blow, a young man about town who was in disgrace with his people and cut off without the customary shilling, was not slow to fall in with Bendoyle's suggestion. Bendoyle had discovered that Umbles had an uncle in Buenos Aires, a very wealthy uncle according to Umbles' own account. Bendoyle's scheme was that Auberon Blow should impersonate this wealthy uncle, whose name was Montague Bartle. The money would be supplied by Bendoyle and Blow to lavish presents and luxuries upon Umbles and his fiancee. When they had become used to the supposed uncle's generosity, the supply was suddenly to cease.

The scheme began to work. Meanwhile the real Montague Bartle arrived with his beautiful daughter Doris. Bartle discovered the plot and let it go on. The sham uncle sought out Umbles and Umbles fell at his feet and worshipped him. Bartle's money provided for a long trip by all concerned to Freeville-on-Sea. There also went the real Bartle. He wanted to see what was going to happen. The gaiety and frivolity of that scene unhinged poor Umbles and he fell in love with a musical artiste named Polly Polino. Bendoyle also found that his feelings towards Peggy were cooler than those he had for Doris, the daughter of the real uncle. Auberon Blow fell in love with Peggy who returned his affections and they all paired off nice and comfy.

Ivor Novello and **Roma Beaumont** in **Perchance to Dream** by Ivor Novello, Hippodrome, April, 1945. Reviewed by James Agate.

Perchance I dreamed at the first night of Mr Novello's new Hippodrome show. Anyway, the following is what the lighter stage's most popular magician induced me to believe that I saw. A Regency Buck, Mr Novello, who is also a highwayman, a cad who will wager £5,000 that he will seduce an unknown cousin within twenty-four hours of her stay under his roof, doubled with a verray parfit gentil knight, prepared to lay wager and a thousand pound pearl necklace at the feet of Purity Unsullied, Miss Roma Beaumont. A cutpurse who dies babbling of reincarnation. Did I spend the rest of dreamtime watching what gross and vulgar spirits would call subsequent developments? Yes. Was time punctuated by aeons of ballet? Yes. Was there a very, very great deal of lush romantic music, scored principally for harp after the manner of that popular composer Herr Mittel Europa? Yes. Or so these things seemed. I vouch for none of them . . .

Is the foregoing a trifle grudging, even bordering on the ungenerous? I think it may be and I hasten to say that the curtain when it went up took with it the entire audience, which remained in its seventh heaven until after three and a half hours the curtain descended and automatically brought the audience down with it. Mr Novello's nonsense had obviously suited their nonsense.

The actor himself? I don't feel he is at home in the age or perhaps the country of Pierce Egan. I feel that his genius requires a steeper setting — a balmier, boshier air, that his spiritual home is the Tyrol. I wonder whether in his next production Mr Novello will wear a feather? I rather think he should.

The Quiz Kid, Lyric, Hammersmith, September, 1959. Reviewed by Bernard Levin in the *Daily Express.*

With a dull thud, another British musical bites the dust.

Johnny Ray at the Hippodrome, October, 1955. Reviewed by Basil Boothroyd in *Punch.*

'You folks', says Mr Ray in a voice scraped raw with song, 'are more generous to me than I deserve.'

The house shrieks indignantly because this is practically abdication, but finding their idol is only introducing his tribute to the band, 'not

Ivor Novello.

only very wonderful musicians, but each one my very dear friend,' it roars obedient acclaim and the band rise to their feet with the sulky air of men who know they are only another man's gimmick. For Mr Ray's gimmick is to effect a touching humility before the gifts divinely bestowed on him. This is no easy trick for an extrovert plus, but he performs it creditably. As he sings his large bony fingers grope for confidence among the spotlights, or nervously smooth the pockets of his costly dinner suit. In approaching a high note, he is the schoolboy cricketer praying to hold a vital catch. He will often hesitate before a phrase, uncertain whether his technique is equal to the task of interpretation.

As the evening wears on, he gathers a little self-esteem. His gestures open out, he falls on a knee and thumps the stage, his hairdo collapses, he begins to get his teeth almost literally into his material, worrying the lyrics like a terrier with an old boot, biting on the sugary phrases as if they were sticks of seaside rock. In an atmosphere of rising hysteria, he gradually expands towards vocal and physical contortions which he knows from experience will drop a spark into the emotional powder barrels out front — an arm thrown up, an interpolated exclamation, a sudden spasmodic shake of the head. The screams mount, the band blasts, those who would like to leave dare not for fear of lynching.

His secret is dark, powerful and obscure. Perhaps to his particular audience his shallows of the spirit seem like deeps. On the other hand, the screamers and the shriekers and long, estatic moaners are clearly getting a separate satisfaction out of their own behaviour. With Johnny Ray, whether you have Mr Emotion embroidered on your sweater or not, screams, shrieks and moans are the done thing. In fact, so much of the performance is contributed from the auditorium that it is as hard to assess its merits as it is to explain its success. On the last score, the ostentatiously worn deaf-aid should not perhaps be overlooked. It hints at a frailty, bravely overcome, and stirs all kinds of half-realised compassions, particularly in those who forget that deaf-aids can be had in much less conspicuous forms nowadays.

Rose Marie, by Harbach & Hammerstein, music by Friml & Stothart, Victoria Palace, August, 1960. Reviewed by Clive Barnes.

Only one joke was applauded: 'We are all going into the fitting room to have a fit.' This kind of brilliance was not sustained.

The Snow Man, a pantomime, 1898. Reviewed by Max Beerbohm.

The Snow Man is not a pantomime to which all children, indescriminately, should be taken by their parents. But all naughty children should be taken to it at once . . . It is well known that naughtiness is alarmingly on the increase. Parents must make a stand. Let them make their stand now, in the Lyceum Theatre. Let all the children who persistently tell fibs, tear their clothes, run away from home, stamp their feet, refuse to say their prayers, steal jam, fidget, make faces, blot their copybooks and slide down the bannisters, be taken, summarily, to see *The Snow Man.* Let them arrive for the rise of the curtain, and be kept there for its fall. Then let them be given fair warning that unless they reform they will be taken to see it again. So will naughtiness be stamped out.

The Sound of Music, by Rodgers and Hammerstein, Palace, May, 1960. Reviewed by T. C. Worsley in the *Financial Times.*

As a patriotic Englishman I devoutly hope my fellow Englishmen will reject this show emphatically. It is common and vulgar.

and by Alan Brien.

Woman's magazine profundities which didn't kindle a spark even from a partisan first-night rush.

and by Robert Muller in the *Daily Mail.*

It is the final fruit of Rodgers and Hammerstein's collaboration, and an over ripe, not to say soggy, old plum it is.

Webster Booth and **Anne Ziegler** in **Sweet Yesterday**, a musical play by Philip Leaver, music by Kenneth Leslie-Smith, Adelphi, June, 1945. Reviewed by James Agate.

Mr Webster Booth and Miss Anne Ziegler sing delightfully and very, very often.

Fings Ain't Wot They Used T' Be, by Frank Norman and Lionel Bart, Theatre Royal, Stratford East, February, 1959. Reviewed by Michael Croft in the *Observer.*

The acting reveals the weakness rather than the strength of Miss Littlewood's method, developing at times into a kind of theatrical secret in which the audience is not supposed to share.

Mel Tormé in **Variety**, Prince of Wales, September, 1956. Reviewed by Derek Monsey in the *Sunday Express.*

Mel Tormé is one of those singers whose success makes me feel that middle age is not just around the corner but a long way behind.

CHAPTER FIVE

Stones
Across the
Atlantic

I had originally intended to have a short section on *current* Broadway. Alas, most of the letters dispatched to American actors and actresses didn't pay dividends. A great many secretaries typed polite little notes to the effect that A was too busy on a meaningful project or B simply couldn't remember (fair enough) — one wrote and said she had just had a lobotomy. Heigho, I should have guessed, for to discuss one's failures in America is considered the worst possible taste. Denholm Eliott once went on a TV chat-show and described in side-splitting detail his latest film, a Smell-O-Vision epic. The net result of which, he said, was to make the cinema smell like Woolworths. The audience and the interviewer were thoroughly discomfited. All of which goes to explain why most of this section has had to be researched — apart from a wonderful few who did divvy up, led by Katharine Hepburn.

Broadway critics have always been famous for their one-liners: the devastating dismissal in half a dozen words which Alexander Woollcott called 'capsule criticism.' George S. Kaufman was the author of the much-quoted line,

Satire is what closes on Saturday night.

Here are some more capsule criticisms that have come my way. *Punch,* in London, of the Oscar Wilde play *Vera* or *The Nihilists,* which opened on Broadway in 1882 and closed within a week, observed that it must have been

. . . vera, vera bad.

Robert Garland, reviewing *Uncle Vanya* by Chekhov in *Journal American,* 1946,

If you were to ask me what *Uncle Vanya* is about, I would say about as much as I can take.

Heywood Broun, reviewing a Broadway comedy:

The play opened at 8.40 sharp and closed at 10.40 dull.

Walter Kerr, reviewing *I Am a Camera* (1954-5):

Me no Leica.

Review of a play called *The Seventh Trumpet* (writer and reviewer unknown), contributed by Peter Cushing, who was in it:

The Seventh Trumpet opened on Broadway last night and blew its last blast.

Robert Benchley (1889-1945) was a pioneer of this genre. As he grappled with the problem of describing plays in a different way for the weekly edition of *Life,* he gradually perfected the art — and his criticisms got shorter. Thus:

Abie's Irish Rose is the kind of play in which a Jewish boy, wanting to marry an Irish girl named Rosemary Murphy, tells his Orthodox father that her name is Rosie Murphesky, and the marriage proceeds . . .

People laugh at this every night, which explains why a democracy can never be a success.

Just about as low as good clean fun can get.

It takes all kinds of people to make a world, and a lot of them seem to like this.

The management sent us some pencils for Christmas; so maybe it isn't so bad after all.

We give up.

Where do people come from who keep this going? You don't see them out in the daytime.

The kind of comedy you eat peanuts at.

In its second year. God forbid.

America's favourite comedy, which accounts for the numbers of shaved necks on the streets.

And that, my dears, is how I came to marry your grandfather.

Dun't esk.

See *Hebrews* 13:8.

Alexander Woollcott (1887-1943), in his essay *Capsule Criticism*, cites the following review of the actor Creston Clarke as King Lear. The reviewer was Eugene Field of the *Denver Post.*

Mr Clarke played the King all evening as though under constant fear that someone else was about to play the Ace.

On another occasion, Woollcott recalls, Field's entire review of a performance of *Hamlet* consisted of 'two melancholy sentences':

So-and-so played Hamlet last night at the Tabor Grand. He played till one o'clock.

However, it isn't only critics who are quoted by Woollcott. Two of the best 'tabloid reviews' of his day were, he says, oral ones spoken by members of the theatrical profession.

One was whispered in my ear by a comely young actress named Tallulah Bankhead, who was sitting incredulous before a deliberate and intentional revival of Maeterlinck's *Aglavane and Slysette,* a monstrous piece of perfumed posturing, meaning exactly nothing. Two gifted young actresses and a considerable bit of scenery were involved, and much pretentious rumbling of voice and wafting of gesture had gone into the enterprise. Miss Bankhead, fearful, apparently, lest she be struck dead for impiety, became desperate enough to whisper.
'There is less in this than meets the eye.'

The second oral gem recorded by Woollcott came from the actor Herbert Beerbohm Tree when he arrived in New York at the eleventh hour to join in the already elaborate rehearsals for *Henry VIII,* in which he was playing Wolsey.

He was expected to survey whatever had been accomplished by his delegates and pass judgement. He approved cheerfully enough of everything until he came to the collection of damsels that had been dragged into the theatre as ladies-in-waiting to the Queen. He looked at them in pained and prolonged dissatisfaction, and then said what we have all wanted to say of the extra-women in nearly every throneroom and ballroom and schoolroom scene since the theatre began:

'Ladies,' said Tree, peering at them plaintively through his monocle, 'just a little more virginity, if you don't mind.'

Dorothy Parker (1893-1967) also had a quick appreciation for the 'oral review' when, as drama critic of the *New Yorker,* she covered the Broadway opening of *The Admirable Crichton* by J. M. Barrie.

'Conciseness is not my gift,' she wrote. 'All my envy goes to the inspired Mr Walter Winchell, who walked wanly out into the foyer after the third act — there are four acts and they are long, long acts — and summed up the whole thing in the phrase,

'Well, for Crichton out loud!'

She was too modest, for she left her own neat example in her review of another play, called *House Beautiful:*

House Beautiful is play lousy.

One-liners get passed around verbally, whatever their origin. With some one is unaware of the date, the play referred to, even the author — yet they stand alone as worthy representatives of the genre. Here's a favourite of mine, just five words, with my sympathy to Mr Natzo:

Guido Natzo was natzo guido.

When *The Solid Gold Cadillac* by George S. Kaufman and Howard Teichmann opened in 1953 a Washington critic wrote,

Drag this tin Lizzie out of town.

A case of tit for tat, since Kaufman is himself a well-known source of brief dismissals of other people's plays. Of one Broadway comedy his comment was,

There was laughter at the back of the theatre, leading to the belief that someone was telling jokes back there.

To Howard Dietz, author of *Between the Devil,* Kaufman remarked, I understand your new play is full of single entendre.

When Gertrude Lawrence (1898-1952), the British revue star,

appeared on Broadway in a play called *Skylark,* he described the event as,

A bad play saved by a bad performance.

Review by Stanley Kauffmann of *The Taming of the Shrew,* as produced by the American Conservatory Theatre in December, 1973.

If a director doesn't really want to do *The Shrew,* this is a pretty good way not to do it.

Finally, Alexander Woollcott sent the following telegram to George and Bea Kaufman on the occasion of their fifth wedding anniversary:

I have been looking around for an appropriate wooden gift and am pleased hereby to present you with Elsi Ferguson's performance in her new play.

Actors in America

By way of introduction to this small collection of personal reviews, I offer three very different views of the acting profession in general.

Walt Whitman (1819-92), poet and occasional drama critic, wrote in the *Brooklyn Eagle,* 1846.

All persons of thought will confess to no great fondness for acting which particularly seeks to 'tickle the ears of the groundlings'. We allude to the loud mouthed ranting style which is much the ambition of some of our players, particularly the younger ones. They take every occasion, in season and out of season, to try the extremist strength of their lungs. If they have to enact passion they do so by all kinds of violent and unnatural jerks, swings, screwing of the nerves of the face, rolling of the eyes, and so on. To men of taste, all this is exceedingly ridiculous.

Which actors do Americans really love best? George Jean Nathan sought the answer to this question in the newspaper obituaries. Here is what he found, published in his *Theatre Book of the Year,* 1949-50.

I have been reading the obituaries and follow-ups of stage folk for something like forty-five years now, and I have still to engage one that in its treatment of a great serious dramatic star shows half the genuine sadness, half the honest tenderness and affection, or one-third the sense of deep loss in the passing that is shown in the instance of a low comic figure whose biggest contribution to dramatic art consists in falling drolly off a rickety bicycle or stumbling over an imaginary something and landing ludicrously on his behind. It was not the greatest Hamlet the American stage had seen who on his death moved the critics to tears; it was a performer whose speciality was making wisecracks while hopping through a whirling rope.

Finally, let us hold up for all to see the profound credo of John Simon, from his book *Singularities* (1964-74). I know an actress (not myself!) who, encountering him by chance in a New York restaurant, quietly and deliberately upturned a plateful of potato salad over him . . .

An important but seldom written about aspect of stage aesthetics is the physical appearance of the performer. Many evils have befallen the theatre in our time, and I dare say that the decline in actors' and actresses' looks is not the most important among them. Neither, however, is it the least important, for all its being the least discussed. In public, that is; in private, one often hears comments about the unbearable exterior of this or that performer . . . There must be beauty in the theatre. One of the many suicidal streaks of our stage is the creeping permissiveness that has allowed the faces and bodies of its women to become eyesores.

Jane Alexander in *Goodbye Fidel,* April, 1980. Reviewed by Douglas Watt in the *New York Daily News.*

* . . . she's about as Latin as a New England boiled dinner.

Lauren Bacall in the film *Confidential Agent,* from the book by Graham Greene. Reviewed by John McCarten in the *New Yorker.*

Note: Though this book is, strictly speaking, about theatre, I've included Lauren Bacall's notice for this film because she contributed it herself in response to my request. For good measure she added a note to the effect that 'The response to my performance in this dud of a film was unanimously negative.'

* It was assuredly no friend of Lauren Bacall's who persuaded her to assume the role of the Honourable Rose Cullen, daughter of Lord Benditch, the English coal baron. Phonetically, Miss Bacall is a lot closer to the Grand Concourse than to Piccadilly Circus, and her conception of how a spoiled young English lady might conduct herself is fashioned of the stuff of outright burlesque. For some reason, perhaps because her sultry stare has been almost as widely publicized as the glance of the Medusa, she keeps her features obstinately immobile even when portraying crises of the first water, and it is only by watching her nostrils carefully for an occasional flare that one can get a clue as to how she's feeling at any particular moment.

Tallulah Bankhead (1902-68) as Cleopatra in *Antony and Cleopatra* by Shakespeare. Reviewed by John Mason Brown.

Tallulah Bankhead barged down the Nile last night as Cleopatra and sank.

John Barrymore as Hamlet, 1925. By Nerman.

John Barrymore (1882-1942) who, at the height of his powers, was widely held to be among the finest actors on either side of the Atlantic. His *Hamlet* reviewed by J. Ranken Towse ran for 101 performances in New York, and the success was repeated at the Haymarket, London.

His performance was not without its synthetic appeal. It was the work of an attractive, earnest and intelligent comedian . . .

Claire Bloom as Hedda in *Hedda Gabler,* Playhouse, New York, March, 1971. Reviewed by Stanley Kauffmann.

. . . she settles for a number of unsubtle readings. When Lövborg and Mrs Elvsted are about to seat themselves, Hedda says coyly, 'I want to sit between you,' with all the subtlety of a truck.

Mrs Patrick Campbell (1865-1940), leading English actress of her day, appeared in many New York productions; in *Aunt Jeannie,* Garden theatre, New York. Reviewed by William Winter.

Mrs Campbell as an elderly siren was effective, but neither bewitchment nor singularity makes a great actress.

Constance Cummings in *Lover Come Back.* Reviewed in the *Los Angeles Examiner.*

* Constance Cummings and Jack Mulhall play the leading parts in *Lover Come Back.* I am afraid it's too late now.

Faye Emerson, discussed by Walter Kerr.

Miss Faye Emerson . . . simply cannot be permitted to endure anything more. It wasn't enough, during one recent season, that Miss Emerson should submit to having her clothes torn off her back, her hair mussed, and her heart broken during the course of a melodrama about brain-washing. She was also forced, once the notices were out, to face the fact that she would have the clothes torn off her back, her hair mussed and her heart broken for only three consecutive appearances. Come Saturday night, she would never again be able to play that stirring eleven o'clock scene in which she stood with one foot on a rickety drawbridge and the other on terra firma while her captor-lover, sobbing on his knees, slowly raised one trembling arm toward a wall-switch that might or might not raise the drawbridge. The drawbridge, to put you out of your suspense, never went up; but the closing notice did.

Jose Ferrer in *Cyrano de Bergerac* by Rostand, March, 1947.

Mr Ferrer likes pauses. He pauses at the slightest provocation. He pauses at the beginning, in the middle and at the end of every line.

Ruth Ford as Temple in *Requiem for a Nun* by William Faulkner, Golden, 1958. Reviewed by Kenneth Tynan.

'What a personality that girl needs!' I said to myself, echoing a famous impromptu of Richard Haydn's.

Edwin Forrest (1806-72), described in the *Oxford Companion to the Theatre* as 'one of the finest American tragic actors of the nineteenth century.' Discussed by William Winter in *Wallet of Time,* 1913.

That which marred his acting, to the judicious, was that which marred his character — his colossal, animal selfishness.

Lillian Gish star of the silent films who turned to the stage in the mid-'twenties, as *Camille* in New Haven (an out-of-town touring date). Reviewed by Alexander Woollcott in the *New Yorker,* 1932.

One has the illusion of watching Camille played by a small town high-school girl. This is part of an abiding immaturity which one finds difficult to describe in such words as will distinguish it from arrested development.

Farley Granger in a musical version of *Pride and Prejudice* by Bo Goldman, on Broadway in the 1950s. Reviewed by Brooks Atkinson.

Farley Granger played Mr Darcy with all the flexibility of a telegraph pole.

Walter Hampden (1879-1956), American actor who was for some time a member of Benson's company in England and returned to New York to make his American debut in 1907.

As Shylock in Shakespeare's *The Merchant of Venice* 1921. Reviewed by O. W. Firkins in the *Weekly Review.*

There are three things to be said at the outset about Mr Hampden's Shylock. It is squalid; it is aged; it is unbalanced and hysterical.

I cannot comment on Mr Firkins' critical abilities, but he sure as hell couldn't count.

Helen Hayes as Cleopatra in *Caesar and Cleopatra* by George Bernard Shaw, 1925. Reviewed by Franklin Pierce Adams.

Fallen archness.

Katharine Hepburn in *The Lake,* 1933. Reviewed by Dorothy Parker.

* Go to the Martin Beck Theatre and watch Katharine Hepburn run the gamut-t-t of emotion from A to B.

and as Rosalind in Shakespeare's *As You Like It,* Court theatre, January, 1950. Reviewed by George Jean Nathan.

Flat and dry of voice, except for a periodically manufactured tremolo that suggests she studied vocal shadings not with Constance Collier but with Al Jolson, inflexible in gesture, and as bare of Shakespearean lilt as Arden's winter trees of foliage, the Bard's heroine becomes merely a schoolgirl's recitation and a lesson learned.

and in *Without Love* by Philip Barry, November, 1942. Also reviewed by George Jean Nathan.

An actress of such strikingly limited ability that, in professional company, she seems almost amateurish, she is nevertheless paradoxically a constantly prehensile and inveigling stage figure. You know she can't act, yet you do not particularly mind. In this respect she resembles a child's toy choo-choo. You know that it is only a poor imitation of the big, real article but it none the less exercises a fascination even for a paternal locomotive engineer.

Charlton Heston in *Design for a Stained Glass Window,* Mansfield theatre, January, 1950. Reviewed by George Jean Nathan.

As (the) husband who sacrifices his faith for worldly gain, Charlton Heston, a pretty fellow whom the moving pictures should exultantly capture without delay, if they have any respect for the dramatic stage, duly adjusts his chemise so the audience may swoon over his expansive, hirsute chest and conducts his prize physique about the platform like a physical culture demonstrator.

James Earl Jones, playing the part of a Tribune in Shakespeare's *Coriolanus* (directed by Gladys Vaughan), Central Park, New York, 1965. Reviewed by John Simon.

Jones sounded like a one-stringed double bass with a faintly Calypso accent, and rolled about like a huge barrel set in motion by a homunculus within.

Clara Morris (1848-1925), whose power for moving an audience was legendary — she filled theatres wherever she went. As Lady Macbeth, discussed by J. Ranken Towse.

Her audacity was largely in excess of her equipment.

Vincent Price as Abraham Lincoln in *Yours, A. Lincoln* by Paul Horgan (based on Otto Eisenschiml's book *Why Was Lincoln Murdered?),* Experimental Theatre Inc, July, 1942. Reviewed by George Jean Nathan.

. . . the Price Lincoln, had Booth not taken the job himself, would have been shot on the spot by every dramatic critic present in Ford's theatre on the fateful night . . .

Jay Robinson in *Buy Me Blue.* Reviewed by Walter Kerr.

Mr Robinson was game, all right. But what is gameness in a man who is suffering from delusions of adequacy?

Flora Robson in *The Damask Cheek* by John Van Druten and Lloyd Morris, October, 1942. Reviewed by George Jean Nathan.

As the ugly duckling who in the end wins her love from the tempting actress, Flora Robson, while expert in a light comedy medium hitherto strange to her, regrettably followed most of the company in maintaining throughout the evening that set stage smile deemed by the acting profession to be an integral factor in the projection of great charm. What, after a steady hour or two, it usually projects is rather a deep-dyed suggestion of great imbecility.

Tommaso Salvini (1829-1916), an Italian actor famous all over Europe, performed Shakespeare with great success in London and the United States. Othello was considered his greatest part and he refused to perform it more than four times in one week. Reviewed, as Othello, by Henry James in *The Nation.*

Salvini's rendering of the part is the portrait of an African by an Italian.

Martha Scott in *Design for Stained Glass Window* by William Berney and Howard Richardson, playing the part of Margaret Clitherow, who preferred death to forsaking the Roman Catholic faith during the period of religious persecution in sixteenth century England, Mansfield theatre, January, 1950. Reviewed by George Jean Nathan.

In the leading role of the sainted martyr, Martha Scott tries vainly to palm off underplaying for spirituality, and the direction seeks futilely to assist her by having the other actors strut, bellow and so overplay that she seems less saintly, as she hopes, than a reluctant attendant at a bull-fight.

Maureen Stapleton in *The Emperor's Clothes* by George Tabori, 1953. Reviewed by George Jean Nathan.

* Miss Stapleton played the part as though she had not yet signed the contract with the producer.

Kay Strozzi in *The Silent Witness* by Jack de Leon and Jack Celestin, April, 1931. Reviewed by Dorothy Parker in the *New Yorker.*

Miss Strozzi . . . had the temerity to wear as truly horrible a gown as ever I have seen on the American stage. There was a flowing skirt of pale chiffon — you men don't have to listen — a bodice of rose-coloured taffeta, the sleeves of which ended shortly below her shoulders. Then there was an expanse of naked arms, and then, around the wrists, taffeta frills such as are fastened about the unfortunate necks of beaten white poodle-dogs in animal acts. Had she not luckily been strangled by a member of the cast while disporting this garment, I should have fought my way to the stage and done her in myself.

Rip Torn, in *Desire Under the Elms* by Eugene O'Neill, Circle in the Square, January, 1963. Reviewed by Robert Brustein.

Torn, playing Eben like a refugee from a Texas lunatic asylum, giggles when he is in despair, stares blankly when he is happy, and spits when he is undecided.

and in *Daughter of Silence,* Music Box, November, 1961. Reviewed by John Simon.

Gazing yearningly out into the audience *à la* Olivier (but somehow always managing to forget to pull his gaze back), throwing lines away like Orson Welles at his slatternliest, and doing his best to look like Henry Daniell's death mask, Mr Torn allows words to revolve wanly in his mouth like a jingling key chain in a bored man's pocket.

Nancy Walker Craig (at the age of twenty) in *Best Foot Forward.* Reviewed by Hedda Hopper.

* Miss Walker reminds me of nothing so much as the Bundle-for-Britain with ears.

Jane White in Shakespeare's *Coriolanus* directed by Gladys Vaughan, Central Park, New York, 1965. Reviewed by John Simon.

As for Miss White, her every look, gesture and move is that of a fishwife suffering in equal measure from neurasthenia and megalomania.

Brandon de Wilde, then a child actor, in *The Member of the Wedding* by Carson McCullers, Empire theatre, January, 1950. Reviewed by George Jean Nathan.

An eight-year-old youngster who glories in the melodramatic name Brandon de Wilde is amusing as the little pest whose monkeyshines bedevil the two principal characters and would doubtless be even more so if one could always make out what he is saying. From where I sat, much of what he mouthed sounded as if it were something out of a modern version of *Prometheus Unbound* by James Joyce.

Norman Wisdom in *Walking Happy,* Lunt-Fontanne, November, 1966. Reviewed by John Simon.

Mr Wisdom, though English, does what most successful American stars have done: every look, every gesture, every intonation of his shrieks (or, perhaps, reeks): 'Love me! Love me! Love me! Look how little, how defenceless, how lovable I am!'

119

Productions — and a few of the people responsible for them

We set the scene for this brief section with two idiosyncratic views from past figures of the American theatre — one an actor and playwright, the other a critic.

John Howard Payne (1791-1852), American actor and playwright.

It is necessary in the production of modern drama to consult the peculiarities of leading players.

Jonathan Oldstyle, critic of the *Morning Chronicle.* An epilogue to one of his reviews in 1801:

To the actors — less etiquette, less fustian, less buckram.
To the orchestra — new music and more of it.
To the pit — patience, clean benches and umbrellas.
To the boxes — less affectation, less noise, less coxcombs.
To the gallery — less grog and better constables.
To the whole house, inside and out — a total reformation.

Amadeus by Peter Shaffer. National Theatre production in New York, January, 1981. Reviewed by Robert Cushman in the *Observer.*

Headline: EXPORTING AMADEUS
A dozen years ago, in an invaluable book called *The Season,* William Goldman analyzed the Broadway phenomenon of the Snob Hit.

'The Snob Hit,' wrote Goldman, 'is rooted in two false beliefs: (1) theatre is "good" for you and (2) British is better. The first accounts for so many Snob Hits being "lofty" in either subject matter or treatment, or both.'

A decline in the British export drive, coupled with rampant protectionism on the part of American Equity, has meant a falling-off in the supply. But the current season has produced a prize specimen. I refer of course to *Amadeus.*

. . . The New York audience, the night I went, gave the play a standing ovation. A cynical friend maintains that Broadway audiences always do this to justify to themselves the mountainous cost of the evening out . . .

The Cherry Orchard by Chekhov, a performance by Stanislavsky's company in 1923, reviewed by John Corbin in the *New York Times.*

Stanislavsky's orchard recalls a line in an English satire on American rural melodrama: 'Don't sell the old 'omestead, Jabez; it's been in the fambly fourteen years.'

The Constant Prince by Pedro Calderón de la Barca, directed by Jerzy Grotowski with the Polish Laboratory of Wroclaw, at a Greenwich Village church, 1970. Reviewed by John Simon.

There is a name in the theatre of our time that is more prestigious than any other. It is perhaps more of an incantation than a name, and even more than an incantation, a magic formula. It is the words 'Jerzy Grotowski', the name of the founder and director of the Polish Laboratory of Wroclaw . . .

(Their) opening bill was Grotowski's adaptation of Julius Slowacki's (the nineteenth century Polish romantic poet's) adaptation of Calderón's *The Constant Prince* . . . The Master was present, at all performances, watching and occasionally making some small adjustment, such as shifting one of the two spotlights a little. He is a piece of walking chiaroscuro: a podgy expanse of very pale face punctuated by blackish glasses (for an eye ailment, we are told); below this, a sizeable stretch of black suit separated from an equally black tie by a white shirt. This is the *ne varietur* uniform, and suggests a cross between a secular priest and a hieratic IBM executive . . .

The five men and one woman in the cast cavort, contort, skip, wallow, prance and dance about. They shrill or rattle off words, unintelligibly even for Poles; they sound like human hurdy-gurdies, whining, shrieking, chanting, howling. The only piece of scenery is a slant-topped slab of wood on which a prisoner is stripped, castrated, and admitted to the group; then another prisoner, the Prince, is brought in. All in white, he is stripped to a white loincloth and tortured by the others, who wear absurd black costumes — a mixture of styles and periods including togas, berets, a cardboard crown, an umbrella, a red cloak that at one point becomes a bullfighter's mantle in a mock *corrida*. The umbrella, like all Grotowskian props, also undergoes metamorphoses, and the whole affair is suggestive of kids discovering a trunk full of clothes and horsing around in them. The gentle and Christ-like Prince does not give in to his tormentors who, by their grotesque millings, hoppings and mumblings around him, supposedly convey that they are as impressed and reverent of him as they are envy- and hate-ridden.

The performers split into little groups and bound and gesticulate about in amorphous imitations of modern dance. They strut, leap and yell in various distorted voices. Much of the shouting is done into the plywood walls or, prone, into the floorboards. There is no attempt at maintaining character; just after the Prince has been tortured, he turns into a living wind machine and provides wind sounds by which the others can be buffeted about. The Prince is finally killed, but his spirit (or in this windy context more accurately, perhaps, his breath) conquers his slayers. I cannot give a more detailed account because (a) hanging over the railing and sandwiched between bodies, I was in no position to take notes; and (b) I was so dumbfounded by the infantilism and coarseness of the proceedings that sheer amazement kept me from even trying . . .

Hamlet by Shakespeare, Cincinnati, April, 1849.

Extract from the diary of William Charles Macready whilst playing Hamlet on tour in America.

Went to rehearsal. Found a most imperfect disgraceful Horatio, who had rehearsed on Saturday and now knew nothing of words or business, one of those wretches who take to the stage as an escape from labour, and for whom the treadmill would be a fitting punishment. Rested. Acted Hamlet to a rather rickety audience, but I tried my utmost, and engaged the attention of at least half the audience. In the scene after the play with Rosencrantz and Guildenstern, an occurrence took place that, for disgusting brutality, indecent outrage and malevolent barbarism, must be without parallel in the theatre of any civilized community. A ruffian from the left side gallery threw into the middle of the stage the half of the raw carcase of a sheep.

Hedda Gabler and **A Doll's House** by Ibsen, directed by Patrick Garland, Playhouse, New York, March, 1971. Reviewed by Stanley Kauffmann.

On the conceptual level, these productions simply don't exist; and in terms of felicitous staging, they are ludicrous. For just one example: when Helmer makes his first entrance in *A Doll's House,* he comes downstage center to Nora, and they *stand* there, close together, face to face, talking that way for at least a full minute, in the middle of their own living-room. I expected them to burst into 'Sweethearts', with full orchestra, at any moment.

Le Misanthrope by Molière, translated by Richard Wilbur. Discussed by Stanley Kauffmann

. . . Here's a random sample of Wilbur's *Misanthrope:*

It's true the man's a most accomplished dunce;
His gauche behaviour charms the eye at once;
And every time one sees him, on my word,
His manner's grown a trifle more absurd.

For two and a half hours?

Richard III by Shakespeare, performed by Theatre Productions Inc, March, 1943. Reviewed by George Jean Nathan.

To the multiplicity of the play's murders, Mr Coulouris and his company added another: that of the play itself. Under the species of acting which they visited upon it, Shakespeare's tragedy was for the most part transformed into something vaguely resembling *Dr Jekyll and Mr Hyde,* without Jekyll.

Romeo and Juliet by Shakespeare, described in her *Diary* by Fanny Kemble (1809-93); she was playing Juliet in the Deep South.

At half-past five, took coffee, and off to the theatre. The play was *Romeo and Juliet*; the house was extremely full: they are a delightful audience. My Romeo had gotten on a pair of trunk breeches, that looked as if he had borrowed them from some worthy Dutchman of a hundred years ago. Had he worn them in New York, I could have understood it as a compliment to the ancestry of that good city; but here, to adopt such a costume in Romeo, was really perfectly unaccountable. They were of a most unhappy choice of colours too, — dull, heavy-looking blue cloth, and offensive crimson satin, all be-puckered, and be-plaited, and be-puffed, till the young man looked like a magical figure growing out of a monstrous, strange-coloured melon, beneath which descended his unfortunate legs, thrust into a pair of red slippers, for all the world like Grimaldi's legs *en costume* for clown. The play went off pretty smoothly except that they broke one man's collar-bone, and nearly dislocated a woman's shoulder by flinging the scenery about. My bed was not made in time, and when the scene drew, half a dozen carpenters in patched trousers and tattered shirt sleeves were discovered smoothing down my pillows and adjusting my draperies.

The last scene is too good not to be given verbatim:

ROMEO: Rise, rise, my Juliet,
    And from this cave of death, this house of horror,
    Quick let me snatch thee to thy Romeo's arms.

Here he pounced upon me, plucked me up in his arms like an uncomfortable bundle, and staggered down the stage with me.

JULIET (*aside*): Oh, you've got me up horridly! — that'll never do; let me down, pray let me down.

ROMEO: There, breathe a vital spirit on thy lips,
    And call thee back, my soul, to life and love!

JULIET (*aside*): Pray put me down; you'll certainly throw me down if you don't set me on the ground directly.

In the midst of 'cruel, cursed fate' his dagger fell out of his dress; I, embracing him tenderly, crammed it back again, because I knew I should want it at the end.

ROMEO: Tear not our heart-strings thus!
    They crack! They break! — Juliet! Juliet! (*dies*)

JULIET (*to corpse*): Am I smothering you?

CORPSE (*to Juliet*): Not at all; could you be so kind, do you think, as to put my wig on again for me? — it has fallen off.

JULIET (*to corpse*): I'm afraid I can't, but I'll throw my muslin veil over it. You've broken the phial, haven't you?
    (*Corpse nodded*)
    Where's your dagger?

CORPSE (*to Juliet*): 'Pon my soul, I don't know.'

Mourn, Washington is Dead, a 'theatrical communication' reviewed by 'Crito' in the *Commercial Advertiser* on 1 January, 1800; George Washington had died on 14 December, 1799.

Thomas Abthorpe Cooper, who features in this review, was an

English actor who went with Wignell to Philadelphia in 1796 and spent the rest of his life in America. He became a firm favourite with the American public and played most of Shakespeare's tragic roles, his best part being Macbeth. However . . .

About six o'clock the band very improperly struck up 'Washington's March'. It was executed in a somewhat slow and lingering manner . . . in about twenty minutes the increasing impatience of the audience was relieved by the curtains drawing up; it arose slowly and discovered the scenery all in black with the words, 'Mourn, Washington is Dead' in large letters painted on a black background. A monody was now spoken by Cooper; he came on with a bow not the most graceful in the world, but with a countenance that seemed to say 'If you have tears prepare to shed them now . . .' His tongue, however, soon counteracted every emotion, for he began to speak in the very tones of Mrs Melmoth, artificial and declamatory, ending his lines with a full cadence of voice . . . Still we were in hopes that as he went on, his feelings would have got the better of his schoolboy rehearsal and have enabled, or rather betrayed him to do the poetry a little more justice; but ah! pitiful to relate; he had hardly exceeded thirty lines when his words stuck in his throat, and he lost all power of recollecting a line further . . . he edged a little nearer the prompter, caught his cue and went on — stopt again — moved on a word — stopt again — the ladies cast down their eyes — he caught another word, and went on — stopt again — the Pit groaned aloud, and a small hiss began to issue from the Gallery — when some good honest fellow got up and clapped his hands, which encouraged our favourite Cooper to start once more, and to go through the piece, consisting in all of perhaps sixty or seventy lines, much to our own as well as his relief. To add that he pronounced it very ill, after the above is, we presume, unnecessary, as no man can ever speak with propriety and effect, whose whole attention is constantly occupied in the sole business of recollection.

Plays and Playwrights

Again, two American views to set the scene.

John S. Sumner, Head of the Society for the Suppression of Vice, New York in the early 1920s, proclaimed:

The Theatre is a sewer!

and on the Power of the Critics, Walter Kerr argues against popular mythology in *Pieces at Eight,* 1952.

It is widely believed that the New York reviewer's verdict on a play is nearly final, and the reviewer is therefore most often painted as a slaughterer of innocents, a man whose principal dedication is to the task of keeping the maximum number of people away from the theatre and the maximum number of plays from succeeding. The reverse would be closer to the truth. One of the first things a New York newspaper critic learns is that he must all but explode with enthusiasm, must in fact seriously outwrite himself if he is to push people into the theatres at all. The fact that he is willing to do so, willing to perjure himself above and beyond his actual respect for the play, willing to employ all those extravagant, overworked, and downright embarrassing adjectives in the cause of theatrical liveliness is the real measure of his devotion to his trade.

Let me take you down through a single day's advertisements in the New York theatrical columns during a season in the 1950s — and the handy quotes that the critics ladled out. One by one, this particular season's plays were 'stunning,' 'magnificent,' 'not to be missed,' 'enormously enjoyable,' 'the stage at its best,' 'exhilarating,' 'as engaging as anything we are likely to see for a long time,' 'enchanting,' 'full of wit, talent, and splendour' and 'extraordinary.' I tell you, old Athens never had a season like this one.

Ask My Friend Sandy by Stanley Young, February, 1943. Reviewed by George Jean Nathan.

It is alleged that one of the most deplorable aspects of contemporary play-reviewing is its habit of either condemning a presentation outright and with no modifications or eulogising it to the skies, also with no modifications. Something, in short, is either totally excellent or totally awful. By way of giving further support to the allegation, which hasn't much basis in fact, let me say, with no reservations whatever, that this farce-comedy of Mr Young's is totally awful.

The Barretts of Wimpole Street by Rudolf Besier, February, 1931. Reviewed by Dorothy Parker in the *New Yorker.*

. . . now that you've got me right down to it, the only thing I didn't like about *The Barretts of Wimpole Street* was the play.

Beyond the Horizon by Eugene O'Neill (his first full-length play), Morosco theatre, November, 1920. Comment by a member of the audience:

An audience goes to the theatre to sit for an hour or so, not for a day. Mr O'Neill seems to think that time is a negligible element in the development of his ideas.

The Cat Screams, a mystery melodrama by Basil Beyea, June, 1942. Reviewed by George Jean Nathan.

The majority of mystery plays, with their disappointing last-minute solutions, are like sitting nervously around for two hours waiting for a telephone call from one's best girl and then at long length suddenly hearing the bell ring, jumping up eagerly to answer it, and finding that it is her mother. This was no exception.

The Cocktail Party by T. S. Eliot, Henry Miller theatre, January, 1950. Reviewed by George Jean Nathan.

I trust I may not be charged with an undue levity when I remark that it might have profited Eliot if he had heard Joe E. Lewis' song, 'Sam, You Made The Pants Too Long', for this exhibit needs considerable shortening to make it dramatically tolerable. As it stands, it is so excessively windy that only by bracing oneself with that hope which ever springs eternal in the reviewer's breast can one drag oneself, after a first act that is more endlessly talkative than an outraged parrot, to return for the second. The allusion to the parrot is apt, since Eliot's observations on human relationships in that initial, interminable act are one long string of cuckooed platitudes . . .

Come of Age by Clemence Dane and Richard Addinsell, City Centre. Reviewed by Walter Kerr.

The authors first introduced us to the seventeen-year-old poet, Thomas Chatterton, at the moment of his suicide in 1770. As we watched, numbly, the lad was summoned from his couch by the offstage voice of Death and told that he had never come of age. He never would come of age, it seemed, until he had 'shared his secret' with a woman — at seventeen he had apparently had little opportunity to do this — and he was now transported to the present time and the fashionable apartment of a high-living, hard-drinking woman of the world. By the time he had felt her jealousy, her rage, and her rather frosty compassion, he had presumably grown up a bit and was ready to die, which he did.

Anyone who had heard any of the interim mooning about the work was prepared for the fact that it was written in rhymed couplets. But nothing could really prepare a man for the paralyzing effect of an entire evening spent listening to choppy, cryptic, and endlessly repetitious forays like:
    That's the worst of it,
        The hunger and the thirst of it.
As if the belligerent beat of the rhymes was not bad enough, we were sometimes tantalized with off-rhymes:
    All this fuss
        About a pinch of dust.
The authors did explain that they had written the play in doggerel as being the most suitable verse form for our time. Our time may not be a happy one, but I am still not convinced that it deserves a play written on the artistic level of the Burma-Shave ads.

The Conference of the Birds, performed by Peter Brook's group from the International Centre for Theatre Research in Paris, Brooklyn Academy of Music, October, 1973. Reviewed by Stanley Kauffmann.

It has very little to do with birds and a great deal to do with glib mystic episode and spurious spiritual insight . . . At the start, a drink

— tea, I suppose — is brewed on stage, then poured into two big bowls that are passed around to be shared by the audience. (Sitting in the back, I missed my sip.) At the end the narrator asked the audience to come up and join hands with the company in a large circle. Dozens did. I left, shocked by this Julian Beck-Judith Malina cheapness in a Brook group. Perhaps they are all still standing there, locked in a new community . . .

The Contrast by Royall Tyler, the first comedy written by an American, John Street theatre, New York, 1787. Reviewed by 'Candour' in the *Daily Advertiser.*

The author has made frequent use of soliloquies, but I must own, I think injudiciously. Soliloquies are seldome so conducted as not to wound probability. If ever we talk to ourselves, it is when the mind is much engaged in some very interesting subject, and never to make calm reflections on indifferent things.

The Dark is Light Enough by Christopher Fry. Reviewed by Walter Kerr.

I wasn't really bent on research. I just happened to overhear a couple of trusting five-year-olds watching television one quiet night.
   'Which guy is the bad guy?'
   'Wait. See who has a moustache.'
   The conversation not only brought me back to the simple, clean-cut, perfectly intelligible world in which I myself grew up, it made me think. What kind of preparation is this for the *real* theatre these kids are going to inherit? As they grow to manhood, and find themselves free to wander the length and breadth of 42nd Street, what is going to happen to their touching conviction that villainy is identifiable?
   . . . There came a point, during a recent season on which I kept tabs, when there were just two moustache plays left on Broadway — and one of them didn't count. The one that didn't count was *The Dark is Light Enough.* In Christopher Fry's verse melodrama a certain Colonel Janik strode fiercely into the drawing-room. His upper lip was decorated, his hooked nose and sunken cheeks were impressively threatening, and he at once behaved abominably to some sweet, soft-spoken people. Confidence returned to you as you watched him: here, you told your believing heart, was a man who would wind up properly, with a slug in his back.
   But no. The whole thing was a trap. Christopher Fry belongs body and soul to the new school of Don't-shoot-him-he-may-be-the-hero dramatics (the variation on this is Don't-let-yourself-like-him-he-may-be-a-lout), and he had no intention of sacrificing this man. He wanted us, as the tumult was dying down, to shed a tear or two for him, to understand that his snarl was a necessary snarl, and to applaud his last-minute rescue from the folk who were trying to get their hands on him. In my time, I'd as soon have saved William V. Mong or Mitchell Lewis from the mob.

The Deputy by Rolf Hochhuth, 1964. Reviewed by John Simon.

The Deputy on Broadway is like one of those comic-strip versions of a literary classic ('My name is Julien Sorel. I just got here!' framed in a balloon above a head), and as the characters bestride the stage you can virtually see the balloons coming out of their mouths.

Give Me Yesterday by A. A. Milne, starring Louis Calhern, March, 1931. Reviewed by Dorothy Parker in the *New Yorker.*

In a shifting, sliding world, it is something to know that Mr A. A. ('Whimsy-the-Pooh') Milne stands steady. He may, tease that he is, delude us into thinking for a while that he has changed, that we are all grown up now . . . and then, suddenly as the roguish sun darting from the cloud, or the little crocus popping into bloom, or the ton of coal clattering down the chute, he is our own Christopher Robin again, and everything hippity-hoppity as of old.

. . . My dearest dread is the word 'yesterday' in the name of a play; for I know that sometime during the evening I am going to be transported, albeit kicking and screaming, back to the scenes and costumes of a tenderer time. And I know, who show these scars to you, what the writing and the acting of these episodes of tenderer times are going to be like. I was not wrong, heaven help me, in my prevision of the Milne work. Its hero is caused, by a novel device, to fall asleep and a-dream; and thus he is given yesterday. Me, I should have given him twenty years to life.

Give Me Yesterday . . . opens in the sunlit drawing-room of the Cavendish Square house of one of those cabinet ministers. The cabinet minister is . . . not happy; his wife is proud, cold, and ambitious; his daughter is a Bright Young Thing; his son has gone Socialist; and, to crown all, it is rumoured that Mowbray is to be appointed to the coveted position of Chancellor of the Exchequer. 'Ah,' I said to myself, for I love a responsive audience, 'so it's one of those plays. All right, it's one of those plays. At least we have no Christopher Robins cocking their heads on the lawn.' For a moment you see, I had forgotten the title, and hope tormented me.

Well. At the end of the first act, the cabinet minister is leaning back in a chintz-covered chair, conning the speech he is to deliver in Yorkshire, and murmuring drowsily, 'The place of my boyhood. Ah, happy days, happy, happy days.' *Then* I knew we were all gone.

In the second act, the cabinet minister has made that speech and is, for the night, back in the little bedroom in Yorkshire where, as a boy, he spent the nights of his holidays. It appears that his boyhood sweetheart, Sally — called, by Mr Louis Calhern, who has gone British or something, 'Selly' . . . had used to occupy the adjoining room, and he had had a nasty habit of tapping on the wall between, to communicate with her. The code was not essentially difficult. There was one tap for 'a', two for 'b' and so on. I ask you, kind reader, but to bear this in mind for rougher times.

The cabinet minister stretches himself out on his old bed, and slips picturesquely into slumber. Darkness spreads softly over the stage, save for a gentle blue beam on Mr Calhern. Music quivers; then come lights. Then there appear two — not one, but two — Christopher Robins, each about eleven years of age and both forced, poor kids, to go quaintsy-waintsy in doings about knights and squires and beauteous maidens . . . For a few minutes, everything is so cute that the mind reels. Then the cabinet minister himself gets into the dream — I do not pretend to follow the argument — and meets up with his boyhood sweetheart, who wears, and becomingly, the dress of her day. And then, believe it or not, things get worse.

The cabinet minister talks softly and embarrassingly to Sally — 'Ah, Selly, Selly, Selly' — but that is not enough. He must tap out to her, on the garden wall, his message, though she is right beside him. First he taps, and at the length it would take, the letter 'I'. Then he goes on into 'l' and, though surely everyone in the audience has caught the idea, he carries through to 'o'. 'Oh, he's not going on into "v",' I told myself. 'Even Milne wouldn't do that to you.' But he did. He tapped on through 'v' and then did an 'e'. 'If he does "y",' I thought, 'I'm through.' And he did. So I shot myself.

It was, unhappily, a nothing — oh, a mere scratch — and I was able to sit up and watch the dream go on . . . All the Cavendish Square characters of the first act march in . . . They force the minister to don a chancellor's robe, and line themselves up between him and his little new-found love. Sadly she vanishes, leaving him wildly shrieking her name . . .

In the next scene, our hero appears with his coat on — to get it over to the audience, one presumes, that he is no longer in bed and asleep — and meets, after all the years, the Selly of his youth, sitting on the steps of the garden wall, just as she used to sit. She is married, for she had had to make something of her life when ambition called him away from her; but she is not, it seems, heppy either. They will fly together, but the cabinet minister, leashed by caution, must first take time to settle his affairs. He will come back for her, he tells her, in a week . . .

The final act takes us all back, two days later, to Cavendish Square. The minister, transformed by love and hope into a new and somewhat stressfully tender man, has started cleaning up his affairs by sending his resignation to the Prime Minister. All seems set for his return to the Real Things of Life. Then comes word that Mowbray is not, after all, to be Chancellor of the Exchequer; and right after that, little to my surprise, arrives the letter from the Prime Minister asking our hero if he won't please come over and be Chancellor. It is the job he always wanted (P.S. He got it) and it comes to him, oh, irony, irony, just at the time he was about to get away from it all. For several minutes, Mr Calhern must, with no other aid than that of his face and his clenching right hand, show us a man torn, a man in agonies of indecision. But he has been too long bound by the thongs of success. ('Success,' people keep remarking, always portentously, throughout the play, 'closes in.') The daring has been squeezed out of him. The play ends with him sitting at his desk, one hand tapping out 'Good-bye dear' — what a man; he must have had woodpecker blood in him! — while the other grasps the pen with which he is to write his acceptance of his Chancellorship.

Now I have gone into this opus at such dreary length not only out of masochism, but from bewilderment. On the morning after its unveiling, the critics of the daily papers went into a species of snake-dance over its magnificence. 'A deeply moving drama on a human topic,' they said . . . Ladies and gentlemen, I have told you the tale of the play they saw. My case rests . . .

And there is the Critic's Device spelled out as clearly as you will ever see it.

Henry IV, Part I by Shakespeare, the Old Vic Company in New York. May, 1946. Reviewed by Earl Wilson in the *Philadelphia Record.*

Dear Earl,

You character, what do you mean preveilling on a dumb chorus kid like myself to cover your Shakespear opening for you?

Simontaneously with my night off I went and mingled with fine people like Paulette Goddard, Ingrid Bergman, Elsa Maxwell, et setra. But I didn't see all the show. Cause for the simple reason I went to sleep.

You weirdy, you didn't tell me the dames would all dress up like it was for their first wedding.

So the first act of this Old Vic, Old Nick or whatever it is from London with Laurence Olivier, why I doze off. Something shining in my eyes woke me up.

It's Paulette Goddard's head with a $185,000 diamond necklace on the back of her head. It's on the back of her head like a tail-light. Get that dame, even the back of her head gets publicity. Why'd she wear a necklace on the back of her head? Maybe so everybody'd see it.

Or is that a catty remark?

'Wake up, baby,' my B.F. says at the end of the first act. 'Some air will bring you to.'

'What happended so far?'

'Nothing,' he says. He regails me with the fact that this is *Henry IV, Part I,* and nothing happens for an hour, as the show's got to run two nights anyway. We piled out to the street.

Talk about your Battle of the Century. This is a battle of the Century Theatre.

I thought since I am in a $12 seat I ought to find out if the show's any good so I listen.

Mary Martin so beautiful with her bangs tells somebody she loves it, and Moss Hart the playwrite loves, and Gene Kelly. Then Georgie Price says 'The play's all double talk. American people are funny. They'll say they love it because they're ashamed to admit they don't understand it.'

Infinitly puzzled by this, I go back and get some laughs out of Falstaff, a Bob Hope character in a Sidney Greenstreet body.

It's the same stampede getting out the second act and I happen to see Lucy Monroe, Mary Margaret McBride and James Sauter taking it on the lam. Somebody asks Mr Sauter where he's going. 'Where do you think?' he says blushing. I guess he means home.

On the sidewalk some characters are yatatayataing about 'Mortimer' in the show. They wonder whether the character is Lee Mortimer or Mortimer Snerd.

'Is there a difference?' says Robert Goldstein.

So Earl the last act is very rapid and I'm just thinking Laurence Olivier is a mean guy and should drop dead when that's what happens — he gets killed by . . . but never mind, I'm not a dame to spoil a story. When he's dead with his red hair hanging down, he looks a little like Danny Kaye, when Danny is alive, I mean.

You should have heard the ovation at the end, Earl. Some people said the cheering was because it was over, but I loved it, and people like that amaze me, and they should drop dead.

Yours in Shakespear,

CONNIE (the Chorus Cutie)

Henrik Ibsen. The worst insult sustained by Ibsen in America was when Madame Helena Modjeska (1840-1909), a Polish actress who emigrated to California in 1876, got hold of *A Doll's House,* renamed it *Thora,* and re-wrote it with a happy ending. In this form it was reviewed by the *Louisville Courier-Journal,* 1883.

. . . finally, through the medium of the children, some indefinite talk about 'religion,' there is a reunion, a rushing together and a falling curtain on a happy family tableau.

Journey's End by R. C. Sherriff, July, 1942. Reviewed by George Jean Nathan.

Journey's End (is) meant to make Englishmen proud of their unassuming fortitude . . . That reticence in general is an attribute of the English character is duly appreciated. But it may be carried too far in drama and Mr Sherriff carries it to the point where it becomes indistinguishable from nitwit lethargy. There are times in his play when, judging from the comportment of his soldiers in their dugout, one can't be sure whether what is going on outside is a war or a Pinero rehearsal.

The Life and Times of Joseph Stalin, produced by Robert Wilson. Brooklyn Academy of Music, 5 and 12 January, 1974. Reviewed by Stanley Kauffmann.

The Life and Times of Joseph Stalin . . . was announced to run from 7 p.m. to 7 a.m. I don't usually review productions I haven't seen completely — I'm told that *Stalin* actually ran until 9 a.m. and 100 people sat through it all — but I would like to comment on the two and a half hours that I saw.

When one enters the old opera house, one sees Queen Victoria standing motionless at stage left. The forestage, right and left, is covered with sand on which various objects are strewn and through which some people's heads poke motionless. High over the audience a wire is strung with some large metal hoops on it. Victoria is immobile while the audience seats itself and waits; then, as the lights dim, she begins a series of Gertrude Steinian utterances. The curtain rises on a stage covered with sand and backed by a blue sky-drop. A large photo of (I think) the young Stalin hangs from the flies but is soon hoisted up. A woman is reading something incomprehensible offstage, and continues throughout. Victoria disappears, two other regally dressed characters appear, then take seats in an audience box. A red-clad runner jogs back and forth across the stage from time to time. Two young women and a man, all stripped to the waist, do a series of dance attitudes. (The pace of these actions, and of almost everything, is very, very slow.) A black youth (male? female?) in Victorian woman's dress is seated, holding a stuffed raven. A chair dangles by a rope from the flies. A man comes down the theatre aisle with a long pole and moves two of the high-strung metal hoops slightly. A man and a boy walk on stage and talk about television. A stout black man in a white suit bounds in and does a lot of pirouettes across the stage. Towards the end of the act, twenty or twenty-five people dressed like stereotype black mammies come out and do slow girations to the Blue Danube Waltz.

This act, called 'The Beach', ran an hour and fifteen minutes; my itemization above is drastically incomplete. After a fifteen-minute intermission, Act Two began with a prelude called 'Victoria Facade' then shifted to 'Victorian Drawing Room.' I left some forty minutes later. There would be five more acts and five more intermissions of fifteen minutes each.

Two points are immediately clear: narrative is not the object; and the title, despite the photo, is irrelevant to anything I saw. (I'm told that, some hours after dawn, there were specific references to Stalin.)

Mourning Becomes Electra, trilogy by Eugene O'Neill, 1931. Reviewed by Alexander Woollcott.

. . . that glum three-decker.

A Red Rainbow by Myron C. Fagin. Reviewed by Walter Kerr.

There was once . . . and for a very short time, an exhibit on Broadway called *A Red Rainbow.* Its title required some explanation. The *Red,* I believe, stood for Communism. The *Rainbow* stood for the light in the heavens on the day Communism took over. The audience stood for more than could possibly be imagined . . .

Thoughts on **Shakespeare** by **Walt Whitman** (1819-92) published in *November Boughs.*

132 | Superb and inimitable as it all is, it is mostly an objective and

physiological kind of beauty the soul finds in Shakspere (sic) — a style supremely grand of the sort, but in my opinion stopping short of the grandest sort, at any rate for fulfilling and satisfying modern and scientific and democratic American purposes.

The Silent Witness by Jack de Leon and Jack Celestin, April, 1931. Reviewed by Dorothy Parker in the *New Yorker*.

You won't have to stay indoors very long this bright spring day. There is but one play about which to tell you, and that will be scarcely the work of five minutes. Then, leaving me here alone in the dingy classroom, out with you into the sweet April sunshine, romping and shouting and skipping! And I hope you all tumble down and break your pretty little faces.

For it is all very well for you. You don't have to labour and ache and strain to bring twigs and feathers and bits of moss to fill up this page. (Somehow those metaphors got mixed while my back was turned; but you know yourself, that is likely to happen to anybody, and there's little use worrying about it at this day and date. I have enough troubles without getting my forehead all over lines with dithering over the English language.) All you have to do is slant a cursory glance at what and how the play was, and then you're through for the day. Perhaps it might be as well to quicken things up and tell you that the drama of the week was *The Silent Witness*; that it is not at all a bad play, though hardly a good play; and give your chance to get off this here and now and leave to practise turning cartwheels for the remainder of my allotted time . . .

Sing Till Tomorrow by Jean Lowenthal. Reviewed by Walter Kerr.

Sing Till Tomorrow had two strikes against it. One was the fact that you couldn't hear the half of it. The other was the half you could hear . . . I should like to record for posterity, however, the fact that at one point in the evening an actor sank into a chair, stared at his opponent, and clearly said, 'You have been sornusolopia.' I have it here in my notes.

Tiger! Tiger! by Edward Knoblock. January, 1919. Reviewed by Dorothy Parker in *Vanity Fair*.

The plot concerns the affair of a Member of Parliament with a cook — an affair which goes on for nearly three years. When, at the end of that time, she decides to leave him, he makes a frightful scene, nearly bursting a blood vessel in his rage and disappointment. It seemed most unreasonable for him to behave in that way; how could he expect a cook to stay in the same situation for more than three years? And he needn't have been so worked up, going around saying that he had nothing to live for, and all that. I know it's the natural way to feel when the cook leaves — but then, there are always the want ads.

Mrs Warren's Profession by George Bernard Shaw. Garrick theatre, New York, October, 1905.

This play was refused a licence by the Lord Chamberlain in England. Two private performances were given by the Stage Society in 1902, but the first public performance was in Connecticut, USA — though it was banned by the police there after one performance. When it opened at the Garrick theatre, New York, the entire cast was arrested — and released on bail — on a charge of disorderly conduct. They were acquitted at the trial some months later. Reviewed by Nym Crinkle in the *New York Herald.*

The limit of stage decency was reached last night in the Garrick theatre in the performance of one of Mr George Bernard Shaw's 'unpleasant' comedies . . . The play is an insult to decency because: —
It defends immorality.
It glorifies debauchery.
It besmirches the sacredness of a clergyman's calling.
It pictures children and parents living in calm observance of most unholy relations.
If New York's sense of shame is not aroused to hot indignation at this theatrical insult, it is indeed a sad plight.

Who's Who in Hell by Peter Ustinov, Lunt-Fontanne, December, 1974.
This play was set in a waiting-room in hell, rather in the manner of *Huis Clos*, and had three characters: an American President, a bit like Nixon; a Russian leader, a bit like Kruschev; and a young American assassin.

Reviewed by Clive Barnes in *The Times.*

Who's Who in Hell . . . has a certain style to it, but the style is virtually all . . . When you come down to it Ustinov is making dangerously feeble jokes about dangerously serious subjects.

Musicals

American audiences are notoriously much less kind, much more demanding and intolerant than the English in their reception of musicals. And in the vanguard, inevitably, we find the critics . . .

Buttrio Square. Reviewed by Walter Kerr.

Buttrio Square was a musical to which all sorts of things had happened. Half of its financing had disappeared during rehearsal. Directors had been switched in mid-stream. It had had to postpone. The acting company had been forced to dig into its own pockets in order to get the curtain up. Then the worst happened: the curtain went up.
Knowing all these things, no one could have gone into the playhouse without crossing his fingers and wishing everyone well.

During the overture you hoped it would be good. During the first number you hoped it would be good. After that you just hoped it would be over.

Jesus Christ Superstar by Tim Rice and Andrew Lloyd Webber, Mark Hellinger theatre, November, 1971. Reviewed by Stanley Kauffmann.

The Christ figure was conventional enough: white gown, long fair hair with a center part, and trim beard. But Mary Magdalene was apparently just out of *Hair,* the Pilate had been watching Basil Rathbone on late-night TV, and the Judas, who was less Iscariot than a reincarnation of St Vitus, revealed himself at last in a sparkling silver jockstrap. They were all surrounded at times by writhing dancers and singers inherited from vintage Cecil B. De Mille . . .

Jews, Catholics, Protestants of the world, relax. The religious crisis of our time is not at the Mark Hellinger theatre, only some of the Jesus Generation. I admit that they are sickening. Imagine a lot of people who think that love means licking everyone like a puppy, that true Christian belief will make life easier!!! Sometimes one does indeed feel like crying, 'Savonarola, where are you, now that we need you?' But *Jesus Christ Superstar* will flow on, if only at syrup's pace. Religion and atheism will both survive it.

Laugh, Town, Laugh — vaudeville produced by M. Wynn, June, 1942. Reviewed by George Jean Nathan.

For such persons as still relish female trapeze performers, including the inevitable one who esteems herself a comedy scream; glue-faced Russians moaning the 'Volga Boatmen's Song'; ventriloquists who twirl plates on long rods the while their dummies squealingly profess to be fearful that the plates will fall off and hit them; female blues singers so vain of their vocal gifts that they render Broadway jukebox songs as if they were operas by Wagner; flamenco dancers, however good, with ferocious scowls, clattering heels that give off the din of a bombing raid on Barcelona, and cataracts of brunette perspiration; equilibrists who indicate their versatility by breaking periodically into what they imagine is a song; and any kind of dog act if only it contains a cute puppy that can stand on its hind legs — for these the show was undoubtedly everything that could be desired.

Marlowe, a rock musical by Leo Rost and Jimmy Horowitz. Rialto, October, 1981. Reviewed by Frank Rich in the *New York Times.*

Connoisseurs of theatrical disaster will still find much amusement in the self-described rock musical that opened last night at the Rialto. In attempting to give us a song-and-dance account of that madcap Elizabethan playwright, Christopher (Kit) Marlowe — the one who had had 'the devil market cornered' — the co-authors, Leo Rost and Jimmy Horowitz, have left no folio undefaced. The insanity begins with the opening scene, in which Queen Elizabeth I despatches a lover with the line, 'Don't forget your codpiece!'

A little later, there's a musical number in which Marlowe, 'Willy' Shakespeare and Richard Burbage get stoned on marijuana provided by Sir Walter Raleigh — who has passed it on from his good friend Pocohontas. Act II reaches its peak when the hero returns from the grave on a cloud of dry-ice smoke. Wearing a silver lame jumpsuit — tight enough to reveal a bulky microphone battery-pack above his navel — he imparts the evening's message in a song called 'The Madrigal Blues': 'Make love to life, and you will find death a friend.'

No, No, Nanette by Mandel Harbach and Irving Caesar, 'sixties revival. Reviewed by John Simon.

No, No, Nanette is trivial, banal, mendacious and stupid beyond the rights of any show, however escapist, to be in this day and age . . .

But what about the songs . . .? Take the most famous, 'Tea for Two'. Melodically, it is almost as simple-minded as the sound of train wheels nocturnal travellers cannot get out of their insomniac brains. One does not come out humming 'Tea for Two' — one runs out pursued, bugged, hummed by it . . .

Regina, a musical by Marc Blitzstein, Forty-Sixth Street theatre, October, 1949. Reviewed by George Jean Nathan.

There is about Blitzstein an obstreperous arbitrariness that discourages sympathy with his ambitions. He remarks, for instance, that 'I wanted to find out how daring it would be to write a musical without one love-scene or passage.' It is less daring than it is gratuitous. It is experiment only for experiment's sake and not with the merit of the experiment uppermost in mind. It is that way with Blitzstein's work in general. I'll bet that, as a small boy, he made violins out of old cigar boxes and butcher-shop string. If he didn't then, he waited to do it, in *Regina,* until now.

Tickets Please! a revue with sketches, Coronet, April, 1950. Reviewed by George Jean Nathan.

Tickets Please! is still another of the revues with a titular exclamation point which may be taken in either one of two ways. I prefer to take it in the other. Though most of the reviewers seem to be eerily enthusiastic about it, my own reaction is largely of an aghast nature . . .

CHAPTER SIX

Classic Roles

Shakespeare's classic roles occupy a unique position in the theatre and its history. Almost from the moment they were written, they have been recognized as the pinacles of the actor's art, the ultimate test by which any serious actor must expect to be judged. Hamlet, Lear, Othello, Macbeth, these are the roles, dominating the plays in which they figure and the whole Shakespearean scene.

Shakespeare offers nothing quite so powerful for actresses — which is presumably why one or two souls have become ambitious enough to venture on the boards as Hamlet. (See following entries for Sarah Bernhardt and Frances de la Tour.) There's no sense in getting indignant about something which has an obvious historical explanation. The plays were written when there were no women acting on the stage: it would be asking a bit much of a boy actor to make him undertake anything on the scale of Lear. The most demanding parts Shakespeare wrote for women are Lady Macbeth and Cleopatra. These I have included.

William Archer (1856-1924) has described much better than I can the special difficulties which beset an actor, or an actress, tackling Shakespeare's major tragic roles.

Shakespeare's Classic Roles William Archer (1856-1924)

We have each our private ideal of Macbeth, Hamlet, Othello, Lear; we have all of us read of, if we have not seen, great performances of these parts; so that every actor who undertakes them has to pass through a triple ordeal, encountering, first, our imagination, kindled by Shakespeare; second, our idealized memory of performances which used to please our, perhaps unripe, judgement; third, our conceptions of the great actors of the past, gathered from the often extravagant panegyrics of contemporaries.

Hamlet

The Play discussed by Jeremy Collier in 1698. He attacked Shakespeare for immodesty in his treatment of Ophelia and compared him, detrimentally, with Euripides . . .

(Phaedra) keeps her modesty even after she has lost her wits. Had Shakespeare secured this point for his young virgin Ophelia, the play had been better contrived. Since he was resolved to drown the lady like a kitten, he should have set her swimming a little sooner. To keep her alive only to sully her reputation, and discover the rankness of her breath, was very cruel.

and by Charles Lamb in 1811.

I confess myself utterly unable to appreciate that celebrated soliloquy in *Hamlet,* beginning 'To be or not to be,' or to tell whether it be good, bad or indifferent, it has been so handled and pawed about by declamatory boys and men, and torn so inhumanly from its living

138

place and principle of continuity in the play, till it has become to me a perfect dead number.

Some productions

Directed by **Tyrone Guthrie**, Old Vic, January 1937. Reviewed by James Agate. Hamlet in this production was played by Laurence Olivier.

The King will be better when Mr Francis Sullivan plays him outside his robes instead of in them and the Queen of Miss Dorothy Dix conveys the impression of not being in the play at all, but of looking in now and again to do a bit of acting. As Ophelia, Miss Cherry Cotterell strikes me as being unripe. Mr Torin Thatcher makes an inaudible Ghost and Mr Frederick Bennett's First Gravedigger is the one gloomy spot in the entire production.

Directed by **Michael Benthall** in Victorian costume, Stratford-on-Avon, April 1948. Reviewed by the *Liverpool Post.*

Was it not absurd that Michael Benthall, the producer, should turn the murdering King of Denmark into a semblance of Albert the Good, and fantastic to put Ophelia in a crinoline, which surely would have buoyed her up when she sought her watery death?

Hamlet has been done in modern dress, and with excuse, did not Shakespeare's own actors play in the clothes of their time? But wantonly to produce the greatest tragedy of England's dramatist in almost the worst costume period of our history is most reprehensible . . .

It was unfair to the players. How could Paul Scofield, in the title role, seem a prince in a Victorian cut-away coat, with drainpipe trousers and soft collar? How — even if the producer had not made him shout with echoes off stage — could Esmond Knight make the Ghost of Hamlet's father seem plausible when dressed like an effigy of the Duke of Wellington? How — but why go on?

Directed by **Laurence Olivier**, National Theatre at the Old Vic, 1963. Reviewed by Ronald Mavor in the *Scotsman.*

Sean Kenny's scenery — the whole stage was taken up by a massive spiral rock, which groaned and writhed about between scenes, shutters opening and closing and sections twisting themselves upon other sections, not to make any particularly recognizable structure but simply to make the great lump look different. Up the ragged rock Horatio would run. Down the rugged rock Hamlet's father would tread as delicately as Agag (and well he might in all that armour). After each seismic convulsion a little bit of the play would appear, only to be stopped by another massive rigour as the concrete elephant gave birth to its metaphysical mice.

Peter O'Toole as Hamlet with Max Adrian as Polonius (and a bit of Sean Kenny's set). Courtesy of Punch.

Footsbarn's Hamlet, an adapted and abbreviated version of the play by the Footsbarn Company from Cornwall, Golden Lane Theatre (Barbican). December, 1980. Reviewed by Robert Cushman in the *Observer.*

The performance lasted only two hours, so much went. The first scene was mimed, crowned by the appearance of a horrifically bony Ghost. 'To be or not to be' was cut entirely (cheeky) and the other soliloquies pared to the bone. All other speeches were made easy. 'Will you listen,' said the Ghost, huffily interpreting the original 'List, list, O list.'

BBC2 production, directed by **Jonathan Miller,** May, 1980. Reviewed by Clive James in the *Observer.*

Elsinore was set in a velodrome . . . you kept expecting a cyclist to streak past on the banking while the Prince was in mid-soliloquy.

The Royal Shakespeare Company at the Aldwych, September, 1981. Reviewed by Robert Cushman in the *Observer.*

At the beginning of *Hamlet* the stage looks like a Build-Your-Own-Elsinore kit.

Some actors in the part of Hamlet

Alan Badel, directed by **Michael Langham,** Stratford-on-Avon, 1956. Reviewed by the *Bristol Evening World.*

Alan Badel's costume resembled that of a comic spaceman with tightly fitting trousers and jutting shoulders, while Harry Andrews' well-spoken King looked like a futuristic cinema commissionaire.

Thomas Betterton (1635-1710), reviewed in Aston's Supplement to Cibber's *Lives of the Actors*, 1740. No date is given for the performance, but it is on record that Betterton went on playing Hamlet throughout his career; his last appearance in the part was on 10 December, 1706, when he was seventy-one years old!

I have often wished that Mr Betterton would have resigned the part of Hamlet to some young actor (who might have personated, if not acted it, better) for when he threw himself at Ophelia's feet, he appeared a little too grave for a young student lately come from the University of Wirtenburg (sic). His repartees seemed rather as apothegms of a sage philosopher, than the sporting plashes of a young Hamlet.

Sarah Bernhardt (1845-1923). Her Hamlet was counted by some among her great successes — not, however, by Max Beerbohm, who reviewed it thus:

I cannot, on my heart, take Sarah's Hamlet seriously. I cannot even imagine anyone capable of more than a hollow pretence at taking it seriously. However, the truly great are apt, in matters concerning themselves, to lose that sense of fitness which is usually called sense of humour, and I did not notice that Sarah was once hindered in her performance by any irrepressible desire to burst out laughing. Her solemnity was politely fostered by the Adelphi audience. From first to last no one smiled. If anyone had so far relaxed himself as to smile, he would have been bound to laugh. One laugh in that dangerous atmosphere, and the whole structure of polite solemnity would have toppled down, burying beneath its ruins the national reputation for good manners. I, therefore, like everyone else, kept an iron control upon the corners of my lips. It was not until I was half-way home and well out of earshot of the Adelphi that I unsealed the accumulations of my merriment.

Richard Briers, while at RADA. Reviewed by W. A. Darlington in the *Daily Telegraph.*

* Richard Briers last night played Hamlet like a demented typewriter.

Richard comments, 'I may not have been a great Hamlet but I was about the fastest.'

Richard Burton at Elsinore, June, 1954. Reviewed by John Barber in the *Daily Express.*

A trumpet blares and on to the stage struts Richard Burton as Hamlet. But he only looks like a film star with the sulks.

Frances de la Tour at the Half Moon, October, 1979. Reviewed by Milton Shulman.

* . . . She speaks most of the poetry on a one-note nasal pitch and, in her final death throes, she tottered about so long I thought she was in danger of being given a breathalyser test.

Albert Finney, Old Vic, 1975. Reviewed by Jason Hillgate in *Theatre*.

Finney's roughneck Hamlet is no prince at all, let alone a sweet prince. More of a 'Spamlet' really.

Robert Helpmann, Stratford-on-Avon, 1948. Reviewed by Kenneth Tynan.

. . . Robert Helpmann . . . gave a very clean-cut and passionless performance — not indeed of Hamlet, but Hamlet's moral tutor at Wittenberg University.

Alec Guinness, directed by **Alec Guinness** and **Frank Hauser**, New, 1951. Reviewed by Beverley Baxter in the *Evening Standard.*

* Mr Alec Guinness is a brilliant actor whose career will not be halted by this failure. But what in the world decided him to play Hamlet with a moustache and a goatee? . . . We were presented with a middle-aged Hamlet instead of the youthful, pitiful, self-infatuated Prince . . .

It is partly a tribute to the success of Mr Guinness in the cinema that we felt last night that Mr Disraeli had come to Elsinore. Here was the note of authority, the strength that evolves from long experience and the calm of maturity. If there was something rotten in the State of Denmark this was the very man to put it right . . .

Charles Macready (1793-1873) recalled by G. H. Lewes.

He was lachrymose and fretful: too fond of a cambric pocket-handkerchief to be really affecting.

Ian McKellen, Cambridge theatre, 1971. Reviewed by Harold Hobson on radio.

* The best thing about Ian McKellen's Hamlet is his curtain-call.

Ian McKellen as Hamlet with James Cairncross as First Grave Digger. Courtesy of Punch.

Laurence Olivier, Old Vic, 1937. Discussed by the eminent psychiatrist, Dr Ernest Jones, in a letter to Tyrone Guthrie, who directed the production.

. . . Temperamentally he is not cast for Hamlet. He is, personally, what we call 'manic' and so finds it hard to play the melancholic part . . . I heartily concur on the severe strictions which have been passed on his gabbling the words, to the ruin of the beautiful and sonorous poetry and philosophy they are meant to convey . . . Hamlet is thinking aloud, not chatting to bystanders.
P.S. You will of course not convey my opinion to Mr Olivier while he is still playing the part.

Which goes to show that there are times when we should ignore psychiatrists, as well as critics!

Esme Percy, Royal Court, February, 1930. Reviewed by James Agate.

When Mr Percy appeared, our eye rested on him with astonishment . . . Hamlet, as his mother reminded us and as Goethe insisted, was fat but, *pace* these authorities, we cannot consent that Hamlet should be cherubic to the point almost of being chubby.

When Hamlet debates the question of being or not being, we ought to feel that the matter has been vexing his bosom ever since his father died. Mr Percy made the speech a metaphysical exercise newly happened upon and delivered it with undergraduate relish and as though he were addressing the Oxford Union. He did not take up arms against his sea of troubles so much as bob up and down upon them like a cork.

David Warner, Stratford-on-Avon, August, 1965. Reviewed by Julian Holland in the *Daily Mail*.

I would as lief the town-crier spoke Shakespeare's lines as hear David Warner. He delivers the soliloquies as though he were dictating to the literary pirates jotting down the first-quarto version of the play.

King Lear

The play, discussed by Nahum Tate (1652-1715) in an introduction to his remodelled version of the text.

. . . a heap of jewels unstrung and unpolished, yet so dazzling in their disorder, that I soon perceived I had seized on a treasure.

In Tate's *King Lear* the Fool was omitted altogether, love scenes were inserted, and Cordelia retired to a cave with her lover during the storm scene (leaving her father to face the pelting of the pitiless storm alone). It ends happily, with Lear restored to his throne. Tate's version was played in place of Shakespeare's for 150 years, until Charles Macready brought back the original with an historic performance at Covent Garden in 1838.

Joseph Warton finds fault with *King Lear* in *The Adventurer,* January, 1754. [Warton's five papers on *The Tempest* and *King Lear,* published in *The Adventurer,* were the first pieces of Shakespearean criticism to be published as a series in a periodical.]

. . . This drama is chargeable with considerable imperfections. The plot of Edmund against his brother, which distracts the attention, and destroys the unity of the fable; the cruel and horrid extinction of Glo'ster's eyes, which ought not to be exhibited on the stage; the utter improbability of Glo'ster's imagining, though blind, that he had leaped down Dover cliff; and some passages that are too turgid and full of strained metaphors; are faults which the warmest admirers of Shakespeare will find it difficult to excuse.

and Charles Lamb in *The Reflector,* 1812.

Lear is essentially impossible to be represented on a stage.

Some productions

Stratford-on-Avon, April, 1883. Reviewed by the *Stratford-on-Avon Herald.*

Headline: AN UNREHEARSED INCIDENT
During a performance of *King Lear* at the Memorial Theatre on Monday evening last an incident occurred which created a good deal of laughter. One of the supernumaries, who was rather slow in making his exit from the stage, allowed one of the scenes to come down upon his head and, continuing its course, he and his spear became separated, he being on one side of the curtain and his weapon on the other. The incident following a scene of great tragic power caused some little relief among the audience.

Stratford Memorial Theatre Company at the Opera House, directed by **George Devine**, Manchester, November, 1955. Reviewed by Alan Bendle in the *Manchester Evening News.*

So devastating are the decorations that the Japanese sculptor, Isamu Noguchi, has imposed upon this production that John Gielgud's Lear is for some time neglected in favour of the Duke, who is wearing indiarubber water-bottles round his waist; the Knight, with a gumboot on one leg and a hockey-pad on the other; and the men draped with sausages. There are also 'things' that descend from heaven, including a large black banana, and at least one hat straight out of *The Mikado.*

King Lear, directed by **Hugh Hunt** with decor by **Reece Pemberton**; Lear was played by Stephen Murray. Old Vic, March, 1951. Reviewed in *Punch.*

A production can turn into a battle between the actors and the scenic effects. In this one, judging by the reviews, the actors lost.

The Old Vic's King Lear is not helped by a set which suggests a corner of a geological museum, occasionally cut off by a slide of old portcullises, like a feudal trap for heffalumps.

and in the *Glasgow Herald.*

This decor, by Reece Pemberton, is fascinatingly bad. Where, the awestruck spectator asks, did Mr Pemberton find that, and that? Why are the attendant soldiery strayed from the horde of Genghis Khan? Why are the wicked sisters got up like the boudoir ladies of Fuseli? Where, and why, did Mr Pemberton come across all that fur?

and by John Barber in the *Daily Express.*

He clutters up the stage with hideous purple rocks, a kind of Forth Bridge of antlers, and swaying totem poles hung with savage fetishes. The fur of a thousand rabbits goes into cumbersome rugs and unsightly caps . . .

Through the darkness and long pauses, between deafening thunderclaps and wind machines, the actors mumble, or shriek like hags. Cordelia, dressed like a charwoman, cannot be heard . . .

The same thing happened in 1958.

King Lear, Old Vic, February, 1958. Reviewed by Milton Shulman in the *Evening Standard.*

Douglas Seale has produced a blasted heath which is nothing if not loud. Banished by his two scheming daughters, Lear has to declaim his curses in competition with some of the most teeth-rattling thunder ever heard in the West End. One felt Lear would gladly have given up his throne for a good pair of ear-plugs.

Some actors in the part of Lear

Edmund Kean, reviewed by William Hazlitt in the *London Magazine,* June, 1820.

Mr Kean chipped off a bit of the character here and there: but he did not pierce the solid substance, nor move the entire mass. Indeed, he did not go the right way about it. He was too violent at first, and too tame afterwards. He sunk from unmixed rage to mere dotage. Thus (to leave the general description and come to particulars) he made the well-known curse a piece of downright rant. He 'tore it to tatters, to very rags,' and made it, from beginning to end, an explosion of ungovernable physical rage, without solemnity, or elevation.

Charles Laughton, Stratford-on-Avon, 1959, directed by **Glen Byam Shaw**. Reviewed by Eric Keown in *Punch*.

. . . If as a Lear it was one of the oddest we have seen the reason lies in the personality and physical attributes of Charles Laughton, who makes no attempt to capture grandeur or majesty. His snow-white hair and beard form an almost complete circle round a pudgy face of the utmost benignity, giving him the air of an innocent Father Christmas . . .

Philip Locke, Young Vic, October, 1980. Directed by **Frank Dunlop**. Reviewed by Victoria Radin in the *Observer*.

There is none of the stiffness of age in this ruler, who minces, struts, flutters his hands and obviously hasn't benefited by the diction lessons of our Queen. His voice at times is a sing-song, at others a growl, at still others a shriek; but always it is slurred. Here is an ageing coquette, who is used to receiving favours, like a courtesan, from his daughters . . . He greets Cordelia's reply of 'Nothing' with a maniacal laugh, and pokes out his tongue as he banishes Kent.

Stephen Murray as Lear, Old Vic, March, 1951. Reviewed by John Barber in the *Daily Express*.

He maintains a gravelly, rasping note, hammering at you until — after two hours without an interval — you rush out thankfully to listen to the traffic.

Laurence Olivier, Old Vic, September, 1946. Directed by himself. Reviewed by Hubert Griffith in the *Sunday Graphic*.

He handicapped himself by wearing a beard and a mane so stupendous that his voice came to me as though he were talking through a tree.

Edmund Kean as Lear.

Charles Laughton as Lear. Courtesy of Punch.

Macbeth

The play. As well as being a huge technical challenge to actors and directors, *Macbeth* has the added disadvantage, in a notoriously superstitious profession, of being considered unlucky. Actors regale one another with tales of broken limbs and other disasters incurred while performing in it, and there is a tradition that one doesn't even mention it by name: it is referred to as 'the Scottish play'.

To set the scene for these reviews I am therefore offering Sybil Thorndike's account of how she and her husband Lewis Casson warded-off trouble from a production in which they were jointly involved.

Dreadful things kept recurring, reaching such frightful proportions that Lewis called me into his room and said, 'Sybil, the devil does work in this play. There is horror behind it. We must do something positive against it.' And together we read aloud the Ninety-first Psalm, which quieted and strengthened us and made us feel normal again.

Some productions

Aldwych, 1920. Reviewed by Herbert Farjeon in *The Shakespeare Scene.*

'The Tragedie of Macbeth' is now being given at the Aldwych theatre: 'the Tragedie of Macbeth', *or something like it.*

From the moment the curtain rises on the Aldwych version one hesitates to identify it with the First Folio, for this is what immediately happens.
First Witch: Ha ha ha!
Second Witch: Ho ho ho!
Third Witch: Hee hee hee!
In support of which it may be claimed that if these words were not written by Shakespeare, then the less Shakespeare he. Certainly they are not to be found in the First Folio, nor are they to be found in any other Folio on God's earth . . .

The weird sisters begin and end the Aldwych *Macbeth* and they are devilish busy all through it, not only on the stage but off. It is safe to estimate that they repeat offstage the chorus quoted above at least thirty times. Whenever any fresh crime is contemplated, whenever it is committed, whenever it is regretted, you hear the weired sisters cry fatefully in the wings, 'Ha ha ha! Ho ho ho! Hee hee hee!' which you might think would satisfy them for the evening, but no! Even when the curtain is down, even when the scenes are being shifted and the playgoer behind you is complaining that the play is too heavy, or that Mr [James Keteltas] Hackett [1869-1926], being only fifty years old, has no need yet to act a man of Macbeth's age (both of which complaints were uttered by the playgoer behind me) — even at these moments, bang in the middle of the long intervals, the myrmidons of Hecate persist in their resolve to wring

our withers, ha ha ha-ing, ho ho ho-ing and hee hee hee-ing while the band assiduously plays.

Modern dress production by Barry Jackson, with Eric Maturin and Mary Merrill, Royal Court, February, 1928. Reviewed by James Agate.

It is not a performance of *Macbeth,* but an essay in self-sacrifice which the actors ought not to have been called upon to make. The spiritual home of Miss Mary Merrill's Lady Macbeth is obviously the more exclusive portions of Finsbury Park. I confess that I never thought to see the speech beginning 'What beast was't then that made you break this enterprise to me?' with the speaker reclining in abandonment and luxury in the arms of her sheikh on an art-coloured divan with a distant gramophone playing the openings of the first act of *Carmen.*

Production directed by John Gielgud, with Ralph Richardson, Stratford-on-Avon, 1952. Reviewed by Kenneth Tynan.

Last Tuesday night at the Stratford Memorial Theatre *Macbeth* walked the plank, leaving me, I am afraid, unmoved to the point of paralysis. It was John Gielgud, never let us forget, who did this cryptic thing; Gielgud, as director, who seems to have imagined that Ralph Richardson, with his comic, Robeyesque cheese-face, was equipped to play Macbeth; Gielgud who surrounded the play's fuliginous cruelties with settings of total black, which is just about as subtle as setting *Saint Joan* in total white; Gielgud who commanded dirty tatters for Macbeth's army and brisk, clean tunics for Malcolm's, just to indicate in advance who was going to win. The production assumed, or so I took it, that the audience was either moronic or asleep; it read us a heavily italicized lecture on the play, and left nothing to our own small powers of discovery. When, in the banquet scene, a real table and some real chairs, chalices, and candelabra were brought on, life intervened for a moment; but once the furniture had gone, we were back in the engulfing, the platitudinous void, with its single message: 'Background of evil, get it?' The point about Macbeth is that the murders should horrify us; against Mr Gielgud's sable scenery they look as casual as crochet-work . . .

Some actors in the part

Edwin Forrest (1806-72), an American tragic actor of considerable standing, idolized in his own country, who visited London in 1836 and again 1845, playing the classic roles of Shakespeare. The first visit was quite successful, the second less so — for which he blamed the machinations of the English actor Charles Macready. Their quarrel was at the root of the subsequent Astor Place riot in New York, from which Macready barely escaped with his life. Reviewed by John Forster.

Our old friend, Mr Forrest, afforded great amusement to the public by his performance of Macbeth on Friday evening at the Princess's. Indeed, our best comic actors do not often excite so great a quantity of mirth . . . The grand feature was the combat, in which he stood scraping his sword against that of Macduff. We were at a loss to know what this gesture meant, till an enlightened critic in the gallery shouted out, 'That's right. Sharpen it!'

Anthony Hopkins, National Theatre at the Old Vic, November, 1973. Reviewed by Felix Barker in the *Evening News*.

This cocky genial fellow sometimes sweats apprehensively and occasionally bellows, but frequently he gives the impression that he is a Rotarian pork butcher about to tell the stalls a dirty story.

I ought to add that I played Lady Macbeth in this production, and got the sort of lukewarm notices which are utterly damning, but not particularly amusing as quotes.

Anthony Hopkins as Macbeth with Diana Rigg as Lady Macbeth. Courtesy of Punch.

Michael Hordern, Old Vic, January, 1959. Reviewed by Alan Brien.

* Michael Hordern as Macbeth is ludicrously enough costumed. Half his time on the stage he cringes like an Armenian carpet-seller in an ankle-length black dressing-gown of fuzzy candlewick while his ruched gold-cloth sleeves sag like concertinas around the tips of his fingers. He would make a sinister Shylock, a frightening Fagin. But this Thane of Cawdor would be unnerved by Banquo's valet, never mind Banquo's ghost . . .

Charles Kean (1811-68), son of Edmund Kean, once played Iago to his father's Othello at Covent Garden. He was much praised for a style of acting known as 'gentlemanly melodrama'. His Macbeth is reviewed by G. H. Lewes in *The Leader,* February, 1853.

When the witches accost him, his only expression of 'metaphysical influence' is to stand still with his eyes fixed and his mouth open . . . In Charles Kean's Macbeth all tragedy has vanished; sympathy is impossible, because the mind of the criminal is hidden from us. He makes Macbeth ignoble, with perhaps a tendency towards Methodism.

Perhaps the barbs which hurt most are those from within the theatrical family . . .

Charles Laughton, Old Vic, 1933-4.
Comment by Lilian Baylis in the actor's dressing-room, as recorded in the authorised biography of Tyrone Guthrie.

Never mind, dear, I'm sure you did your best. And I'm sure one day you may be quite a good Macbeth.

Charles Macready (1793-1873).
Leigh Hunt wrote of his Macbeth:

It wants the Royal warrant.

Of all the Macbeths in the last fifty years, Peter O'Toole's took the mightiest tumble of them all. It did, however, play to packed houses for the entire run.

Peter O'Toole, Prospect Theatre Company production, September, 1980. Reviewed by Irving Wardle in *The Times.*

Mr O'Toole . . . strides on in what one first takes to be the last stages of battle fatigue. His walk is an exhausted lunge, his voice thick, hoarse, and full of abrupt sledge-hammer emphases. But as he begins, so he continues. His manner on the stage is not that of a man in an intricate, danger-fraught situation, but that of someone who owns the place. He walks around the stage as if he were inspecting a property he has just recently acquired; pinching a cheek here and there, tossing commands over his shoulder, but not paying much attention to the small fry.

His verse speaking consists of a heavy lurch from beat to beat, delivered in measured, sustained tone, and depending on prolonged phrasing within a single breath. Arresting to begin with, if only as total departure from modern verse convention, it grows extremely monotonous and blots out the sense. Its tonal range varies between arrogance and torment, allowing him no chance to show Macbeth's guile or diplomacy; let alone the unstained national hero of the first scenes. 'Fail not our feast,' he thunders at Banquo, from which the victim might have known what was coming.

and by Michael Billington in the *Guardian*.

He delivers every line with a monotonous tenor bark as if addressing an audience of deaf Eskimos . . . It was P. G. Wodehouse who memorably said that the 'Tomorrow and tomorrow and tomorrow' speech has got a lot of spin on it but, as delivered by Mr O'Toole, it is hit for six like a full toss.

and by Robert Cushman in the *Observer*.

His performance suggests that he is taking some kind of personal revenge on the play.

Peter O'Toole as Macbeth. (In rehearsals for this production, the play was always referred to as the 'Harry Lauder Show'.) Courtesy of Punch.

Ronald Pickup played Macbeth in his final term public production at RADA. *The Times Literary Supplement* said:

* . . . This Lady Macbeth understandably committed suicide to escape the ranting of her husband, played by Ronald Pickup.

James Quin (1693-1766), English actor, played leading Shakespearean roles, first at Lincoln's Inn Fields theatre, then at Covent Garden and Drury Lane. The latter part of his career was spent in rivalry with Garrick, of whom he once said, 'If the young fellow is right, I and the rest of the players have all been wrong.'

His Macbeth is reviewed by Francis Gentleman.

Mr Quin, whose sole merit in tragedy was declamation, or brutal pride, was undescribably cumbersome in *Macbeth*; his face, which had no possible variation from its natural grace, except sternness and festivity, could not be expected to exhibit the acute sensations of this character; his figure was void of the essential spirit, and his voice far too monotonous for the transitions which so frequently occur; yet, wonderful to be told, he played it several years with considerable applause.

Ralph Richardson, Stratford-on-Avon, 1952. Reviewed by Kenneth Tynan.

. . . His feathery, yeasty voice, with its single spring-heeled inflexion, starved the part of its richness; he moved dully, as if by numbers, and such charm as he possessed was merely a sort of unfocused bluffness, like a teddy-bear snapped in a bad light by a child holding its first camera. Sir Ralph, who seems to me to have become the glass eye in the forehead of English acting, has now bumped into something quite immoveable. His Macbeth is slovenly; and to go further into it would be as frustrating as trying to write with a pencil whose point has long since worn down to the wood.

Some Lady Macbeths

As with Macbeth, so with Lady Macbeth. Caryl Brahms wrote in *The Times,* 1 August 1966:

. . . though there are many ways of acting Lady Macbeth, we may well conclude that the role is unactable.

Mrs Patrick Campbell (1865-1940). Her Lady Macbeth incurred a penalty to which actresses now, at least, are no longer subjected — a personal letter from Shaw, enumerating her shortcomings.

Blunder 1. You should not have played the dagger scene in that best evening dress of Lady Macbeth's, but in a black wrap like a thundercloud with a white face.
Blunder 2. You should not have repeated Macbeth's exit business — you should have gone off like a woman of iron.

Blunder 3. You should not have forgotten that there was blood on your hands and on his, and that you dared not touch one another for fear of messing your clothes with gore.

Mary Knepp or **Knipp** (? -1677), early English actress and a friend of Nell Gwynn. According to Samuel Pepys she was a gay and lively woman, at her best in comedy — as one might gather from his description of her Lady Macbeth in his *Diary.*

She was most comical and natural when she walks forth sleeping (the which I can testify, for Mrs Pepys also walks forth sleeping at some times) and did most ingeniously mimick the manner of women who walk thus.

Flora Robson, Old Vic, 1933-4. Reviewed by James Agate in the *Sunday Times.*

[She] has the mechanics of the part well in hand and perfectly conveys what we might call the Lady's business side. But Lady Macbeth requires more than a strict attention to business.

Simone Signoret in a production direction by **William Gaskill**, Royal Court, October, 1966. Reviewed by Alan Brien in the *Sunday Telegraph.*

Simone Signoret's Lady Macbeth, a conical, bell-tented matron who moves on wheels like a draped Dalek surmounted by a beautiful Medusa head, speaks with a monotonous French accent punctuated by American vowels.

and by Thomas Quinn Curtiss in the *New York Times.*

Simone Signoret's Lady Macbeth was in need of both subtitles and microphones.

Sarah Siddons (1755-1831). Reviewed by John Taylor in the *Morning Post,* February, 1785.

. . . In the taper scene she was defective; her enunciation was too confined . . . the faces she made were horrid and even ugly, without being strictly just or expressive. She appeared in three . . . dresses. The first was handsome and neatly elegant: the second rich and splendid, but somewhat pantomimical, and the last one of the least becoming, to speak no worse of it, of any she ever wore upon the stage. Lady Macbeth is supposed to be *asleep* and not *mad*; so that custom itself cannot be alleged as a justification for her appearing in *white satin.*

Peg Woffington (1714-60) played opposite Garrick and was for a while his mistress. Critics of her time generally refer to her voice as being too harsh. Reviewed by Francis Gentleman.

Mrs Woffington was extremely well received, and really did the part as well as her deplorable tragedy voice would admit.

Irene Worth, Stratford-on-Avon, June, 1962.

Up to the sleepwalking scenes . . . Miss Worth was a cosy lady, all curves where she should have been angles of steel.

Othello

The play discussed by George Bernard Shaw in the *Saturday Review,* May, 1897.

Othello . . . is pure melodrama. There is not a touch of characterization that goes below the skin . . . To anyone capable of reading the play with an open mind as to its merits, it is obvious that Shakespeare plunged through it so impetuously that he had finished it before he had made up his mind as to the character and motives of a single person in it.

Some productions

Directed by **Franco Zeffirelli**, Stratford-on-Avon, October, 1961. Reviewed by Bernard Levin.

For the eye, too much; for the ear, too little; for the mind, nothing at all.

That is the verdict on this long-awaited *Othello,* the last Stratford production of the current Shakespeare season. And so much was expected from it.

Has it not Sir John Gielgud playing, for the first time in his career, what he once told me was the only great classical part he had never played but long wished to?

And is it not directed by the great Zeffirelli, who conquered the Old Vic, Covent Garden, and Glyndebourne in a single season, and wanted only the Royal Shakespeare scalp for his belt?

Then what went wrong? Mr Zeffirelli must step forward for the blame — all of it.

No hot Italian realism here: the director has clearly decided that the scenery's the thing.

I have never seen so many *objects* on any stage in my life. There are flags and banners, piles of books, trunks and chests, rolls of carpet, jewel boxes, documents and maps, more steps than Odessa ever dreamed of, stone walls that certainly do a prison make, sticks of sealing wax, a backdrop after Veronese and bronze doors a long way after Ghiberti; and seventy times seven pillars without a drop of wisdom. (They rock when anybody leans on them; and, if it comes to that, the stone walls sway in the slightest breeze) . . .

Some actors in the part of Othello

Harry Andrews, Stratford-on-Avon, 1956. Reviewed in the *Financial Times*.

It is in the early part of the play that Mr Andrews is most at a disadvantage. In his rather prosaic fashion, he looks and sounds like an outstanding member of the British General Staff, sunburned after a tour of the Middle East . . . The voice occasionally allows itself a Churchillian growl of emphasis, but otherwise the conception is all manly reticence.

Charles Fechter (1824-79), a French actor who as a young man played romantic parts in Paris; he was the first Armand in *La Dame aux Camellias*. In the 1850s he moved to London, where he was much admired, although his English was never very good. G. H. Lewes said that Fechter's Hamlet was one of the best he had seen. Here, however, he is reviewing the Othello.

His performance of Othello . . . had not one good quality. False in conception, it was feeble in execution. He attempted to make the character natural, and made it vulgar . . . Othello is grave, dignified, a man accustomed to the weight of great responsibilities, and to the command of armies; Fechter is unpleasantly familiar, paws Iago about like an over-demonstrative schoolboy; shakes hands on the slightest provocation; and bears himself like the hero of a French *drame,* but not like a hero of tragedy.

John Gielgud discussed by Eric Keown in *Punch,* October, 1961.

Sir John Gielgud is not a natural Othello, and one sees why he has resisted the part so long.

Anthony Hopkins, with Bob Hoskins as Iago, BBC2 production directed by **Jonathan Miller**, October, 1981. Reviewed by Clive James in the *Observer.*

. . . there was the question of why Othello looked so white. The play is replete with lines saying how black he is. He has a sooty bosom. Mr Hopkins had a suet bosom, which isn't the same thing. Also Iago carried on like the most untrustworthy man in the world, which made Othello a fool to trust him. Would you buy a used handkerchief from this man?

Laurence Olivier, National Theatre production at the Old Vic, April, 1964. Reviewed by Alan Brien in the *Sunday Telegraph*.

There is a kind of bad acting of which only a great actor is capable. I find Sir Laurence Olivier's Othello the most prodigious and perverse example of this in a decade . . . Sir Laurence is elaborately at ease, graceful and suave, more like a seducer than a cuckold. But as the jealousy is transfused into his blood, the white man shows through more obviously. He begins to double and treble his vowels, to stretch his consonants, to stagger and shake, even to vomit, near the frontiers of self-parody. His hips oscillate, his palms rotate, his voice skids and slides so that the Othello music takes on a Beatle beat.

Laurence Olivier as Othello. Courtesy of Punch.

Paul Scofield, Olivier, National, directed by **Peter Hall**, March, 1980. Reviewed by Robert Cushman in the *Observer*.

Paul Scofield delivers the last three speeches of *Othello* . . . very simply and affectingly. Earlier he administers to Desdemona a crackling slap on the face. The rest of the time he is sonorously somnolent . . .

156 | and in the *Field*

He comes with the stiff swagger of a peacock and an equally awkward accent, which makes him sound less like a Moor and more like a man wrestling with the new set of National Health teeth.

and by Peter Jenkins in the *Spectator*.

His black man's form of speech was most peculiar and reminded me of Hutch, who used to sing at Quags in an accent that got lost somewhere between Jamaica and Berkeley Square. His idea of a black man's movement consisted of a kind of Firbankian prancing which, in moments of deep anguish, came to resemble an orangutan choreographed by Sir Frederick Ashton.

Robert Stephens, Regent's Park, June, 1976. Reviewed by Ned Chaillet in *The Times*.

Robert Stephen's Othello suffers from a make-up that sweats off in drops like blood and, by hiding his facial expressions, forces him to act entirely with his voice and body. His body, unfortunately, is clad in a chest-baring toga and, for some reason, Mr Stephens frequently adopts a posture where he stands with his bare feet wide apart and holds his hands rigidly away from his side. He is then limited to conveying his torment in regular shudders and frequent falls.

Antony and Cleopatra

The play discussed by G. B. Shaw in the *Saturday Review*, May, 1897.

Antony and Cleopatra is an attempt at a serious drama. To say that there is plenty of bogus characterization in it — Enobarbus, for instance — is merely to say that it is by Shakespeare.

Some actresses in the part of Cleopatra

Janet Achurch (1864-1916), best remembered as one of the first English actresses to play Ibsen. She also played leading roles in Shakespeare, touring with Frank Benson's company. Queen's theatre, Manchester, March, 1897. Reviewed by George Bernard Shaw in the *Saturday Review*.

Of the hardihood of ear with which she carries out her original and often audacious conceptions of Shakespearean music I am too utterly unnerved to give any adequate description. The lacerated discord of her wailings is in my tormented ears as I write, reconciling me to the grave. It is as if she had been excited by the Hallelujah Chorus to dance on the keyboard of a great organ with all the stops pulled out.

Glenda Jackson, directed by **Peter Brook** at Stratford-on-Avon, October, 1978. Reviewed by Milton Shulman in the *Evening Standard.*

. . . dressed in a number of chic outfits more suggestive of Chelsea than the Nile, Miss Jackson's danger of succumbing to absolute passion was no closer than Mrs. Thatcher's likelihood of weeping at Cabinet meetings.

Except for her final death scene with Antony, she gave me the impression that he didn't really appeal to her.

and by Robert Cushman in the *Observer*

Glenda Jackson meanwhile is still Elizabeth I . . .

Vanessa Redgrave, directed by **Tony Richardson**, with Julian Glover as Antony. Bankside Globe, August, 1973. Reviewed by Irving Wardle in *The Times.*

With the two mighty lovers, the question is of how far their anti-heroic playing is deliberate . . .

'I am dying, Egypt, dying,' remarks Julian Glover, just to let her know.

'Rogue, thou hast lived too long,' shrieks Vanessa Redgrave, pursuing the offending messenger with a coke bottle.

and

By the end, with a long showy gown added to her red wig and arch, self-mocking manner, she has come to resemble no one so much as Danny la Rue — a dubious interpretation of the word 'queen'.

Janet Suzman, RSC at Stratford-on-Avon, 1972.

* Where Shakespeare had written the word 'O', she favoured us with an extended imitation of a hurrying ambulance.

and in the television version, reviewed by Clive James.

* I occupied the spare time in several of her speeches by counting her teeth.

CHAPTER SEVEN
Directors, Productions, Sets and Theatres

This section embraces production, the sets, the theatre itself and the director, who makes it all happen.

It will be observed that in the older reviews the word 'producer' is used where we would say 'director'. The terminology has changed. I have kept naturally the old terminology in the old reviews.

Shakespeare's **All's Well that Ends Well** directed by **Tyrone Guthrie**, Stratford-on-Avon, 1959. Reviewed by Kenneth Tynan.

All's Well That Ends Well, the first Stratford production I saw this year, is directed by Tyrone Guthrie with his familiar, infuriating blend of insight and madness. On the one hand we have the great conductor, the master of visual orchestration, conceivably the most striking director alive when there are more than six people on the stage; on the other hand we have his zany *Doppelgänger,* darting about with his pockets full of fireworks, and giving the members of the orchestra hot-feet whenever genuine feeling threatens to impend . . .

Shakespeare's **Antony and Cleopatra** directed by **Jonathan Miller,** BBC, May, 1981. Reviewed by Clive James in the *Observer.*

Jonathan cuts a tremendous dash as a director. Unfortunately Shakespeare cuts an even more tremendous dash as a playwright, so there is not as much room as there might be for a director to express his individuality. Jonathan gave another Phaidon production of paintings this time hailing from Venice, with a particular emphasis on Veronese and Tiepolo. You could marvel at the miracles of lighting while the actors got on with murdering the verse.

Beau Geste by P. C. Wren, directed by **Basil Dean**, His Majesty's, January, 1929. Reviewed by Hannen Swaffer in the *Daily Express.*

. . . Mr Dean has put the sweat of the desert into it all, and the battle and the horror.

It was so realistic that right at the end, when the hero was given a 'Viking's funeral', the stage fireman, thinking it was a real fire, actually turned the hose on the scene! An LCC inspector urged him on, while the safety curtain was lowered a few seconds before it should have been.

This was realism with a vengeance!

A Bell for Adano by Paul Osborn, based on a novel by John Hersey, September, 1945. Reviewed by James Agate.

Why must all the actors bellow like sealions conversing with walruses on the further side of an ice flow in a blizzard?

Sean Kenny's sets for **Blitz!** by Lionel Bart, Adelphi, 1962. Reviewed by Kenneth Tynan.

. . . A bookmaker repeatedly quoted by James Agate once said that Marie Lloyd had a heart as big as Waterloo station. *Blitz!* is as big as Waterloo station, but it has no heart.

It does, however, have Sean Kenny's scenery, and herein may lie its true significance. Belasco and Novello went pretty far in the direction of spectacular realism; but in *Blitz!* there are distinct signs that the sets are taking over. They swoop down on the actors and snatch them aloft; four motor-driven towers prowl the stage, converging menacingly on any performer who threatens to hog the limelight; and whenever the human element looks like gaining control, they collapse on it in a mass of flaming timber.

In short, they let the cast know who's boss. They are magnificent, and they are war: who (they tacitly enquire) needs Lionel Bart? I have a fearful premonition of the next show Mr Kenny designs. As soon as the curtain rises, the sets will advance in a phalanx on the audience and summarily expel it from the theatre. After that, the next step is clear: Mr Kenny will invent sets that applaud.

Peter Brook and Peter Hall. Discussed by Kenneth Tynan in the *Observer,* 1957.

Having closely compared Peter Brook's production of *Titus Andronicus* with Peter Hall's production of *Cymbeline,* I am persuaded that these two young directors should at once go into partnership. I have even worked out business cards for them:

Hall & Brook Ltd, the Home of Lost Theatrical Causes. Collapsing plays shored up, unspeakable lines glossed over. Wrecks salvaged, ruins refurbished: unpopular plays at popular prices. Masterpieces dealt with only if neglected. Shakespearean juvenilia and senilia our speciality: if it can walk, we'll make it run. Bad last acts no obstacle: if it peters out, call Peter in. Don't be fobbed off with Glenvilles, Woods or Zadeks: look for the trademark — Hall & Brook.

Faust by Goethe, directed by **Henry Irving** (who acted the part of Mephistopheles), Lyceum, 1887. Reviewed by Henry James in the *Century Magazine.*

We attach the most limited importance to the little mechanical artifices with which Mr Irving has sought to enliven *Faust.* We care nothing for the spurting flames which play so large a part, nor for the importunate lighting which is perpetually projected upon somebody or something. It is not for these things that we go to see the great Goethe . . . We even protest against the abuse of the said lighting effect: it is always descending on someone or other, apropos of everything and nothing; it is disturbing and vulgarizing, and has nothing to do with the author's meaning. That blue vapours should attend on the steps of Mephistopheles is a very poor substitute for his giving us a moral shudder. That deep note is entirely absent from

Mr Irving's rendering of him, though the actor, of course, at moments displays to the eye a remarkably sinister figure. He strikes us, however, as superficial — a terrible fault for an archfiend.

The Force of Habit, by Thomas Bernhardt, Lyttelton, November, 1976. Reviewed by Irving Wardle in *The Times.*

What a waste of talent, and everybody's time. Not to mention money: how much, I wonder, did it cost to install that full-sized, artfully dilapidated lorry to stand unused by the side of Timothy O'Brien and Tazeena Firth's caravan?

and in the *Daily Mirror.*

It is said that the quickest way to empty a theatre is to yell 'Fire'.

Another method, slightly slower, is to put on the current National Theatre production of *The Force of Habit.*

The Force of Habit *with Oliver Cotton as Clown, Philip Locke as Garibaldi and Gawn Grainger as Juggler. Courtesy of* Punch.

Shakespeare's **Henry V**, directed by **F. R. Benson** (who played the name part), Lyceum, 1900. Reviewed by Max Beerbohm in the *Saturday Review.*

Mr F. R. Benson is an Oxford man, and he is in the habit of recruiting his company from his university. Insomuch that, according to the *Daily Chronicle,* 'the influence of university cricket has been seen in many provincial towns visited by Mr Benson's company.'

Alertness, agility, grace, physical strength — all these attributes are obvious in the mimes who were, last week, playing *Henry the Fifth* at the Lyceum. Every member of the cast seemed in tip-top condition — thoroughly 'fit'. Subordinates and principals all worked well together. The fielding was excellent, and so was the batting. Speech after speech was sent spinning across the boundary, and one was constantly inclined to shout 'Well *played,* sir! Well played *indeed!*' As a branch of university cricket, the whole performance was, indeed, beyond praise. But, as a form of acting, it was not impressive.

The Hitch Hiker's Guide to the Galaxy, directed by **Ken Campbell**, Rainbow, July, 1980. Reviewed by Irving Wardle in *The Times.*

I fear Mr Campbell has piloted his voyagers into a black hole.

An Italian Straw Hat by Eugene Labiche and Marc-Michel, adapted by Thomas Walton, directed by **Denis Carey**, Old Vic, December, 1952. Reviewed in the *Tatler.*

The ladies of the Old Vic are really not pretty enough to dance the Can-can. Lurking in their ranks there may well be an overpowering Lady Macbeth, or a tender Desdemona, but one searches their somewhat peaked faces and dowdy hair in vain, for any sign of a Frou-Frou or a Nanette. Since they are chosen for their intellectual and emotional potentialities, rather than for shapeliness of limb, the elevation of their skirts, as they romp their way through this still vigorous farce, tends to produce a lowering of the spirits.

Julius Caesar by Shakespeare, His Majesty's, 1932. Reviewed by Herbert Farjeon.

A massive company has been assembled at His Majesty's theatre to restore what is called 'the Tree tradition' with an overwhelming production of *Julius Caesar,* which I hardly need tell anyone who knows anything about the Tree tradition means plenty of lictors and vestal virgins or, to sum the matter up in the base vernacular, *Julius Caesar* with knobs on.

The Tree Tradition it was that gave us *A Midsummer Night's Dream* with real rabbits scuttling across the stage and a whole set of wings of different colours for Titania. It was the Tree tradition that arranged appropriate rumbles of thunder when Desdemona was smothered in order to make the proceeding really impressive. In short, it was the Tree tradition that buried the light of Shakespeare under a bushel of spectacle and called it Swan of Avon . . .

For this tribute to the memory of a dead manager rather than a live playwright, all the heavyweights in London from Mr Oscar Asche downwards seem to have flocked together . . . The company is rather like a football team consisting entirely of full-backs. The lines of blank verse succeed each other like bowls bowling down a bowling alley. The actors . . . seem mesmerized by their own voices. The nimble flame of Shakespeare is extinguished by the hooves of elephants. Here once again is the awful Shakespeare we ought to like.

As for the crowd, it is massive and vociferous and suggestive in some of its effects of a sort of Chu-Chin-Caesar. Whether the super who shouted 'Shut Up!' during Anthony's funeral speech was told to, or whether he just lost his head, it was a jolly moment — even jollier, I thought, than the moment when Casca and Cassius sheltered from the streaming rain under a red lamp in what looked like the entrance to a real old Roman night club.

King John by Shakespeare, directed by **Peter Potter**, Old Vic, September, 1961. Reviewed by Bernard Levin in the *Daily Express*.

I verily believe that if *King John* contained the line 'Pass the mustard' it would, in this version, have gone 'Hum-hum-hum-ho-ho PASS — he-he-gurgle-gurgle THE tralalala (i' faith) tum-ti-tum MUSTARD deedle deedle-deedle-ha-ha-ha-ha-ha-ha-ha.' (Trumpets without.)

The result, all too predictably, was three hours that passed like thirty.

Let's Pretend, St James's, December, 1938. Reviewed in the *Daily Mail*.

The scenery — and there's tons of it — declared a kind of sit-down strike on the revolving stage the producer had planned to whizz round before the eyes of the audience before many of the scenes . . . Well, when they came to do it at last night's dress rehearsal, the revolving stage revolved beautifully — but the scenery just stayed put. That is to say, odd corners of it clung to any old curtain or pillar, anything to remain facing the seats where the audience were to have been tonight.

Now the audience won't be there because after the umpteenth try it was decided to postpone the production . . .

Revolves are notoriously hazardous. I remember one occasion at Stratford during Two Gentlemen of Verona *the stage hands operating the machinery had obviously taken a drop too much with the result that the revolve accelerated wildly and anyone brave enough to step on was promptly sent spinning off.*

The Merchant of Venice by Shakespeare, directed by **Komisarjevsky**, Stratford-on-Avon, 1932. Reviewed by L.L.H. in the *Daily Express*.
Headline: CRAZY NIGHT AT STRATFORD.

The craziest production of Shakespeare's *The Merchant of Venice* that I ever saw opened at Stratford's famous new Memorial Theatre tonight. Komisarjevsky the famous Russian producer and the first guest producer to be given a free hand in this theatre, was responsible.

He produced the play against a background of fantastic Venetian scenery of his own design.

The pillars of St Mark's leaned drunkenly against a nightmare Venetian tower, surrounded by a confusion of flying bridges. The set was riotously out of perspective and bathed in a pink glow.

When he needed a change of scene, he split the set in half and slid it into the wings on moving stages in full view of the audience.

Then there was a third stage resembling a roof garden raised in the middle to a height of eight or ten feet. On this, half way between heaven and earth, he made Portia and Nerissa play their parts.

Always when the changes were made the scenery swayed tipsily. One of the bridges was so placed that every time the acting took place on it, only two thirds of the audience could see what was happening.

He began and ended the play with a dance of grotesque figures to music by Bach, and dressed his actors, sometimes farcically, with an extravagance of plumes, ruffs and cloaks.

All the company tried to make it Shakespeare, but Komisarjevsky made it Stratford's Crazy Night.

A Midsummer Night's Dream by Shakespeare, Covent Garden, 1816. Reviewed by Hazlitt.

We have found to our cost, once and for all, that the regions of fancy and the boards of Covent Garden are not the same thing. All that is fine in a play, was lost in the representation. The spirit was evaporated, the genius was fled; but the spectacle was fine: it was that which saved the play. Oh, ye scene-shifters, ye scene-painters, ye machinists and dress-makers, ye manufacturers of moon and stars that give no light, ye musical composers, ye men of the orchestra, fiddlers and trumpeters and players on the double drum and loud bassoon, rejoice! This is your triumph; it is not ours: and ye full-grown, well-fed, substantial, real fairies . . . We shall remember you: we shall believe no more in the existence of your fantastic tribe . . .

A Midsummer Night's Dream by Shakespeare, directed by **Augustin Daly**, Daly's, July, 1895. Reviewed by George Bernard Shaw.

The Two Gentlemen of Verona has been succeeded at Daly's Theatre by *A Midsummer Night's Dream*. Mr Daly is in great form. In my last article I was rash enough to hint that he had not quite realised what could be done with electric lighting on the stage. He triumphantly answers me by fitting up all his fairies with portable batteries and incandescent lights, which they switch on and off from time to time, like children with a new toy. He has trained Miss Lilian Swain in the part of Puck, until it is safe to say that she does not take one step, strike one attitude, or modify her voice by a single inflection that is not violently, wantonly and ridiculously wrong and absurd. Instead of being mercurial, she poses academically like a cheap Italian statuette. Instead of being impish and childish, she is elegant and affected. She laughs a solemn, measured laugh like a heavy

German Zamiel; she announces her ability to girdle the earth in forty minutes in the attitude of a professional skater and then begins the journey awkwardly in a swing, which takes her in the opposite direction to that in which she indicated her intention of going.

Another stroke of Mr Daly's is to make Oberon a woman. It must not be supposed that he does this solely because it is wrong, though there is no other reason apparent. He does it partly because he was brought up to do such things and partly because they seem to him to be a tribute to Shakespeare's greatness which, being uncommon, ought not to be interpreted according to the dictates of common sense. A female Oberon, and a Puck who behaves like a page boy earnestly training himself for the post of footman recommend themselves to him because they totally destroy the naturalness of the representation and so accord with his conception of the Shakespearean drama as the most artificial of all forms of stage entertainment.

A Midsummer Night's Dream by Shakespeare, directed by **Tyrone Guthrie**, Old Vic, 1952. Reviewed by the *Muswell Hill Record.*

The setting of Tyrone Guthrie's production of *A Midsummer Night's Dream* at the Old Vic is as delicate and decorative as the design for a lavender box. But Mr Guthrie's fairies totter around like a bunch of elephants on an ice rink.

A Midsummer Night's Dream by Shakespeare, directed by **Michael Langham**, Old Vic, 1960. Reviewed by Norman Phelps in the *Daily Post.*

Michael Langham could not make his mind up apparently, whether this was a funny play or an office party.

A Midsummer Night's Dream by Shakespeare, directed by **Michael Langham**, Old Vic, 1961. Reviewed by Eric Keown in *Punch.*

Mr Langham has decided that something must be done to brighten the misunderstandings of the lovers in the forest, and so turns the tussle between Hermia and Helena into a rugger movement, the two men as hard-working backs keeping them apart. It's clear that, had she been a man, Judi Dench with her astonishing speed and agility would have been an England fly-half. I grant it is amusing, but I have an old-fashioned feeling it is not quite Shakespeare.

A Midsummer Night's Dream by Shakespeare, directed by **Peter Brook**, Royal Shakespeare Company, February, 1971. Reviewed by Stanley Kauffmann.

. . . the white emptiness suggests an inappropriate cross between an operating room and Avedon's studio in *Vogue.*

A Midsummer Night's Dream *with Alan Howard as Oberon, Sara Kestelman as Titania, John Kane as Puck and Philip Locke as Quince. Directed by Peter Brook. Courtesy of* Punch.

Much Ado About Nothing by Shakespeare, directed by **Henry Cass**, Old Vic, 1934. Reviewed by Herbert Farjeon in *The Shakespeare Scene.* Headline: Much-a-Disney.

The gentlemen in this production of *Much Ado* are dressed in Elizabethan costume. That sounds like a good foundation, but it is no foundation at all for the ladies are dressed like ladies in late eighteenth century portraits by Gainsborough and Hero is seen preparing for her nuptials while she discusses the details of an Elizabethan costume in a boudoir that might have been decorated for Lady Teazle.

Mr Cass, the producer, says he did this because the periods chosen seemed to him 'the most attractive and suitable for each sex.' This however is not his only defence. These mixed costumes, says Mr Cass, remove the play from any definite time and place and make it what it really is, a masque.

If Mr Cass thinks that *Much Ado* is really a masque, he is mistaken about masques and mistaken about *Much Ado* . . . And why seek to remove from any definite place a play in which the opening line runs 'I learn in this letter that Don Pedro of Arragon is comes this night to Messina'? Why treat Don John and Co. like Peter Pan pirates unless *Much Ado* is really a play for tots? Why dress the Friar like a High Priest of the Greek Church unless *Much Ado* is really a play for loonies? As for the treatment of Dogberry and his watchmen, I limit myself to recalling the fact that they enter in front of a back cloth of rooftops and chimney pots with cats dangling watches and a general air of Mickey Mousery that savours of the sort of comic picture postcard one would blush to receive even from one's old nurse.

Much Ado About Nothing by Shakespeare, directed by **Denis Carey**, Old Vic, October, 1956. **Peter Rice**'s set, reviewed by John Barber in the *Daily Express*.

The scenery — looking like a boy's fork dipped into brown Windsor soup — wobbled until its false flowers shook.

Pericles by Shakespeare, directed by **John Coleman**, Stratford-on-Avon, April, 1900. Reviewed in the *Leamington Chronicle*.

Sitting near me were two ladies, one of whom had a single volume edition of Shakespeare, in which she endeavoured to follow the progress of the play. At last she put the book aside, remarking to her companion. 'The play on the stage seems to be quite different from the book.'

The Provok'd Wife by Vanbrugh, directed by **Peter Wood**, Lyttleton, November, 1980. Reviewed by Robert Cushman in the *Observer*.

I wonder if Peter Wood was scared as a child by a particularly bad production of Restoration comedy.

When he directs one of them himself he seems to have in his mind the memory of two actors on an empty stage in pretty clothes just talking, talking, talking.

Mr Wood has no intention of letting this happen in his own productions, which are extremely busy . . .

Richard II by Shakespeare, directed by **F. R. Benson** (1858-1939) at the Stratford Festival, 1896. Described by Constance Benson.

There was very nearly a tragedy one night in the last act. FRB used to have the curtain up on a street scene, with a man hanging from the gallows. By some mistake, the rope was tied round the poor offender's neck and not (as rehearsed) round his arms. Fortunately some dreadful gurgling noises attracted the attention of the stage manager, who quickly snatched the poor man from the jaws of death. The wardrobe master afterwards soundly rated the half-strangled 'super' for making a commotion on stage.

It should be explained that 'supers' were local amateur actors, hired to swell the ranks of touring companies.

Richard II by Shakespeare, directed by **Ralph Richardson** with Alec Guinness in the name part, New, 1947. Reviewed by Kenneth Tynan.

. . . Sir Ralph, I begin to think, has a common-place mind behind all that marketable technique; a mind mole-like in its earthiness. He tries to make Mr Guinness bellow, which is like casting a clipped and sensitive tenor for Boris Godounov; he would have him speak at the top of a voice whose peculiar quality it is to have no top. Richard is a character part; he is not one of Corneille's waxwork grandees. The key to him is the line: 'O that I were as great as is my grief!' If he were, he might be a tragic figure. But the circumstances are wrong, and he remains merely a misfit. Sir Ralph's production, fettered to the textual footnotes, gave us nothing of this. The Richard we saw — to abandon guess work about the Richard we might have seen — was a mercurial prig; in silence, smugly prim, in speech, ardently royal. If you can imagine Bloomsbury turned full-throated monarchist, you have some idea of the intellectual climate around him. At his best (in the deposition scene), Mr Guinness recalled to me a phrase of Henry James's about a 'Bohemian wanting tremendously to be a Philistine'. . . .

Richard III by Shakespeare, directed by **Colin George**, Old Vic, March, 1962. Reviewed by Bernard Levin in the *Daily Express.*

There is a learned man at present trying to discover whether dolphins can talk. When he has finished this study, he might consider investigating whether producers can think.

On the evidence of this disastrous production by Mr Colin George, it seems unlikely.

The Romans in Britain by Howard Brenton, directed by **Michael Bogdanov**, Olivier, National, October, 1980.

This play was greeted with considerable moral outrage chiefly because, as reported in the *Daily Express:*

The highlight (lowlight?) . . . of the distasteful proceedings was the downstage sodomisation of a live Ancient Brit by a beefy Roman footsoldier.

Sir Horace Cutler, Conservative leader of the GLC sent a telegram of protest to Sir Peter Hall and commented to the *Daily Telegraph:*

One expects more responsibility from the National Theatre. It is not some Soho hovel.

Mrs Mary Whitehouse did not go to the play but expressed her vociferous disapproval from a BBC van parked outside the theatre. She also told the *Guardian:*

One is concerned about protecting the citizen, and in particular young people. I am talking about men being so stimulated by the play that they will commit attacks on young boys . . .

and reviewed by Ned Chaillet in *The Times.*

Michael Bogdanov's direction is probably right to make the action blatant and explicit at the risk of offence for a work of such violent imagination would be even worse presented coyly. But when a Celt has a violent struggle with a stuffed woolly dog, the whole thing seems a joke.

Chris Dyer's set for Shakespeare's **Romeo and Juliet**, directed by **Trevor Nunn**, Aldwych, July, 1977. Reviewed by Irving Wardle in *The Times*.

Never have I felt more impatient with them for failing to shin down the balcony (an easily scalable structure by Chris Dyer) and eloping to Mantua together.

and by Sheridan Morley in *Punch,* April, 1976 (when it opened at Stratford).

The two lovers, played by Ian McKellen and Francesca Annis, are not only star-crossed but visibly into their thirties which makes one wonder during duller moments why they aren't out looking for work or worrying about their children's education.

The Taming of the Shrew *with David Sucket as Grumio, Jonathan Pryce as Petruchio and Paolo Dionisotti as Katharina. Courtesy of* Punch.

The Taming of the Shrew by Shakespeare, directed by **Michael Bogdanov** for the RSC, Stratford-on-Avon, May, 1978. Reviewed by John Barber in the *Daily Telegraph*.

The theatre drunk started demonstrating in the auditorium . . . swore at the attendants trying to show him out, and eventually climbed on the stage where he overturned pillars, tore down curtains and wrecked scenery.

People started walking out. Not, however, those who recognized Jonathan Pryce.

He was doubling two roles: that of the wife-taming Petruchio . . . and the boozy Christopher Sly, the tinker before whom — in Shakespeare's original — the comedy is acted by a troupe of strolling players.

At the beginning of Michael Bogdanov's production, the text is drastically re-written to fit modern dress. As usual at this theatre the audience revel in these modish gimmicks. Petruchio (whose name is mispronounced throughout) arrives on a motorbike.

A brass band marches around playing 'Kiss Me Kate'. His wedding takes place with a flurry of umbrellas. Her father tots up money on a computer which catches fire . . .

Romeo and Juliet with set by Chris Dyer, Marie Kean as Nurse, Francesca Annis as Juliet, Ian McKellen as Romeo and Michael Pennington as Mercutio. Courtesy of Punch.

Ken Rowell's decor for Shakespeare's **The Taming of the Shrew**, directed by **Denis Carey**, December, 1954. Reviewed by Milton Shulman in the *Evening Standard*.

The decor by Ken Rowell would lead you to suppose that Padua was built by window dressers. The costumes look as though they have been pulled out of Christmas crackers, and one hat worn by Petruchio may have come about by an explosion in an ostrich farm.

The Tempest by Shakespeare, Covent Garden, 1815. Reviewed by Hazlitt.

As we returned some evenings ago from seeing *The Tempest* at Covent Garden, we almost came to the resolution of never going to another representation of a play of Shakespeare's as long as we lived; and we certainly did come to this determination, that we would never go *by choice*.

The Tempest by Shakespeare, Sadler's Wells, January, 1934. Reviewed by James Agate in the *Sunday Times*.

Proceeding by elimination, let me run over one or two things which couldn't be anybody's reasons for liking this production. Certainly not the scenery, which consisted of an almost bare stage sparsely furnished with logs constructed out of pink Edinburgh rock, an igloo or wigwam made out of the raffia used by Miss Cicely Courtneidge for her production numbers, and three screens similarly fringed. Nor yet the costumes, since Prospero's magic robes would have shamed the Queen of Carnival at that town obviously hinted at in the lines:

> The approaching tide
> Will shortly fill the reasonable shore,
> That now lies foul and muddy.

To wit, Southend. Miranda's frock did not help, since it could obviously be worn with only envious comment at any tennis-club dance . . . and as Iris, Ceres and Juno, Mesdames Margaret Field-Hyde, Flora Robson and Evelyn Allen look like goddesses from the Forest of Elizabeth Arden.

The Tempest by Shakespeare, directed by **Peter Brook**, Drury Lane, 1957. Reviewed by Robert Wraight in the *Star*.

No doubt with the object of appealing to the modern child, Mr Brook has given the enchanted island a space age touch. A sputnik moon hangs in the sky, the goddess Juno arrives by space ship and Shakespeare's opening 'sweet airs' are like the sound track of a science fiction film with an X certificate. It all adds up to a rather superior panto. But it is rather hard on the Bard.

and by the *Daily Herald*. Headline: IT'S PANTO BY SHAKESPEARE.

Shakespeare came back to Drury Lane last night. Peter Brook's production of *The Tempest* may seem an odd show for Christmas. It is not. Under our boldest producer the play becomes a gorgeous pantomime — with above average dialogue. Prospero's desert island revenge is related with a load of magic, a flying ballet and trap doors. If it wasn't for the bawdy bits you could take the children.

Abd' elkader's set for Shakespeare's **The Tempest** directed by **Clifford Williams**, Stratford-on-Avon, April, 1963. Reviewed by Roger Gellert in the *New Statesman*.

The moving strips that transport plastic rocks, trees and hardly less plastic actors, mopping, mowing; Prospero's mushroom podium, on which he rises like a giant Wurlitzer; the pawnbroking trio of balls that hang from the thunder cloud, and detonate with all the elemental grandeur of Rice Krispies. These are gimmicry run mad, not magic.

Leslie Hurry's sets for Shakespeare's **Timon of Athens** Old Vic, September, 1956. Reviewed by Milton Shulman in the *Evening Standard*.

A set that might have been left behind by a Wolverhampton production of *Babes in the Wood*.

and by Kenneth Tynan in the *Observer*.

Leslie Hurry's settings are as coarse as his costumes, a dissonance of sequins, Pepsi-cola purple and dessicated mud.

Toys in the Attic by Lillian Hellman, directed by **John Dexter**, Piccadilly, 1960. Reviewed by Mervyn Jones in *Tribune*.

John Dexter's production exhibits his usual inspired inattention to detail.

and by Bernard Levin in the *Daily Express*.

Mr John Dexter's production consists of a series of pregnant pauses, none of which, unfortunately, are ever brought to bed.

The Winter's Tale by Shakespeare, BBC, February, 1981. Reviewed by Clive James in the *Observer*.

The Winter's Tale was worthily done, but one gets uncomfortable for the actors when they are surrounded by cubes and cones. You can't quell the fear that if one of them sits on a cone instead of a cube, the blank verse will suffer.

Theatres

Bad notices are not the preserve of actors, productions and plays: from time to time they are also lavished upon the buildings in which it all happens. People whose feelings run high about theatre mind very much about the house which contains it, the decor they must inhabit during intervals and even (as with Shaw) the ambience that attaches itself to a particular theatre and that can be shattered by a change of policy on the part of the management.

Here is a critique of the original 'new' theatre, opened at Stratford-on-Avon in 1879, described in the *Daily News*.

The theatre, which is what was called by Mr Pepys 'a new old-fashioned hall', stands beside the glassy Avon. Like a king in a play who, when he appears in great majesty, is racking his brain to say his part, this building is not completely satisfactory. It is a three-piled medley of architectural titbits, in which the Chateau of Montaigne is seen striving with an Elizabethan country house, although the Victorian builder has the best of it.

This theatre was rebuilt after the First World War and reopened in 1932, to a chorus of protests from which I selected the following.

The new **Shakespeare Memorial Theatre**, discussed in a letter signed A. Cripps, Worthing, in the *Daily News Chronicle*.

There is only one thing that can be said in favour of the new Memorial Theatre at Stratford. It is a tremendous, overwhelming argument against war.

Only a nation that has been bludgeoned by four years' incessant warfare into a state of insensitivity — mental, moral and (one might almost say) physical — could possibly have allowed itself to put up a structure of such unspeakable hideousness: and in such a spot!

Here's a special kind of nostalgia, for the loss of a theatre's bad reputation.

The Independent Theatre, March, 1895. Described by George Bernard Shaw in his review of *A Man's Love* in the *Saturday Review.*

The Independent Theatre is becoming wretchedly respectable. Nobody now clamours for the prosecution of Mr Grein under Lord Campbell's Act, or denounces myself and other frequenters of the performances as neurotic, cretinous degenerates. This is not as it should be.

The Chichester Festival Theatre, discussed by Kenneth Tynan in his review of an early production there — *The Broken Heart* by John Ford. This review took the form of an open letter addressed to Sir Laurence Olivier.

. . . Chichester is a product of our gullibility: instead of letting the whole audience see the actors' faces (however distantly), we now prefer to bring them closer to the actors' backs. The Chichester stage is so vast that even the proximity argument falls down: an actor on the opposite side of the apron is farther away from one's front-row seat than he would be from the twelfth row of a proscenium theatre — where in any case he would not deliver a crucial speech with his rear turned towards one's face.

The Olivier Theatre when it was first opened, was described by Sheridan Morley as:

a space which might seem over-large for a full-scale revival of Ben Hur on ice.

and Leigh Hunt took fierce exception when Drury Lane was invaded, as he saw it, by Chinese bad taste. Comment in the *Examiner*, September, 1817.

. . . we protest vehemently against the saloon. They have absolutely filled it with Chinese pagodas and lanthorns, *adorned* with monsters and mandarins, and shedding a ghastly twilight! Nothing can be more puerile and tasteless. All the world knows that though the Chinese are shrewd people in some things, they are very stupid and disgusting in others, matters of taste included; and if the world did not know it, these Chinese lanthorns would be sufficient to enlighten it!

and our **National Theatre** building, designed by Sir Denys Lasdun, gave rise to the *bon mot* (quoted by Gillian Widdicombe in the *Observer,* February, 1982).

. . . the best view of London is from the National Theatre, because from there you can't see the National Theatre.

Miscellany

Whilst researching I have come across odd bits and pieces that fit no particular category, but are perhaps relevant to the theme of this book. Or just funny. For 'Miscellany' you may also read 'Author's Whim'.

William Hazlitt (1778-1830) wrote:

Poetry and the stage do not agree well together!

Sydney Smith (1771-1845), co-founder of the *Edinburgh Review,* lectured in moral philosophy and became a canon of St Paul's. He said to Mrs Groat, when she tried to lure him into the theatre:

All this pleasure inspires me with the same nausea I feel at the sight of rich plum cake or sweetmeats; I prefer the driest bread of common life.

No Stone, No Turn
John Chamberlain, whose theatrical company was the first to stage most of Shakespeare's plays, wrote as follows in a letter to Sir Dudley Carleton, 1619.

The funeral (of the Queen) is put off to the 29th of next month, to the great hindrance of our players, which are forbidden to play so long as her body is above ground.

Annual Report
Kenneth Tynan in the *Observer,* July, 1956.

Which reminds me: the Vic is about to break up for the hols, and it is time for prize-giving. The Michael Hordern Memorial Cup for teamwork is shared between Messrs. Gwillim and Francis. Paul Rogers retains, for the second year running, the Trustees' Trophy for Versatility under Fire. The Gielgud Medallion, an embossed gold larynx, goes to John Neville, who continues next term as Head of the school. After several hung juries, the Governors have decided against awarding the Olivier Laurel-Wreath: Richard Burton led on the last ballot, but the requisite majority was not obtained . . .

You can even discuss a Play without seeing it . . .
Peter Pan, Scala, December, 1961. Reviewed by Bernard Levin in the *Daily Express.*

Having been advised that *Peter Pan* was back again at the Scala Theatre, this year with Miss Anne Heywood as Peter and Miss Jane Asher (a memorable 'Alice' on records) as Wendy, I had no doubt that it was once again everything it should be.

What is more, I thought it would be a pity to risk disillusion by actually going to see it.

Thus the management is pleased, I am pleased, my readers are, I trust, pleased, and in general, as Sir Winston once said, all legitimate interests are in harmony.

. . . and you can even review a Play when you have pretended to see it.
From the *Satirist,* 1807.

In our first number we promised our readers a review on reviews, a critique upon critiques. These are various illiberalities practised by some newspaper writers.

The *British Neptune* (nay, start not, reader, there actually is such a paper) vaunted itself to be a glorious and impartial journal whose criticism you might depend upon, till one fatal day when *The Constant Couple* came under the lash of its editor. This spoiled all: for he chose to abuse Messrs Elliston, Dowton, Palmer and Barrymore, in their respective parts, when lo and behold, the play had not been represented.

The *Morning Herald* has, in the course of a month, mentioned Mr Holland as having played Pizarro, when he never came upon the stage, and very good naturedly poetised Mr Bannister for his comicalities in Jobson, when Mr Dowton had undertaken the part at short notice; who in his turn gets commended in the *Morning Post* for his acting in *All in the Wrong,* which happens to be a play in which he has no part.

Georg Solti

Many years ago when I was contemplating this book I sat next to Sir Georg at dinner and told him about it. He immediately volunteered this contribution, which is more than can be said for the well known and, dare I say it, rather pompous actor who was sitting on my right. Re Mozart's *Figaro,* in an American provincial newspaper.

He conducted the second act Finale with a smile on his face — it would have been better if he had cut his throat.

Actors aren't the only ones to suffer

Ibsen at the first performance of his play *Rosmersholm* at Augsburg, April, 1886. Described by someone who was with him in the audience.

He witnessed the performance with weeping and gnashing of teeth. Seated in the front of the stalls he winced in pain at every word uttered from the stage; with both hands clutching the plush of the orchestra rail, he groaned ceaselessly: 'Oh, God! Oh, God!' In the third act John Rosmer conceived the grotesque idea of appearing with elegant piqué spats over shining polished calfskin boots. When the man appeared, Ibsen reeled as though struck, and clasped my arm. 'Look, look at that!' The Rosmer he had created was wearing bright yellow spats. We were convinced that Ibsen would prohibit the whole performance at the last moment, with some vehement outburst, but then, suddenly, he straightened himself, and, with a gesture as though to brush away a bad dream, said, 'I must forget my original conception. Then it isn't too bad.' And, with quiet resolve, he adopted this attitude.

and here is Shaw conjuring up a similar scene.

Théàtre de l'Oeuvre de Paris performing Ibsen's *Rosmerholm* and *The Master Builder* at the Opera Comique, London, March, 1895. Reviewed by George Bernard Shaw.

M. Lugné-Pöe and his dramatic company called L'Oeuvre came to us with the reputation of having made Ibsen cry by their performance of one of his works. There was not much in that: I have seen performances by English players which would have driven him to suicide.

Positively last appearances?

Hope Booth, young actress of the late nineteenth century. Reviewed by George Bernard Shaw.

I must somewhat tardily acknowledge an invitation to witness a performance at the Royalty Theatre by Miss Hope Booth, a young lady who cannot sing, dance or speak, but whose appearance suggests that she might profitably spend three or four years in learning these arts, which are useful on the stage.

The Wicked Earl by Walter Hackett (a new play in which a retired actor, Cyril Maude, came back from the west country to say good-bye to the London stage). His Majesty's, February, 1927. Reviewed by Hannen Swaffer in the *Daily Express.*

The play is not more than so-so . . . It was amusing to see Mr Maude as a wicked train robber and delightful to admire him in immaculate evening dress in the Earl's Norfolk home . . . However, it was chiefly pleasant to remember that as after all Mr Maude is only sixty-four we have really a chance to say goodbye to him in better plays.

On **Mrs Siddons'** return from retirement to play Lady Macbeth at Covent Garden, June, 1816. Reviewed by Hazlitt.

Players should be immortal, if their own wishes or ours could make them so; but they are not. They not only die like other people, but like other people they cease to be young, and are no longer themselves, even while living . . . Mrs Siddons retired once from the stage: why should she return to it again? She cannot retire from it twice with dignity; and yet it is to be wished that she should do all things with dignity. Any loss of reputation to her is a loss to the world. Has she not had enough of glory? . . . The enthusiasm she excited had something idolatrous about it . . . does she think we have forgot her? Or would she remind us of herself by showing us what *she was not*? Or is she to continue on the stage to the very last, till all her grace and all her grandeur gone, shall leave behind them only a melancholy blank?

    . . . If it was reasonable that Mrs Siddons should retire from the stage three years ago, certainly those reasons have not diminished since . . . [She] always spoke as slow as she ought: she now speaks slower than she did . . . The machinery of the voice is too ponderous for the power that wields it. There is too long a pause between each sentence, and between each word in each sentence . . . The stage waits for her . . .

Lastly, if Mrs Siddons has to leave the stage again, Mr Horace Twiss will have to write another farewell address for her: if she continues on it, we shall have to criticize her performances. We know not which of these two evils we shall think the greatest.

Miss Piggy
This is the worst notice that Miss Piggy could be persuaded to produce. Miss Piggy in *The Muppet Movie.* Reviewed by Martin Malina in the *Montreal Star.*

She may be the screen's sexiest new star since Marilyn Monroe.

The Translator's Hazard — there's always a bilingual critic to check up on you. *Don Juan* by Molière, translated by John Fowles. Discussed by Irving Wardle in *The Times.*

From a hasty check with the original, Mr Fowles' translation achieves its literary grace at some cost to textual accuracy. 'Everything's arranged for my loins to have their meat', his Juan remarks, where Molière's simply announces that he is off on an 'enterprise amoureuse'.

The Society of Damned Authors
In a letter to the Editor of the *Spectator* in 1811, Lamb announced the foundation of a Society of Damned Authors, membership being confined to authors who shared the experience of having a performance of at least one of their works hissed by a rejecting audience. He described the tenets of the Society as follows:

That the public, or mob, in all ages, have been a set of blind, deaf, obstinate, senseless, illiterate savages. That no man of genius would be ambitious of pleasing such a capricious, ungrateful rabble. That the only legitimate end of writing for them is to pick their pockets and, *that failing,* we are at full liberty to vilify and abuse them as much as ever we think fit.

On the first night of Lamb's disastrous play *Mr H* he is said to have joined in the hissing of the audience in the hope that no one would recognise him as the playwright.

The audience attacked for pretentiousness
At *An Ideal Husband* by Oscar Wilde, New York, November, 1918. Reviewed by Dorothy Parker in *Vanity Fair.*

Somehow, no matter how well done an Oscar Wilde play may be, I am always far more absorbed in the audience than in the drama. There is something about them that never fails to enthrall me. They have a conscious exquisiteness, a deep appreciation of their own culture. They exude an atmosphere of the *New Republic* — a sort of Crolier-than-thou air. 'Look at us,' they seem to say. 'We are the cognoscenti. We have come because we can appreciate this thing —

we are not as you, poor bonehead, who are here because you couldn't get tickets for the Winter Garden.' They walk slowly down the aisle and sink gracefully into their seats, trusting that all may note their presence, for the very fact of their being there is proof of their erudition. From the moment of the curtain's rise they keep up a hum of approbation, a reassuring signal of their patronage and comprehension. 'Oh, the lines, the lines!' they sigh . . .

And Stupidity
At *Reunion in Vienna* by Robert E. Sherwood. Lyric, January, 1933. Reviewed by James Agate in the *Sunday Times*.

The essence of this play is wit, and there is not power either in Nature or outside it to make wit endurable to the English play-goer . . .

This piece is so witty and wise, so completely suited to the grown-up mind, and so full of theatre as the French understand theatre, both in high comedy and in Palais-Royal farce, that in my opinion it is doomed to failure.

And for Frivolity
by Walter Kerr in 1952.

The ability to sleep through a Broadway performance is usually attributed to cocktails, but this, I think, is a canard. Women have been known to lap up not only their own Martinis but substantial portions of their husbands' and still sit giddily alert through three long acts. The power of the male to remain erect in an evening suit while achieving a state of delightful oblivion is unique . . . The male has learned how to deal with a theatre which has, for some time now, been principally designed for his wife.

While the old boy dozes off, his wife's eyes dart restlessly over the stage that has been set for her. She checks the fashionable living-room interior for helpful hints in homemaking. She wonders whether tonight's arrangement of bookshelves would do for that reshuffling of her husband's den she has in mind. She checks the draperies critically. She contemplates the placement of the sofa. She makes a note of the tea service. She frowns at the rather nervous dab the ingénue has just made at grouping some flowers in a vase. She sets her lips grimly as the outspoken comedy maid unsuccessfully tidies an antimacassar.

Of course she studies the gowns — usually by Valentina — and wonders whether brassieres mightn't be better after all. She awaits each entrance of the principal actress breathlessly: to see what she will be wearing. The acts of the play are, for her, divided into the turquoise with the flair (Act one), the scalloped beige (Act Two), and That Peach Monstrosity (Act Three).

Each coiffure as it appears is examined, taken down, rinsed, reset, and this time properly modelled to the face it adorns. Later she can tell you everything you want to know, and quite a bit you don't, about colour clashes, bone structure, and the inadequate concealment of avoirdupois.

From time to time she attends to the play. These times usually have something to do with love . . .

Audience Participation
In a fragment of one of Antiphones' comedies, c. 336 BC, a playwright complains of the rigours of comedy:

The writer of tragedy is a lucky fellow! The audience always knows the plot as soon as his play begins. All the poet has to do is give a jog to their memories. He just says 'Oedipus': they know all the rest — father, Laius; mother, Jocasta; daughters, sons, what's to come and what is past. If he but utter one word 'Alcmeon', the very children at once repeat: 'He went mad and killed his mother; in a minute Adrastus will come in in a rage and go out again . . . . . .' We can't do that, we have to invent everything — new names, the action before the play begins, the present situation, the climax, the opening. If a comic character forgets any of this, he's hissed off the stage, but a tragic character can forget as much as he likes.

Audiences haven't changed. I remember playing Lady Macbeth in a matinée for schoolchildren, and they all joined in lustily for the 'I have given suck' speech.

Even critics sometimes get sympathy
Gordon Craig on Kenneth Tynan in a conversation between the two men, recorded in Tynan's book *Curtains.*

You have the right face for a critic . . . You have the look of a blooming martyr.

. . . And they get bad notices.
Peter Ustinov, on the BBC radio programme, *The Critics,* February, 1952.

They search for ages for the wrong word, which, to give them credit, they eventually find.

Insurance Cover?
From the *Life of Garrick* by Thomas Davies, 1808.

The first effort of his talents was exerted at Ipswich, as Aboan, in the play *Oroonoko,* a part in which his features could not easily be discerned: under the guise of a black countenance he hoped to escape being known, should it be his misfortune not to please.

Carried away by his part
From the *Symposiacs* of Plutarch (AD 46-120)

They tell this of Aesop that whilst he was representing in the theatre Atreus deliberating the revenge of Thyestes, he was so transported beyond himself in the heat of the action, that he struck with his sceptre one of the servants who was running across the stage, so violently that he laid him dead upon the place.

Too shy

Skin Deep by Ernest Enderline, Criterion, May, 1928. Reviewed by Hannen Swaffer.

The young author of last night's new play, *Skin Deep*, was too shy to make his call. When they had searched for him in vain, Athene Seyler said, in explanation, 'He comes from Manchester.'

. . . and judging by the rest of the review, was on the first train back there.

Another kind of Miracle play

Any modern actor who has complained of the discomforts of touring should take note of this extract from Agustin De Rojas — *The Entertaining Journey* c. 1595. I quote it at length, because of its extraordinarily vivid picture of the strolling players' life.

He and his side-kick, Solano, having already suffered many vicissitudes were now stuck without money in a small provincial town. This last episode must have proved too much for poor old Solano, for I can't think of another instance where an actor has left in the middle of a performance . . .

One day we heard a drum beat and a boy announced that excellent comedia *Los Amigos Trocados*, to be performed that night in the town hall. We spoke to the boy and he took us to the autor (actor/manager). I don't know whether it grieved him to see us so ragged, but finally he embraced us, and after we had related our hardships to him, we dined, and he bade us rid ourselves of our fleas, so that they might not cling to the costumes, for we were to act in the comedia. That night, in fact, we took part, and the next day he made an agreement with us to act in his company. He now gave me a part to study in *The Resurrection of Lazarus*, and to Solano the role of the resurrected saint. Everytime the comedia was played, the author took off a garment in the dressing-room and loaned it to Solano, charging him especially to let no fleas get into it. When the play was ended Solano returned to the dressing-room, took off the costume, and donned his old clothes. We continued this life for more than four weeks, eating little, travelling much, with the theatrical baggage on our backs, and without ever making the acquaintance of a bed. Going this way from village to village, it happened to rain a good deal one night so, as it was only a short league to where we were going, the director told us to make a litter of our hands and carry his wife, while he and the other two men would carry the baggage of the company, the boy taking the drum and other odds and ends. In this way we reached our destination, completely worn out, foot-sore and covered with mud; indeed we were half dead, for we were serving as pack-mules. Arrived in the village, the director immediately requested permission to play, and we acted Lazarus. Solano and I put on our borrowed clothes, but when we arrived at the passage concerning the sepulchre, the director, who took the part of Christ, said several times to Lazarus, 'Arise, Lazarus! surge!

surge!' and seeing that he did not arise, approached the sepulchre, believing Solano had fallen asleep. He found, however, that Lazarus had indeed risen, body and soul, taking his clothes with him. Seeing the fix we were in, I took the road to Zaragoza without, however, finding any trace of Solano, nor the director or his clothes, nor the spectators of Lazarus, who they doubtless thought had ascended to heaven.

From the Thespians' Dictionary

The following excerpts are taken from *The Thespian Dictionary; or Dramatic Biography* printed in 1805. Nothing like it in this century has been similarly undertaken, and judging by the frankness of its disclosures, that's perhaps just as well. Nonetheless the book gives a very real sense of what the theatre was like in the eighteenth century — the partisanship of the audiences, supporting their favourite actors, actresses and playwrights, much like the football fans of today. They were as violent and vociferous as any modern fanatic, and it was not uncommon for theatres to be closed for three or more days in an attempt to quell the rioting.

Actors and actresses too were not averse to conducting rows on stage — see Mrs Rogers and Mrs Hamilton — and though one feels grateful for the decorum that prevails nowadays, what zest they all displayed!

Mr. Brown Actor. His memory was frequently treacherous; but he had, on this occasion, a peculiar *laugh* which always put the audience into good-humour, and gave himself sufficient time for recollection.

Oh yes, we all know that one.

Mr. Burton Actor. He appeared for the first time at Market Street, Herts, in the character of David in *The Rivals*. We say appeared, for, though extremely perfect in his part, fright had prevented all utterance, and his brother performers, anticipating the meaning of his motions, were obliged to declare to the audience what they knew he *intended to say.*

Colley Cibber. Cibber, like the generality of successful dramatists, who are chiefly indebted to managerial power for their fame, was jealous of all rival authors — he never encouraged young writers; for it was his delight, according to his own phrase, 'to crush those singing birds'.

Susanna Cibber. When Mr Whitehead's comedy, *School for Lovers,* was in preparation (1762) and the performers assembled at Mr Garrick's house with the author, it was suggested by some person present that the age of Celia, the character intended for Mrs Cibber, which was sixteen, would be better altered to two or three and twenty, and Mrs Cibber's opinion was asked about it. She was then reading her part with her spectacles on her nose, and after a little deliberation said, she liked the character better as it was, and desired it might remain as it stood. She was at this time more than fifty years old.

Mr Crawford. Actor/Manager. His wife would never appear on the stage till she was paid, and her husband was frequently obliged to send to, and collect the money she demanded, from the doorkeepers. The band likewise mutinied, and the poor manager, one night he was to play Othello, there being no musicians in the orchestra, offered to play on the violin himself, between the acts, which proposal being cheerfully accepted by the audience, he played that night the double part of Moor and Fiddler, and his performance in the orchestra was more applauded than that on the stage.

Charles Farrel. Actor. He excelled in Harlequin, and at the advanced age of seventy-five danced the Highland broad dance; the sword wounding him in the thigh, from a false step perhaps, did not make him desist, and though the blood streamed on the stage, he persevered.

Mrs Hamilton and a Mrs Bellamy were rivals, and yet had agreed to appear in each other's benefit performances. The rot set in when Mrs Hamilton didn't turn up to pay her dues to Mrs Bellamy, so Mrs B. played it tit for tat.

Mrs Hamilton. Upon Mrs Hamilton's entrance she was saluted in a warmer manner than she wished, and was prevented for some time from speaking by that most disagreeable of all sounds to the dramatic ear, hisses! At length, upon the tumult ceasing a little, she advanced and addressed the audience in the following Demosthenian style: 'Gemmen and Ladies, I suppose as how you hiss me because I did not play at Mrs Bellamy's benefit. I would have performed, but she said as how my audience stunk, and were all tripe people.' When the fair speechifier had got thus far, the pit seemed one and all transformed at her irresistible oratory, for with one voice they encored her, crying out, 'Well said, Tripe,' a title she retained till she quitted the theatre.

Hollingsworth. One evening, between the play and farce, peeping, according to custom, through the aperture in the curtain, he received an apple with a penknife stuck in it, near his eye.

John Philip Kemble. Though not so happy in comedy, he was remarkable for his risibility, and the most trifling incident would spoil his serious countenance in tragedy. During his first performance in Dublin of Mark Anthony (*All for Love*), he happened to look up, and perceiving a pedantic old figure, who was leaning over the upper box, with a listening trumpet to his ear, he began to smother a laugh, but no longer able to contain himself, to the great astonishment of the audience, his laugh became loud and immoderate, and it was some time before he was able to finish the character.

Known as 'corpsing', this desire to laugh on stage at inappropriate moments can be a nightmare.

James Quin. The last time of his appearance on the stage was on the 19th March, 1753, on which night the stage, pit and boxes were all at the advanced price of five shillings. The next year, finding himself disabled in some measure by the loss of his teeth from renewing his former assistance, he declined it altogether saying, in his usual blunt manner, 'By G—, I will not whistle Falstaff for anybody.'

Mrs Rogers. After standing out a long siege of amorous courtship from Wilks, at last yielded up the fortress. Though ardent, Wilks's passion for Mrs Rogers proportionally cooled, and the lady's temper not readily submitting to this, produced much bitterness and disagreement. They were, however, obliged often to play the lovers on the stage, particularly the parts of Jaffier and Belvidera, in which there are scenes of much tenderness. Wilks bore up the character of the lover with much seeming, but Mrs Rogers was so incapable of stifling her resentment in the embraces that she gave Jaffier, that she ever and anon left visible and bloody marks of her jealousy. This, however painful to Wilks, was sport to the audience, and the play for this reason was much frequented.

Henry Thornton. As an actor, he boasts of that merit which constitutes a good country performer, for he can bustle through a part with considerable ease, though unacquainted with the author's words. As an instance of Mr Thornton's ability to avoid total disaster, the story is told how one night at Gosport, while representing Biron in the tragedy *Isabella*, he died without handing over the letter which unravels the plot. As he lay prostrate in the final scene, one of the other actors whispered to him: 'Mr Thornton, the letter!' 'The letter!' Thornton then rose up, took the letter out of his bosom, and said, 'One thing I had forgot through a multiplicity of business. Give this letter to my father. It will explain all' — and lay down again in the arms of death.

Scorpions' Corner
— when critics, writers and actors turn on each other.

An early example, from the *Poetics* of Aristotle (384-322 BC)

The comparision of tragic and epic imitation may also be compared to what the modern actors are in estimation of their predecessors; for Myniscus used to call Callipides, on account of his intemperate action 'the ape', and Tyndarus was censured on the same account.

Shakespeare. He was, by all the evidence, well liked by his contemporaries in the theatre. His success with audiences attracted remarkably little envy and malice. However, here is a fellow-playwright, one of the 'university wits' of the day, who was not too pleased by it . . .

Robert Greene, in *A Groatsworth of Wit*, 1592.

. . . there is an upstart crow, beautified with our feathers, that with his tiger's heart wrapt in a player's hide, supposes that he is well able to bumbast out a blank verse as the best of you: and being an absolute *Johannes factotum*, is in his own conceit the only Shake-scene in a country.

and Lord Byron (1788-1824) in a letter to James Hogg, March, 1814.

Shakespeare's name, you may depend on it, stands absurdly too high and will go down. He had no invention as to stories, none whatever. He took all his plots from old novels, and threw their stories into a dramatic shape, at as little expense of thought as you or I could turn his plays back again into prose tales. That he threw over whatever he did write some flashes of genius, nobody can deny: but this was all. Suppose any one to have the dramatic handling for the first time of such ready-made stories as Lear, Macbeth etc and he would be a sad fellow, indeed, if he did not make something very grand of them. (As) for his historical plays, properly historical, I mean, they were re-dressings of former plays on the same subjects, and in twenty cases out of twenty-one, the finest, the very finest things, are taken all but verbatim out of old affairs. You think, no doubt, that 'A Horse, a horse, my kingdom for a horse!' is Shakespeare's. Not a syllable of it. You will find it all in the old nameless dramatist.

and George Bernard Shaw (1856-1950)

Shakespeare wrote for the theatre because, with extraordinary artistic powers, he understood nothing and believed nothing. Thirty-six big plays in five blank verse acts, and . . . not a single hero! Only one man in them all who believes in life, enjoys life, thinks life worth living, and has a sincere, unrhetorical tear dropped over his death-bed; and that man — Falstaff. What a crew they are — fools, clowns, drunkards, cowards, intriguers, fighters, lovers, patriots, hypo-chondriacs, who mistake themselves (and are mistaken by the author) for philosophers, princes without any sense of public duty, futile pessimists who imagine they are confronting a barren and unmeaning world when they are only contemplating their own worthlessness, self-seekers of all kinds, keenly observed and masterfully drawn from the romantic-commercial point of view . . .

George Bernard Shaw by Matt.

Thomas Davies, Garrick's first biographer, on Garrick:

I have never heard him speak warmly in the commendation of any actor, living or dead.

Fanny Kemble (1809-93) on acting with Charles Macready. Extract from her *Diary*.

He growls and prowls and roams and foams around the stage, in every direction, like the tiger in his cage, so I never know which side of me he means to be, and keeps up a perpetual snarling and grumbling so that I never feel sure that he has done and that it is my turn to speak.

Charles Macready on John Kemble (1757-1823).

He was a first-rate actor in second-rate parts.

W. S. Gilbert (1836-1911) librettist, to **Herbert Beerbohm Tree**, actor, after his first performance as Hamlet:

My dear fellow, I never saw anything so funny in my life, and yet it was not in the least bit vulgar.

Sarah Bernhardt of **Mrs Patrick Campbell**, as quoted by James Agate in the *Sunday Times,* December, 1933.

In my hearing Sarah Bernhardt said of one of the greatest English actresses of our time, 'Elle a beaucoup de talent, la petite Campbelle!'

What I wouldn't give to have heard Bernhardt's delivery of this line.

Henrik Ibsen.
Comment by Strindberg in 1884:

I begin to hate Ibsen after *An Enemy of the People*; there's something insufferably aesthetic about him.

James O'Neill, actor, to his son, Eugene, after seeing the latter's play *Beyond the Horizon* at the Morosco theatre, November, 1920:

It's all right, Gene, if that's what you want to do, but people come to the theatre to forget their troubles, not to be reminded of them. What are you trying to do — send the audience home to commit suicide?

Unjustinian
In the sixth century the Byzantine Emperor Justinian married Theodora, a highly-praised mimic from San Vitale. He published an edict permitting a nobleman to marry an actress provided she renounced her profession.

I don't think the status of actresses has ever quite recovered from this blow.

Juliet plays Tennis — not strictly theatre, but I can't resist it. Herbert Farjeon, in *The Shakespeare Scene.*

. . . may I call your attention to the most remarkable stage direction ever printed in any edition of Shakespeare? It occurs in the motion picture version of *Romeo and Juliet*, price two dollars, published by

Metro-Goldwyn-Mayer, and it's to be found in the scene where Juliet is waiting impatiently for the Nurse's return from Romeo. Here Juliet says,

'from nine to twelve
Is three long hours, yet she is not come.
Had she affections and warm youthful blood,
She would be swift in motion as a ball.'

Then comes the Metro-Goldwyn-Mayer stage direction:
She imitates the stroke of a racket.

Talking Back. Arnold Bennett in an article in the *Academy*, Feb, 1901.

Upon the conclusion of the first performance of *Arms and the Man* at the Avenue theatre, Mr Shaw was called before the curtain by an audience of enraptured *dilettanti*. At the very moment of the author's appearance, a lone man in the gallery gave utterance to a loud and inimical 'Boo!' Mr Shaw nonchalantly raised his head, 'And with a look of all sweet accord' remarked,

'I rather agree with you, my friend.'

Ralph Richardson once electrified a first-night audience and other members of the cast by stepping out of character in mid-scene and turning towards the auditorium with the question, 'Is there a doctor in the house?'

Somebody in the audience stood up.

'Doctor,' said Sir Ralph, 'isn't this play awful?'

An Actor goes on Eternal Tour
Epitaph on the grave of Thomas Jackson — actor — buried in Gillingham, Norfolk.

Sacred to the memory of Thomas Jackson, comedian, who was engaged Dec. 21st 1741 to play a comic cast of characters in this great theatre, The World, for many of which he was prompted by nature to excel. The season being ended — his benefit over — the charges all paid — and his account closed, he made his exit in the tragedy of Death on the 17th of March 1798, in full assurance of being called once more to rehearsal, where he hopes to find his forfeits all cleared — his cast of parts bettered — and his situation made agreeable by Him who paid the great stock debt for the love he bore to performers in general.

Bibliography

Most of the reviews in this book were originally published in newspapers and periodicals. When quoting them I have given the name of the writer and, when it was known to me, the original source. But when quoting from collected editions of a critic's work, from an anthology or from a straight book of criticism, I have frequently omitted the source — to avoid tedious repetition. Reviews which are quoted without source may be found in the books listed below.

James Agate *The English Dramatic Critics,* anthology, Arthur Barker, 1932.
　　　　　　First Nights, Ivor Nicholson and Watson, 1934.
　　　　　　More First Nights, Gollancz, 1937.
　　　　　　The Amazing Theatre, Harrap, 1939.
Constance Benson *Mainly Players,* Butterworth, 1926.
Fanny Burney *Diary,* 1778.
Allen Churchill *The Theatrical,* McGraw Hill, New York, 1975.
Jeremy Collier *A Short View of the Immorality and Profaneness of the English Stage,* 1698.
Herbert Farjeon *The Shakespeare Scene,* Hutchinson, c 1943.
John Forster and George Henry Lewes *Dramatic Essays,* Walter Scott, 1896.
James Forsyth *Tyrone Guthrie, a biography,* Hamilton, 1976.
William Hazlitt *A View of the English Stage,* 1818.
Leigh Hunt *Dramatic Essays,* 1894.
Clive James *Visions Before Midnight,* Cape, 1977.
Stanley Kauffmann *Persons of the Drama,* Harper and Row, New York, 1976.
Walter Kerr *Pieces at Eight,* Max Reinhardt, 1952.
The Works of Charles and Mary Lamb, 7 vols., edited by E. V. Lucas, Methuen 1903-5.
George Henry Lewes *On Actors and the Art of Acting,* 1875.
Charles Macready *Diaries,* Macmillan and Co., 1975.
George Jean Nathan *Theatre Books of the Year,* Alfred Knopf, New York.
Samuel Pepys *Diaries,* Henry B. Wheatley, 1893-6.
William Prynne *Histrio mastix,* 1642.
George Bernard Shaw *Our Theatres in the Nineties,* 3 vols., Constable and Co., 1932.
John Simon, *Singularities,* Random House, New York, 1964.
J. Ranken Towse *Sixty Years of Theatre.*
Kenneth Tynan *He That Plays The King,* Longmans, 1950.
　　　　　　Curtains, Longmans, 1961.
　　　　　　Tynan Right and Left, Longmans, 1967.
　　　　　　A View of the English Stage, Davis-Poynter, 1975.
Victorian Dramatic Criticism, selected by George Rowell, Methuen, 1971.
William Winter *The Wallet of Time.*
Alexander Woollcott *The Portable Woollcott,* Viking Press, New York, 1946.

Index